Graphic Novels for Young Readers

**Recent Titles in
Genreflecting Advisory Series**

Diana Tixier Herald, Series Editor

Graphic Novels for Young Readers

A Genre Guide for Ages 4–14

Nathan Herald

Genreflecting Advisory Series

Diana Tixier Herald, Series Editor

AN IMPRINT OF ABC-CLIO, LLC
Santa Barbara, California • Denver, Colorado • Oxford, England

Library of Congress Cataloging-in-Publication Data

Herald, Nathan.
  Graphic Novels for Young Readers : A Genre Guide for Ages 4-14 / Nathan Herald.
     p. cm. -- (Genreflecting Advisory Series)
  Summary: "This genre guide to graphic novel reading interests helps librarians
  and teachers choose titles appropriate for children and 'tweens"-- Provided by publisher.
  Includes bibliographical references and index.
  ISBN 978-1-59884-395-8 (acid-free paper) 1. Graphic novels--Juvenile literature--Bibliography.
  2. Children--Books and reading--United States. 3. Preteens--Books and reading--
  United States. I. Title.
  Z5956.C6H47 2011
  [PN6710]
  741.5'9--dc22   2010044947

ISBN: 978-1-59884-395-8

15 14 13 12 11   1 2 3 4 5

This book is also available on the World Wide Web as an eBook.
Visit www.abc-clio.com for details.

Libraries Unlimited
An Imprint of ABC-CLIO, LLC

ABC-CLIO, LLC
130 Cremona Drive, P.O. Box 1911
Santa Barbara, California 93116-1911

This book is printed on acid-free paper ⬭
Manufactured in the United States of America

To Jack, Mark, and Patrick. One of the greatest gifts parents can give their children is the gift of knowledge. Thanks for being my target audience.

Contents

Acknowledgments

A lot of authors have said that the hardest part of writing is knowing who to thank; and now I have the honor of wracking my brains trying to name names without sounding like a total schmuck.

First off, this book would not even have been conceived if it were not for the efforts of my editor, Barbara Ittner—not only has she been a guiding force in this book, but she now stands as the gold standard that all future editors I may work with will have to measure up against.

The <u>Genreflecting Advisory Series</u> editor also deserves recognition—not only for helping out with the occasional suggestion for the book, but helping out throughout my entire life. Diana Herald not only got me in touch with Barbara, but also got me in touch with some of the greatest books I have ever read. Thanks, Mom.

If it were not for the unflagging faith of my wife, there were several times that I would have probably thrown in the towel and quit. Her patience, resolve, and nerve helped to cajole, prod, and motivate me, especially when I couldn't see the book for the pages. Melissa, I owe you a huge debt of gratitude that I don't think I can ever fully repay.

To my cheering squad across the valley—thank you all for your support and kind words. I can't name you all, but here's to a few that I can think of right off hand: Dad, your humor and faith in me have helped more than you know; "Buzz" Tobin, Pawel Obotz, Danny Snow, and the Markert Men—Steve "Big Guy" and Matt, you guys make my day job bearable; thank you for all of your support. Will Arbaugh, Michael Zimmerle, and Robert Archer—three distinctly disparate people, three unique world views, three very close friends that I would be lost without, even if we don't get to spend much time together.

Finally, to everyone out there whom I've met face to face, or digitally, I appreciate your input and suggestions, even if I didn't use them.

Introduction

Graphic novels have become a huge commodity in the publishing world. In this era of visual media, the standard book format has been taking a severe beating. Society has become so accustomed to having stories told via pictures that it sometimes seems the written word is having a difficult time competing.

Although graphic novels have been around for a while (some say close to 200 years),[1] it wasn't until the past twenty-five years that they really began to come into their own in the United States. With such series as <u>The Watchmen</u>, <u>The Dark Knight Returns</u>, and <u>A Contract with God</u>, readers and critics alike realized that graphic novels weren't just for kids. Well-written, adult-themed stories could be and were being created through a visual medium that utilized drawn, nonsequential images with text, presenting a story in a way that was not possible with just one medium.

On the other side of the world, another society had been using the comic book form since the 1950s. By the early 2000s Japan's comic book production may have been only 22.6 percent of the entire publishing schedule, but it made up a full 38.2 percent of all sales copies in Japan (Fusanosuke).[2] To put this in perspective, in America in 2002, the total market share of comic books was approximately .011 percent.[3] To say that the comics industry is a strong part of the Japanese culture is like saying librarians like books.

Why bring up Japan? Well, Japan produces manga, Japanese comics, which have taken the United States by storm over the past ten years. Who out there has not heard of such titles as <u>Pokémon</u>, <u>Dragonball Z</u>, or <u>Naruto</u>? The simple fact is that just like the British invasion of music in the 1960s, the Japanese manga invasion has won over Western audiences today.

Not that this is a bad thing. Manga promotes a multiculturalism that standard Western-style comics fail to do, simply because manga is culturally different for Western readers. It requires effort to understand why people act a certain way in these books, as opposed to how they would act in a Western-style comic. A working knowledge of certain cultural conventions inherent to both societies is required to appreciate the work in its entirety. Fans of manga—especially younger readers— consider this a bonus. Not only are their reading tastes cosmopolitan, but they are also privy to a lot of information that adults do not have.

Over the past several decades, the popularity of graphic novels has grown tremendously. In 2007 graphic novel sales in the United States and Canada were $375 million, a 12 percent rise from 2006 and quintuple the sales in 2001.[4] A number of guides to graphic novels have been published—some for fans and general readers, some specifically for librarians. In 2005 Libraries Unlimited published Mike Pawuk's definitive guide, *Graphic Novels: A Genre Guide to Comic Books, Manga, and More.* This guide is geared to librarians who serve adult and teen readers. However, younger readers read graphic novels, too. Where is the genre guide that can help children find the graphic novels they will enjoy? *Graphic Novels for Young Readers* seeks to fill that gap.

Purpose and Audience

This guide focuses on graphic novels for children ages four to fourteen. It covers over 600 titles for young readers, from preschoolers through eighth graders, spanning close to forty years of graphic novels published for younger audiences.

The book is designed specifically for librarians in school and public libraries who serve young readers, as well as teachers who work with these age groups. Finding good books to pair up with readers can be a daunting task; this book seeks to make that task easier. In addition, it is hoped that this guide will dispel the idea that graphic novels are nothing more than basic escapist fantasy, fit only for bookstores and bedrooms.

Granted, the graphic novel has come a long way, but the stigma still lies in wait for the unsuspecting librarian who may not be "up" on what is "good reading." Although graphic novels for younger audiences were originally born out of the needs of an untapped market, its creators quickly cast off the shackles of profiteering and focused on writing great stories for interested audiences.

Scope, Methodology, and Selection Criteria

Titles annotated in this guide were chosen for their ease of access, target audience, content (age appropriateness), and educational factors. Selections were based on personal experience, suggestions from target audiences, reviews from associations and businesses that deal with graphic novels, and sometimes even the authors and artists themselves.

The focus is on titles published in the last decade, with older titles still popular with young readers included as well.

I have made every attempt to provide balanced and thorough coverage for the designated age range, with the most reliable information possible—any errors found within the text are mine.

Organization and Features

Like other books in the Genreflecting series, entries in this book are arranged by major genre, and then by popular subgenres and themes. Keep in mind that these are books aimed at younger readers, the majority of whom are not looking for the minutia that differentiate one <u>Batman</u> series from another. Also, with younger readers there is not as much contention about a series being in one genre or another (as it can be the case among older readers), and the final decision about which chapter they were to go into was mine.

Entries are organized alphabetically by title. Those that can fit into more than one genre are cross-referenced in the appropriate genres. Series titles are boldfaced and underscored and include an introductory annotation followed by an indented list of individual titles in alphabetical order, also annotated. Individual, freestanding titles are listed separately, are not indented, and are also annotated. Bibliographic information provided for all entries includes title, author and illustrator names, publisher, date, number of pages, and ISBNs. Suggested reading levels are indicated at the end of the bibliographic entry using the following icons:

GR. PK-2	Grades PreK–2	**GR. 2-7**	Grades 2–7
GR. PK-5	Grades PreK–5	**GR. 2-8**	Grades 2–8
GR. K-2	Grades K–2	**GR. 3-5**	Grades 3-5
GR. K-3	Grades K–3	**GR. 3-7**	Grades 3-7
GR. K-4	Grades K–4	**GR. 3-8**	Grades 3-8
GR. K-5	Grades K–5	**GR. 4-6**	Grades 4-6
GR. K-8	Grades K–8	**GR. 4-7**	Grades 4-7
GR. 1-7	Grades 1-7	**GR. 4-8**	Grades 4-8
GR. 1-8	Grades 1–8	**GR. 5-8**	Grades 5-8
GR. 2-4	Grades 2–4	**GR. 6-8**	Grades 6-8
GR. 2-5	Grades 2–5	**GR. 7-8**	Grades 7-8
GR. 2-6	Grades 2–6		

For those titles that have received awards, this symbol appears at the beginning of the entry   , and the award is named at the end of the annotation.

The organization of this book allows the user to find "similar" titles to those that young readers enjoy—simply find the book the young reader likes and look for the titles listed near it. It also helps librarians make selections for their children's collections—from completing series to developing a more balanced graphic novel collection for young readers.

This book is by no means a complete guide to the genre. As with any printed book, by the time the manuscript has returned from the printer, some of the information is outdated, and many more titles have come out. Keeping up on graphic novels can challenge even the most avid readers.

One of the best ways to keep up on current titles is to speak with local comic book shop owners. They usually have the most up-to-date information available. If you live in an area without a shop, Diamond Comics (the preeminent distributor of comics in the United States) maintains a Web site (http://www.previewsworld.com) that previews all new titles coming out, along with other "fanboy" (an industry term that has multiple meanings; use with caution!) information that patrons may be interested in. If you're not sure whether there is a retailer in your area, you can always consult http://www.comicshoplocator.com to find the nearest seller of comic books and graphic novels.

Because graphic novels are so popular with today's young readers, it is vital that librarians and educators become acquainted with the genre. This book attempts to lay the groundwork for such an acquaintance. Ultimately, it seeks to connect young readers with the books they will enjoy.

Notes

1. The History of Comic Books, available at http://www.inventors.about.com/od/csartinventions/a/comics.htm (accessed October 4, 2010); Scott McCloud, Understanding Comics: The Invisible Art (New York: HarperCollins, 1994), 17.

2. Japanese Manga: Its Expression and Popularity, available at http://www.accu.or.jp/appreb/09/pdf34-1/34-1P003-005.pdf (accessed October 4, 2010).

3. U.S. Census Bureau, Information Sector Services—Estimated Revenue 2000–2002, available at http://census.gov/prod/2004pubs/04statab/infocomm.pdf (accessed October 12, 2010); cbgxtra.com, "2002 Order Estimates for Diamond Comic Distributors, available at http://cbgxtra.com/cbgs-2002-order-estimates-for-diamond-comic-distributors (accessed October 12, 2010).

4. ICv2 Confab Reports 2007 Graphic Novel Sales Rise 12%, available at http://www.publishersweekly.com/pw/by-topic/1-legacy/24-comic-book-reviews/article/8185-icv2-confab-reports-2007-graphic-novel-sales-rise-12-.html (accessed October 4, 2010)

Chapter 1

Action and Adventure

Fists flying and kicks being thrown, superheroes, people, and all kinds of other creatures racing around in all manner of vehicles using weapons on each other—these are hallmarks of the action and adventure genre. Though the titles listed in this collection may not be as intense or violent as their counterparts for older readers, they still can get the pulse racing and create the urge to pile up the pillows on the floor and start diving off the bed. However, action and adventure stories are not exclusive to the cape and cowl set; in fact, in graphic novels the heroes of action and adventure titles are just as often nonhuman as they are traditional heroes.

Superheroes

Ever since the mid-1940s, when Superman appeared on newsstands, there has been a long-standing demand for stories about superheroes. Over the years these superheroes have come and gone, taken turns as good guys and bad, been killed off and resurrected time and again. Superheroes are quite often a young reader's first introduction to graphic novels.

Since Alan Moore's *Watchmen* in the mid-1980s, superheroes have undergone a sort of metamorphosis, resulting in some darker, albeit deeper, heroes who may not always be a shining example of decency. From Batman's turn toward a darker and grittier feel, to the feral monstrousness of the *X-Men*'s Wolverine, comic characters have a definite edge to them that may cause most parents to think twice before letting their kids loose at the comic book store.

The titles in this section have been limited to those that are kid friendly. Therefore, many titles are collections of early stories first published during the "Comics Code Era" that helped create the 1960s camp classic *Batman* with Adam West.

Even though this chapter is limited to "safer" titles, there is still a large showing of entries that will grab the interest of even the most reluctant readers.

The Adventures of Daniel Boom aka Loud Boy: Vol 1. Sound Off! **Written by D. J. Steinberg. Illustrated by Brian Smith. Grosset & Dunlap, 2008. 96pp. ISBN-10: 0-4484469-8-7. ISBN-13: 978-04484469-8-1. GR. 3-5**

> Almost ten years old, Daniel was born without an "indoor voice." In fact, his voice is strong enough to shatter glass. When he goes to a new school, he meets several other kids with other "social issues" (throwing tantrums, fidgeting, etc.) that turn out to be superpowers!

Avengers and Power Pack Assemble! **Written by Marc Sumerak. Illustrated by Gurihiru. Marvel Comics, 2006. 96pp. ISBN-10: 0-7851215-5-2. ISBN-13: 978-07851215-5-8. GR. 3-8**

> The Power Pack joins forces with Earth's Mightiest Heroes in this fun-filled romp.

BATMAN

Originally created as a more human counterpart to Superman, Batman is one of the most iconic characters in the world. Billionaire playboy Bruce Wayne saw his parents gunned down as a young boy, and that experience made him travel the world, turning his mind and body into a nearly superhuman tool to combat criminals.

Much darker in theme than Superman, Batman has and seems to continue to captivate male readers of all ages, but stories for younger readers are more difficult to come by. Evil and often psycho villains like the Joker, Killer Croc, Poison Ivy, and Two-Face make the Batman stories particularly violent and disturbing. Often if a reader is not interested in Superman, you can hook him or her with Batman.

What follows is a list of known kid-friendly titles in the <u>Batman</u> series.

Batman: War on Crime. **Written by Paul Dini and Alex Ross. Illustrated by Alex Ross. Dc Comics. 1999. 64pp. ISBN-10: 1-5638957-6-5. ISBN-13: 978-15638957-6-0. GR. 5-8**

> Batman faces the challenge of attempting to save a child from following the same obsessed path that he himself once went down, while his alter ego, Bruce Wayne, must decide how to invest in a neighborhood that could have much more far-reaching implications than the Dark Knight could ever imagine.
>
> **Parental Advisory:** gun violence

Batman Adventures.

> The <u>Batman Adventures</u> was created to tie in with the then-new *Batman: The Animated Series*. Drawn in the same style as the television show, the books followed the same story lines that appeared in the animated series. The stories created for the animated series follow their own story line and may run counter to the traditional DC canon.

Batman: Arctic Attack. Written by Robert Greenberger. Illustrated by Jason Kruse. Stone Arch Books, 2010. 56pp. ISBN-10: 1-4342156-1-X. ISBN-13: 978-14342156-1-1. **GR. 3-6**

> When Robin discovers that the polar ice caps are melting and it's not due to global warming, he and Batman must travel to the Arctic to fight Ras-Al-Ghul.

Batman: Mad Love. Written by Paul Dini. Illustrated by Bruce Timm. DC Kids, 1995. 63pp. ISBN-10: 1-5638924-4-8. ISBN-13: 978-15638924-4-8. **GR. 3-8**

> The Joker and Harley Quinn are up to something, and it's up to Batman to stop them before tragedy strikes. One of the more popular Batman books for younger readers.

The Batman Adventures. Written by Kelley Puckett and Martin Pasko. Illustrated by Ty Templeton. DC Kids, 1993. 144pp. ISBN-10: 1-5638909-8-4. ISBN-13: 978-15638909-8-7. **GR. 2-6**

> The original animated series on the Kids WB! network gets a comic book treatment. These stories are self-contained and don't attempt to make any changes to the Batman canon. They are direct adaptations of the Emmy Award–winning series produced by Warner Brothers Animation.

Batman Adventures: Dangerous Dames and Demons. Written by Paul Dini. Illustrated by Bruce Timm. DC Kids, 2003. 192pp. ISBN-10: 1-5638997-3-6. ISBN-13: 978-15638997-3-7. **GR. 4-8**

> More animated adventures are collected from the original cartoon series. This book also collects and reveals the history of "Harley Quinn," the Joker's former psychiatrist and new girlfriend/sidekick. Also included are two *Batman Adventures Annuals*, and the *Batman Adventures Holiday Special*.

Batman Adventures Vol. 1: Rogues' Gallery. Written by Ty Templeton, Dan Slott, and Scott Peterson. Illustrated by Rick Burchett, Ty Templeton, Tim Levins, and Terry Beatty. DC Kids, 2004. 112pp. ISBN-10: 1-4012032-9-9. ISBN-13: 978-14012032-9-0. **GR. 2-7**

> The animated series *Batman Adventures* gets print treatment in this kid-friendly format. Also available in a "learn to read Spanish" format from Berlitz. Contains the stories "No Asylum," "Free Man," "My Boyfriend's Back," and "Need to Know."

Batman Adventures Vol. 2: Shadows & Masks. Written by Ty Templeton, Dan Slott, and Scott Peterson. Illustrated by Rick Burchett, Ty Templeton, Tim Levins, and Terry Beatty. DC Kids, 2004. 112pp. ISBN-10: 1-4012033-0-2. ISBN-13: 978-14012033-0-6. **GR. 2-7**

> The continuing adventures of the Dark Knight in a kid-friendly format, with age-appropriate stories: more action, less atmosphere,

and easier to understand story lines. Also available from Berlitz in a "learn to read Spanish format." Stories include "Shot to the Heart," "Liar, Liar," "Playing with Matches," "Two Minute Warning," and "A Bat in the House."

Batman Beyond. Written by Hilary J. Bader. Illustrated by Joe Staton, Rick Burchett, and Terry Beatty. DC Kids, 2000. 144pp. ISBN-10: 1-5638960-4-4. ISBN-13: 978-15638960-4-0. **GR. 2-5**

> *Batman Beyond* sends the series into the future approximately thirty to forty years. Bruce Wayne is long retired, and Gotham has begun to fall into a steep decline—so a new Batman takes up the mantle, under the guidance of Bruce Wayne. This is the only graphic novel of the failed cartoon series aimed at a younger audience. The series never was able to get its footing, but it did produce an interesting story or two.

The Batman Strikes! **GR. 3-6**

Yet another graphic novel tie-in to an animated series, The Batman Strikes! parallels the story lines of the animated series *The Batman,* which was designed as a stand-alone series that does not follow any established story lines from the DC universe, movies, or previous animated shows. Although the graphic novels have not won any awards, the television series won two Emmys and an Annie (the International Animated Film Association).

The Batman Strikes! Vol. 1: Crime Time. Written by Bill Matheny. Illustrated by Christopher Jones and Terry Beatty. DC Kids, 2005. 104pp. ISBN-10: 1-4012050-9-7. ISBN-13: 978-14012050-9-7.

> The latest kid-friendly version of Batman is collected here from the Cartoon Network. All the characters have been updated, with probably the Joker getting the biggest makeover. Follows the story lines of the Cartoon Network series *The Batman!*

The Batman Strikes! Vol. 2: In Darkest Knight. Written by Matthew K. Manning. Illustrated by Bill Matheny. DC Kids, 2005. 104pp. ISBN-10: 1-4012051-0-0. ISBN-13: 978-14012051-0-2.

> More stories from the Cartoon Network series. Batman defends Gotham City from villains such as Catwoman, Mr. Freeze, Firefly, the Joker, and Man-Bat.

The Batman Strikes! Vol. 3: Duty Calls. Written by Bill Matheny and J. Torres. Illustrated by Christopher Jones and Terry Beatty. DC Kids, 2007. 144pp. ISBN-10: 1-4012154-8-3. ISBN-13: 978-14012154-8-4.

> The last stories from the Cartoon Network series. The Batman again protects Gotham City from a who's who of his famous foes: the Joker, the Penguin, Bane, Catwoman, Clayface, and the Riddler, among others. However, the Batman has a new partner on the force, Detective Yin.

Billy Blaster. `GR. 1-5`

Billy Blaster is the nine-and-a-half year old hero of Zone City. In addition to protecting the city, Billy is an inventor and student. Joined by his friends Wu Hoo, the Ninja Wizard, and Rika, the Japanese Super-Heroine, Billy must defend the universe from all sorts of bad guys.

The Billy Blaster series has a handy glossary at the back for words used in the book, as well as writing prompts and discussion questions.

Billy Blaster: Attack of the Rock Men. Written by David Orme. Illustrated by Peter Richardson. Stone Arch Books, 2009. 40pp. ISBN-10: 1-4342127-3-4. ISBN-13: 978-14342127-3-3.

> Billy Blaster has joined the newest gaming craze: Rock Men! When kids start showing up brainwashed, it's up to Billy to stop the dangerous man behind this plot.

Billy Blaster: Ice Caves of Pluto. Written by David Orme. Illustrated by Peter Richardson. Stone Arch Books, 2009. 40pp. ISBN-10: 1-4342127-5-0. ISBN-13: 978-14342127-5-7.

> Traveling to Pluto with Wu Hoo, Billy discovers his alien friends frozen stiff in their ship! Can Billy free them and then get everyone out again?

Billy Blaster: Mind Thief. Written by David Orme. Illustrated by Peter Richardson. Stone Arch Books, 2009. 40pp. ISBN-10: 1-4342127-6-9. ISBN-13: 978-14342127-6-4.

> A nefarious wizard is stealing minds, and Billy must work fast to stop him. His problems are compounded after the wizard kidnaps Wu Hoo.

Billy Blaster: Mutants from the Deep. Written by David Orme. Illustrated by Peter Richardson. Stone Arch Books, 2009. 40pp. ISBN-10: 1-4342126-9-6. ISBN-13: 978-14342126-9-6.

> Toxic waste is being dumped into the ocean by evil sailors, and their acts are creating monsters! Can Billy stop the pollution and the giant mutant jellyfish, or will they steal all of the town's candy?

Billy Blaster: Red Wolf. Written by David Orme. Illustrated by Peter Richardson. Stone Arch Books, 2009. 40pp. ISBN-10: 1-4342126-7-X. ISBN-13: 978-14342126-7-2.

> Billy's Friend Wu Hoo visits Zone City for a wizard convention, but the wizards are acting strange. Could the evil Red Wolf be behind it?

Billy Blaster: The Frozen Men of Mars. Written by David Orme. Illustrated by Peter Richardson. Stone Arch Books, 2009. 40pp. ISBN-10: 1-4342127-2-6. ISBN-13: 978-14342127-2-6.

> On a trip to Mars, Billy and Wu discover three scientists who have been frozen for centuries. Will they be thawed out in time to save Earth?

Billy Blaster: The Lost City. Written by David Orme. Illustrated by Peter Richardson. Stone Arch Books, 2009. 40pp. ISBN-10: 1-4342126-8-8. ISBN-13: 978-14342126-8-9.

> People in Zone City are disappearing! Does a man from the Middle Ages named Arthur have something to do with it?

Billy Blaster: Time Warriors. Written by David Orme. Illustrated by Peter Richardson. Stone Arch Books, 2009. 40pp. ISBN-10: 1-4342127-1-8. ISBN-13: 978-14342127-1-9.

> Billy and Wu face off against Taro, an ancient scientist who is stealing weapons from the future. The two travel back to stop Taro, but will they be able to return to their own time?

Billy Blaster: Water Pirates from Outer Space. Written by David Orme. Illustrated by Peter Richardson. 40pp. Stone Arch Books, 2009. ISBN-10: ISBN-13: 978-14342126-7-2.

> Earth's oceans and lakes are shrinking, and it's up to Billy Blaster to find out where the water is going, and who, or what, is taking it.

BuzzBoy. `GR. 4-8`

A superhero's sidekick who never grew up, Buzzboy now watches too much TV, feasts on junk food, and is possibly Earth's only hope. Teaming up with a young sorceress who has a penchant for sarcasm and a reformed mad scientist who quit being evil to focus on baking; Buzzboy and his unlikely group of heroes must now face off against other unlikely villains.

Buzzboy: Trouble in Paradise. Written and illustrated by John Gallagher. Sky Dog Press, 2002. 144pp. ISBN-10: 0-9721831-0-8. ISBN-13: 978-09721831-0-9.

> A new antihero for a new generation, Buzzboy must face his former mentor, Lord Ultra, over the fate of the world.

Buzzboy 2: Monsters, Dreams & Milkshakes. Written and illustrated by John Gallagher. Sky Dog Press, 2004. 144 pp. ISBN-10: 0-9721831-1-6. ISBN-13: 978-09721831-1-6.

> In this second installment, the diner-dwelling hero faces off against such threats as all-star wrestling aliens from Mars, nightmare ghouls inhabiting dreamland, and—horror of horrors—his biggest challenge yet: true love!

Go Girl! `GR. 3-6`

> Once upon a time, Janet Goldman was the flying superhero Go-Go Girl. As time often does, Go-Go Girl eventually hung up her costume and settled down to a more pedestrian life, including raising a daughter. Lindsay, Janet's daughter inherited Janet's flying ability. This series is hailed as a must read for girls. (Lulu Award)

Go Girl! Written by Trina Robbins. Illustrated by Anne Timmons. Dark Horse Comics, 2002. 88pp. ISBN-10: 1-5697179-8-2. ISBN-13: 978-1567179-8-1.

> Lindsay is the daughter of the once-famous superhero Go-Go Girl and has started following in her mother's footsteps. Now she's fighting crime and righting wrongs, with some occasional help from her mom.

Go Girl! Vol. 2: The Time Team. Written by Trina Robbins. Illustrated by Anne Timmons. Dark Horse Comics, 2004. 96pp. ISBN-10: 1-5930723-0-9. ISBN-13: 978-15930723-0-8.

> Doc, the school genius, has created a time machine out of an exercise bike. Thanks to Heather the Cheerleader, Doc, Lindsay (aka Go Girl!), and Heather are now trying to outrun T. rexes and alien spaceships.

Go Girl! Vol. 3: Robots Gone Wild! Written by Trina Robbins. Illustrated by Anne Timmons. Dark Horse Comics, 2006. 184pp. ISBN-10: 1-5930740-9-3. ISBN-13: 978-15930740-9-8.

> Go Girl faces off against realistic video game monsters and a robot that looks just like her but has the mind of a master criminal. Go Girl!'s sidekick takes up sleuthing by herself in a small side story.

Invincible. GR. 5-8

> High school senior Mark Grayson is just like every other kid his age: he has a part-time job, has a hard time understanding girls, and sleeps late on Saturdays. His dad, Omni-Man, just happens to be the most powerful superhero on Earth. How can he hope to live up to the standards his dad has set? (Later books in the series cover more adult situations.)

Invincible Vol. 1: Family Matters. Written by Robert Kirkman. Illustrated by Cory Walker. Image Comics, 2003. 120pp. ISBN-10: 1-5824032-0-1. ISBN-13: 978-15824032-0-5.

> What would you do if your father was the most powerful superhero on Earth? What if you had all the problems of being a normal teenager on top of that? Girl problems and part-time jobs are going to pale in comparison to what is next for Mark: his own superpowers!

Invincible Vol. 2: Eight Is Enough. Written and illustrated by Robert Kirkman. Image Comics, 2004. 128pp. ISBN-10: 1-5824034-7-3. ISBN-13: 978-15824034-7-2.

> Mark thought he had it tough being the son of the Earth's most powerful superhero, but now, in addition to planning for college, he has to face off against aliens, girlfriends, and robot zombies. He also has to figure out who killed the preeminent superhero group, The Guardians of the Globe.

JUSTICE LEAGUE

First appearing in the 1960s, the Justice League is a group of DC superheroes who work together to protect Earth from villains. The original characters were Superman, Batman, Wonder Woman, Flash, Green Lantern, Aquaman, and the Martian Manhunter. Over the years the ranks have swelled or deflated by superheroes coming and going as writers see fit. Several incarnations have been spun off from the original concept, including America, Europe, International, Task Force, Elite, and Extreme Justice.

The Saturday morning television staple *Justice Friends* (1973–1986), which ran for thirteen years, was based on the Justice League, as was the animated TV series *Justice League* (2001–2004), which was then built into *Justice League Unlimited* (2004–2006). All have proven how popular this series is.

Justice League Adventures. GR. 2-7

A print version of the popular Cartoon Network series that ran for several seasons, Justice League Adventures collects selected episodes and presents them in an easy-to-read format especially aimed at younger or reluctant readers.

Justice League Adventures Vol. 1: The Magnificent Seven. Written by Various. Illustrated by Various. DC Kids, 2004. 112pp. ISBN-10: 1-4012017-9-2. ISBN-13: 978-14012017-9-1.

Batman, Superman, Green Lantern, Wonder Woman, and the rest of the Justice League have their abilities and skills tested as they rescue a small African nation from a cabal of superpowered criminals, prevent Chronos from destroying the space–time continuum, and protect the world from a quartet of space-traveling freedom fighters.

Justice League Adventures Vol. 2: Friends and Foes. Written by Various. Illustrated by Various. DC Kids, 2004. 112pp. ISBN-10: 1-4012018-0-6. ISBN-13: 978-14012018-0-7.

More stories from the television show. The Justice League continues its adventures, this time recruiting a young suburban girl as its newest member; take on the villainy of the emotion-controlling Psycho-Pirate; and search for a traitor who has managed to infiltrate its own ranks.

Justice League Unlimited series. GR. 2-7

After DC and Cartoon Network wrapped the first series of *The Justice League,* they decided to expand and introduce other DC superheroes along with the original "founders," who now work from a suborbital station monitoring events on Earth. The subsequent television series was spun off into a graphic novel series as well.

Justice League Unlimited: Heroes. Written by Adam Beechen, Mike McAvennie, and Bill Williams. Illustrated by Carlo Barberi, Rick Burchett, Leigh Gallagher, and Sandford Green. DC Kids, 2009. 144pp. ISBN-10: 1-4012220-2-1. ISBN-13: 978-14012220-2-4.

> Another seven stories from the television series. Now monitoring Earth from its orbital headquarters, the Justice League faces off against attacks from aliens, sorcerers, supervillains, and any other threat that might arise.

Justice League Unlimited: The Ties That Bind. Written by Adam Beechen and Paul Storrie. Illustrated by Carlo Baberi, Rick Burchett, Leigh Gallagher, and Sandford Green. DC Kids, 2008. 144pp. ISBN-10: 1-4012169-1-9. ISBN-13: 978-14012169-1-7.

> The Justice League faces off against various baddies in outer space, the Old West, and at Christmas!

Justice League Unlimited Vol. 1: United They Stand. Written by Adam Beechen. Illustrated by Carlo Barbieri, Walden Wong, and Ethen Beavers. DC Kids, 2005. 104pp. ISBN-10: 1-4012051-2-7. ISBN-13: 978-14012051-2-6.

> This book marks the shift from the original seven characters to the full complement of DC heroes. The expanded group now faces off against those who threaten Earth, in the stories "Divide & Conquer," "Poker Face," "Small Time," "Local Hero," and "Monitor Duty."

Justice League Unlimited Vol. 2: World's Greatest Heroes. Written by Adam Beechen. Illustrated by Carlo Barbieri, Walden Wong, and Ethen Beavers. DC Kids, 2006. 104pp. ISBN-10: 1-4012101-4-7. ISBN-13: 978-14012101-4-4.

> The Justice League encounters the Oldest Green Lantern, journey to deep space to face off against Darkseid, and end up in Camelot to face off against Morgaine Le Fay.

Justice League Unlimited Vol. 3: Champions of Justice. Written by Adam Beechen. Illustrated by Carlo Barbieri, Walden Wong, and Ethen Beavers. DC Kids, 2006. 104pp. ISBN-10: 1-4012101-5-5. ISBN-13: 978-14012101-5-1.

> Two Flashes face off against the Mirror Master, while Red Tornado faces a crisis. The JLA also goes on a journey into Limbo with Deadman.

Magic Pickle. **Written and illustrated by Scott Morse. Graphix Nooks, 2008. 112pp. ISBN-10: 0-4398799-5-7. ISBN-13: 978-04398799-5-8.** `GR. 2-6`

> He's small, he's green, and he's pickled! Weapon Kosher, aka the Magic Pickle, has been in suspended animation for several decades. Imagine his surprise (and Jojo Wigman's chagrin) when he bursts through her bedroom

floor. See Magic Pickle fight evil produce! See Jojo try and explain to her friends a flying pickle! Wince at bad puns!

Marvels. **Written by Kurt Busiek. Illustrated by Alex Ross. Marvel Comics, 2008. 248pp. ISBN-10: 0-7851278-4-4. ISBN-13: 978-07851278-4-0.** `GR. 5-8`

Check out thirty-five years of Marvel superheroes and villains through the camera lens of Phil Sheldon, a newspaper photographer who has witnessed the major battles throughout the years. A must read for the die-hard fanboys and those new to comics as well. (Harvey Award)

Other Editions

Marvels (UK Edition). **Panini (UK) Ltd., 2008. 216pp. ISBN-10: 1-9052399-7-1. ISBN-13: 978-19052399-7-9.**

> The British edition of the original story.

Marvels. **Written by Kurt Busiek. Illustrated by Alex Ross. Marvel Comics, 2010. 248p. ISBN-10: 0-7851428-6-X. ISBN-13: 978-07851428-6-7.**

> A new edition for a new generation. The latest edition contains tons of extras, including much of Busiek's early work, a new story, pages from Ross's sketchbooks, and a guide to the many cameos placed throughout the story.

Marvels 10th Anniversary Hard Cover. **Marvel Comics, 2004. 400pp. ISBN-10: 0-7851138-8-6. ISBN-13: 978-07851138-8-1.**

> Follow a worm's-eye view of the Marvel universe over thirty-five years as told through the photographic lens of Phil Sheldon, a newspaper photographer who has experienced "the Marvels"—superheroes from the Marvel Universe—from the ground level. It also includes interviews with the author and illustrator, a cover gallery, and other extras.

Mo and Jo, Fighting Together Forever. **Written by Jay Lynch. Illustrated by Dean Haspiel. Toon Books 2008. 40pp. ISBN-13: 978-0-9799238-5-2. ISBN-10: 09799238-5-9.** `GR. K-2`

A brother and sister (Mo and Jo) constantly fight with each other, so when a superhero gives them his costume (full of superpowers), they fight so much about it that it tears in half! Now only half as strong, can they work together to defeat the villains?

New Mutants Vol. 1: Back to School. **Written by Nunzio Defilippis and Christina Weir. Illustrated by Keron Grant. Marvel Comics, 2005. 152pp. ISBN-10: 0-7851124-2-1. ISBN-13: 978-07851124-2-6.** `GR. 4-8`

Once known as the X-Men in training, the New Mutants are asked to come back to Professor Xavier's School for Gifted Children to teach a new crop of students. What will the "New Mutants" do when they're considered the "Old Mutants?"

Note: A second story arc was written following the continuing exploits of the New Mutants, but has yet to be collected into book format. The series was then scrubbed for a reset of the entire Marvel Universe.

Power Pack: Day One. **Written by Fred Van Lente. Illustrated by Gurihiru and Colleen Coover. Marvel Comics, 2008. 104pp. ISBN-10: 0-7851300-7-1. ISBN-13: 978-07851300-7-9.** `GR. 4-8`

Alex, Julie, Jack, and Katie Power are four regular kids, on a regular day, experiencing regular kid things. In twenty-four hours, everything that they know and are familiar with will change, from alien abduction to dealing with super powers. The Power kids will never be the same again!

Sidekicks: The Transfer Student. **Written by J. Torres. Illustrated by Takeshi Miyazawa. Oni Press, 2002. 96pp. ISBN-10: 1-9299984-0-6. ISBN-13: 978-19299984-0-1.** `GR. 4-8`

Terry Highland's dad was a super hero sidekick, and now she's showing the same powers. Unfortunately, at her new school, the Shuster Academy, you're not allowed to use your powers, or you'll be expelled! What is she going to do when three ruffians by the names of "Biff," "Bam," and "Pow" show up and want to stir up trouble?

SPIDER-MAN

One of the most recognizable superheroes, Spider-Man has been a fan favorite since his debut in the mid-1960s. In fact, according to the book *Spider-Man the Icon* by Steve Saffel, his popularity was such that when he first appeared in the last issue of the failing comic book series <u>Amazing Fantasy</u>, Spider-Man became so popular, he was given his own series.

Something about Spider-Man makes him extremely appealing. Unlike other superheroes, he wasn't born to it; his family wasn't murdered, spurring him into becoming a stalker of the night; and he definitely did not come from another planet. When he started out, he was just a geeky high school kid who was only noticed by bullies.

When you think about it, it's amazing what one radioactive spider can do. Instead of dying of venom poisoning, Peter Parker developed incredible skills that mimicked a spider. He soon found he could climb walls, shoot webbing, and lift three to four times his own weight. Well, what kid wouldn't love to have these abilities?

Over the years Peter Parker has undergone a lot of changes, including an entire series reset in the early 2000s, completely rewriting his early years. The series listed here deals with the "New" Spider-Man.

Ultimate Spider-Man series. `GR. 4-8`

In 2000 Marvel finished up its "housecleaning" story line about the evil supermutant called Onslaught. In the course of the series, the human heroes of the Marvel Universe "sacrificed" themselves by stepping into a rift in the universe. This move allowed Marvel to reset the story lines of several brands. As of this writing, Marvel is drawing the Ultimate line to a close, but the series has taken on an extremely dark, non-kid-friendly tone.

Ultimate Spider-Man: Ultimate Collection Vol. 1. Written by Brian Michael Bendis. Illustrated by Mark Bagley. Marvel Comics, 2007. 352pp. ISBN-10:0-7851249-2-6. ISBN-13: 978-07851249-2-4.

This volume follows Spider-Man from getting his powers and graduating from high school, to facing off against the Green Goblin and even the Kingpin. This massive edition collects the entire first year of the revamped Ultimate Spider-Man series.

Ultimate Spider-Man: Ultimate Collection Vol. 2. Written by Brian Michael Bendis. Illustrated by Mark Bagley. Marvel Comics, 2009. 344pp. ISBN-10: 0-7851288-6-7. ISBN-13: 978-07851288-6-1.

Follow Spider-Man's exploits through his second year. The Green Goblin has returned and knows who Spider-Man really is. Will Peter go along with the psychopath to save the two most important people in his life, Mary Jane and Aunt May?

SUPERMAN

The most recognizable and venerable superhero in the world, Superman is known to most American kids from a young age. From his creation in the 1930s by writer Jerry Siegel and illustrator Joe Shuster to the current conglomeration of artists and writers who work on several different titles under the *Superman* franchise, the Man of Steel has been through a lot of changes in his lifetime.

Originally from the doomed planet of Krypton, Kal-El was placed inside a ship set to take off right before the planet was destroyed. The ship crash-landed in the farmland of Kansas, where the young child was found by a poor but forthright farmer and his wife. The child is renamed Clark and raised by the Kents as their only son. Clark eventually grows up and moves to Metropolis, where he lives two lives: his "fake" life, that of the mild-mannered reporter, Clark Kent, and his real-life persona, Superman.

Over the years Superman has faced madmen, monsters, and invaders from outer space, as well as other super heroes. He has also married his true love, Lois Lane, and has been killed—once.

In September 2009 DC redefined Superman with the release of *Superman: Secret Origins*. As of this writing, the canon is defined by <u>Superman: The Man of Steel</u>, and *Superman: Birthright*.

The sampling of titles that follows gives an extremely brief overview of Superman's exploits, specifically chosen for younger audiences.

<u>Superman: The Man of Steel.</u> `GR. 4-8`

Following the housecleaning of the DC Universe with the *Crisis on Infinite Earths* story line that allowed DC to remove a lot of useless or pointless characters from its books, it was decided that Superman needed to be redefined for a new generation of readers. <u>The Man of Steel</u> series effectively rebooted the series, starting out with Superman's origins and powers, as well as redefining Superman's archnemesis, Lex Luthor, his love interest, Lois Lane, and his alter ego, Clark Kent.

Superman: The Man of Steel Vol. 1. Written by John Byrne. Illustrated by John Byrne and Dick Giordano. DC Comics, 1991. 152pp. ISBN-10: 0-9302892-8-5. ISBN-13: 978-09302892-8-7.

This book collects the original six-issue miniseries that redefined Superman for a new generation. Starting with the destruction of his home world, Superman deals with the hazards of being a superhero, meeting people of a similar bent (Batman), and the discovering the joys of having an archnemesis (Lex Luthor).

Superman: The Man of Steel Vol. 2. Written by John Byrne and Marv Wolfman. Illustrated by John Byrne and Jerry Ordway. DC Comics, 2003. 224pp. ISBN-10: 1-4012000-5-2. ISBN-13: 978-14012000-5-3.

This marks the start of monthly story lines from <u>The Man of Steel</u> books. In this volume, Superman faces off against Metallo and discovers his weakness. Superman also teams up with the Teen Titans for a stint, and Lex Luthor's insane humor is featured.

Superman: The Man of Steel Vol. 3. Written by John Byrne and Marv Wolfman. Illustrated by John Byrne and Jerry Ordway. DC Comics, 2004. 208pp. ISBN-10: 1-4012024-6-2. ISBN-13: 978-14012024-6-0.

Superman faces off against a psychotic 'Nam veteran who can materialize his weapons out of thin air and a mummy, Morgaine Le Fay (with the help of the Demon Etrigan); he finally teams up with Hawkman to repel an alien invasion.

Superman: Bizarro Is Born! **Written by Louise Simonson. Illustrated by Erik Doescher. Stone Arch Books, 2010. 56pp. ISBN-10: 1-4342156-7-9. ISBN-13: 978-14342156-7-3.** `GR. 2-6`

Lex Luthor has cloned Superman, but something has gone wrong. The new Superman looks weird, and he's got some bizarre ideas about Truth, Justice, and the American way.

Superman: Peace on Earth. **Written by Paul Dini and Alex Ross. Illustrated by Alex Ross. DC Comics, 1998. ISBN-10: 1-5638946-4-5. ISBN-13: 978-15648946-4-0.** `GR. 4-8`

Superman faces his most difficult opponent since Doomsday: Hunger on a global scale. Unfortunately, he quickly discovers that some problems are not nearly as easy to solve as others. Can the Man of Steel feed the world without causing international strife?

Teen Titans Go! `GR. 2-7`

Another popular franchise from DC Comics gets the "kid treatment." Originally started as a television series on the Cartoon Network, *Teen Titans* assembled a group of five teens from different backgrounds (an alien, a cyborg, a sorceress from a different dimension, a shape-shifting mutant, and a vigilante's sidekick) to fight crime. An incredibly popular series, especially with younger boys, Teen Titans Go! brings the animation style of the television series to the printed page, collecting both television episodes and original content that showcases these pubescent heroes and their dangerous, deadly, and decidedly wacky villains.

Teen Titans Go!: Titans Together! Written by J. Torres. Illustrated by Todd Nauck and Lary Stucker. DC Kids, 2007. 144pp. ISBN-10: 1-4012156-3-7. ISBN-13: 978-14012156-3-7.

The Titans face a weapon that causes transmutations, scary books, Robin's archenemy Slade, Red X, switched up superpowers, and a Secret Santa program.

Teen Titans Go! Vol. 1: Truth, Justice, Pizza! Written by J. Torres. Illustrated by Todd Nauck, Tim Smith, and Lary Stucker. DC Kids, 2004. 112pp. ISBN-10: 1-4012033-3-7. ISBN-13: 978-14012033-3-7.

The Titans face off against members of The Hive, Beast Boy discovers it's not a good idea to cry wolf, Cyborg questions his leadership abilities, Raven develops the zit from heck, and Starfire enlists Cyborg and Beast Boy to get Robin to take her out for Valentine's Day.

Teen Titans Go! Vol. 2: Heroes on Patrol. Written by J. Torres and Adam Beechen. Illustrated by Todd Nauck, Udon Studios, and Lary Stucker. DC Kids, 2004. 112pp. ISBN-10: 1-4012033-4-5. ISBN-13: 978-14012033-4-4.

A couple of provisional members are fighting, and it's up to the Titans to sort it all out. Then Starfire's evil sister shows up with a challenge for her sister.

In another story, the wicked half-stack Gizmo has some new toys to try out on the Titans, while Aqualad continually prevents them from stopping a sea monster. This volume also has the "infamous" "Naked City" story line, in which implied nudity occurs toward the end of the story.

Teen Titans Go! Vol. 3: Bring It On! Written by J. Torres. Illustrated by Todd Nauck and Lary Stucker. DC Kids, 2005. 104pp. ISBN-10: 1-4012051-1-9. ISBN-13: 978-14012051-1-9.

Terra, another provisional character, is "captured" by Robin's nemesis, Slade, and then Mumbo, the magical malefactor uses his tricks to distract the Titans while he runs amuck. On Halloween, Beast Boy has to look after a Mr. Wolf, who has a strange affliction under the full moon. Later, Speedy and the Titans face off against Plasmus, who has managed to get into toxic sludge again. Finally, a new villain has kidnapped The Killer Moth's daughter Kitten, and it's up to Robin to save her, regardless of whether he wants to or not.

Teen Titans Go! Vol. 4: Ready for Action! Written by J. Torres. Illustrated by Todd Nauck and Lary Stucker. DC Kids, 2005. 104pp. ISBN-10: 1-4012051-1-9. ISBN-13: 978-14012051-1-9.

Starfire befriends a lost child at the mall, only to discover he is more than what he appears. Titan associate Hot Spot deals with anger management. Cyborg faces off against an old opponent, concert goers become zombies, and it's attack of the chibis (Japanese for small person, in this case with small bodies and oversized heads!

Tiny Titans. `GR. PK-2`

A delightful spin-off of Teen Titans that is aimed at younger audiences who may not be ready for the full rough and tumble of the regular series. (Eisner Award)

Tiny Titans Vol. 1: Welcome to the Treehouse. Written by Art Baltazar and Franco. Illustrated by Art Baltazar. DC Comics, 2009. 144pp. ISBN-10: 1-4012207-8-9. ISBN-13: 978-14012207-8-5.

The Teen Titans are reimagined as toddlers in this funky new series aimed at younger readers. See what kind of troubles the "Tot Titans" can get into at Sidekick Elementary.

Tiny Titans Vol. 2: Adventures in Awesomeness. Written by Art Baltazar and Franco. Illustrated by Art Baltazar. DC Comics, 2009. 144pp. ISBN-10: 1-4012232-8-1. ISBN-13: 978-14012232-8-1.

The adventures of the "Tot Titans" continue in this second book, which looks at the Titans as small kids living life at Sidekick Elementary.

Tiger Moth. `GR. 1-5`

An interesting take on the traditional superhero finds Tiger Moth, a martial arts warrior, and his friends fighting evil insects in the streets and classrooms of their buggy world. An anthropomorphic insect with a blue costume and red wings, Tiger Moth acts like a slacker, but when there is danger around, he is no slouch.

Tiger Moth: Insect Ninja. Written by Aaron Reynolds. Illustrated by Erik Lervold. Stone Arch Books, 2007. 40pp. ISBN-10: 1-5988905-7-3. ISBN-13: 978-15988905-7-0.

> Tiger Moth, a young superhero skilled in martial arts, is tasked with finding a missing painting.

Tiger Moth: Kung Pow Chicken. Written by Aaron Reynolds. Illustrated by Erik Lervold. Stone Arch Books, 2008. 40pp. ISBN-10: 1-4342-045-5-3. ISBN-13: 978-14342045-5-4.

> Tiger Moth has been captured! It's now up to Kung Pow and his little sister, Amber, to save Tiger moth.

Tiger Moth: The Dragon Kite Contest. Written by Aaron Reynolds. Illustrated by Erik Lervold. Stone Arch Books, 2007. ISBN-10: 1-5988905-6-5. ISBN-13: 978-15988905-6-3.

> To celebrate the Chinese New Year, the local community holds a kite-flying contest, but when the Fruit Fly Boys try to cheat, it's up to Tiger Moth to stop them.

Tiger Moth: The Dung Beetle Bandits. Written by Aaron Reynolds. Illustrated by Erik Lervold. Stone Arch Books, 2007. 40pp. ISBN-10: 1-5988931-7-3. ISBN-13: 978-15988931-7-5.

> Did Stinky McCree beetle-nap a bunch of Dung beetles? Tiger Moth is on the case!

Tiger Moth: The Fortune Cookies of Weevil. Written by Aaron Reynolds. Illustrated by Erik Lervold. Stone Arch Books, 2007. 40pp. ISBN-10: 1 -5988931-8-1. ISBN-13: 978-15988931-8-2.

> Strange messages are appearing in fortune cookies, and it's up to Tiger Moth and his gang to figure out why.

Tiger Moth: The Pest Show on Earth. Written by Aaron Reynolds. Illustrated by Erik Lervold. Stone Arch Books, 2008. 40pp. ISBN-10: 1-4342045-4-5. ISBN-13: 978-14342045-4-7.

> Tiger Moth and Kung Pow decide to take a break and check out the new carnival in town. Can they derail this evil funfest before having to face off against the mastermind behind the trouble under the big top, Wing Kong?

Wonder Woman: The Spirit of Truth. **Written by Paul Dini and Alex Ross. Illustrated by Alex Ross. DC Comics, 2001. 64pp. ISBN-10: 1-5638986-1-6. ISBN-13: 978-15638986-1-7.** `GR. 4-8`

Stepping away from the traditional "rock'em-sock'em" format of Wonder Woman, Dini and Ross chose to study Wonder Woman and how the rest of the world perceives her. A good story for girls about how it's not important what you wear, but what you do.

Zinc Alloy.

Zach Allen loves nothing more than reading comic books, and his greatest wish is to be like his favorite superheroes. It seems unlikely that will happen—until one day he discovers instructions on how to build a high-tech robot suit. Now that he has a giant robot, will he use it for good, or will he get revenge on all those bullies?

Zinc Alloy: Coldfinger. Written by Donald Lemke. Illustrated by Douglas Holgate. Stone Arch Books, 2010. 40pp. ISBN-10: 1-4342158-6-5. ISBN-13: 978-14342158-6-4. `GR. 2-5`

Zack and his family are on winter vacation in the mountains, but Johnny the bully tricks Zack into entering the ski contest. On top of that, an evil villain is building a giant freeze ray! Can Zack defeat the villain *and* win the trophy?

Zinc Alloy: Revealed! Written by Donald Lemke. Illustrated by Douglas Holgate. Stone Arch Books, 2009. 40pp. ISBN-10: 1-4342076-3-3. ISBN-13: 978-14342076-3-0. `GR. 1-5`

Zack Allen has revealed that he is actually the superhero Zinc Alloy, and now he's the coolest kid at school! But what happens when he takes off the suit?

Zinc Alloy: Super Zero. Written by Donald Lemke. Illustrated by Douglas Holgate. Stone Arch Books, 2009. 40pp. ISBN-10: 1-4342076-2-5. ISBN-13: 978-14342076-2-3. `GR. 1-5`

Zach Allen has to decide whether or not to do the right thing: Will he get revenge on the bullies, or will he become Zinc Alloy?

Zinc Alloy vs. Frankenstein. Written by Donald Lemke. Illustrated by Douglas Holgate. Stone Arch Books, 2009. 40pp. ISBN-10: 1-4342118-8-6. ISBN-13: 978-14342118-8-0. `GR. 1-5`

After a good deed goes bad, Zinc is chased out of town by an angry mob. Hiding out in an abandoned house on the edge of town, Zach faces his toughest challenge yet, a robotic Frankenstein.

Traditional Adventure

Though similar in overall theme to the superhero genre, the heroic adventure can be distinguished by the type of characters. Where a superhero story features a larger than life character who is often costumed and possesses superhuman abilities, protagonists in heroic adventures are (mostly) normal people (usually children or teens in these stories) who happen to fall into fantastic situations. CrossGen's Sephie from Meridian is probably the closest to crossing over into superhero territory with her special abilities, but other characters like Alex Rider are basically normal people who have extraordinary adventures without fantastic powers.

Titles in this section have become quite popular with young readers who prefer their action with a little more realism and fewer campy sound effects.

Alex Rider. GR. 4-8

Alex Rider, a fourteen-year-old orphan, has just discovered that his uncle (and guardian) has died in a suspicious car accident. After investigating, Alex discovers that his uncle worked for MI6—the British equivalent of the CIA—and they now want him to pick up where his uncle left off. This series originally manifested in traditional book form and film. The graphic novel series is based more on the movie scripts than the book, but it's still a thrill a minute.

Alex Rider: Point Blank. Written by Anthony Horowitz and Antony Johnson. Illustrated by Kanao Damerum and Yuzuru Takasaki. Philomel, 2007. 144pp. ISBN-10: 0-3992502-6-3. ISBN-13: 978-03992502-6-2.

> In the second Alex Rider graphic novel adaptation of the children's series, Alex is sent to a private school in Switzerland to investigate the school's headmaster.

Alex Rider: Skeleton Key. Written by Anthony Horowitz and Antony Johnson. Illustrated by Kanao Damerum and Yuzuru Takasaki. Walker Books Ltd., 2009. 176pp. ISBN-10: 1-4063134-8-3. ISBN-13: 978-14063134-8-2.

> After Alex runs afoul of a Chinese triad gang, he flees to an island near Cuba. Unfortunately for Alex, an insane Russian General has plans to rewrite history, explosively! This edition is only available in Europe at this time.

Alex Rider: StormBreaker. Written by Anthony Horowitz and Antony Johnson. Illustrated by Kanao Damerum and Yuzuru Takasaki. Philomel, 2006. 144pp. ISBN-10: 0-3992463-3-9. ISBN-13: 978-03992463-3-3.

> Alex discovers that his dead uncle was a super spy, and now he must undertake the mission that killed his uncle.

Alison Dare: Little Miss Adventures. **Written by J. Torres. Illustrated by J. Bone. Oni Press, 2008. 96pp. ISBN-13: 978-14352748-6-0. ISBN-10: 1-4352748-6-5.**

> Allison Dare, the daughter of an archaeologist/adventurer (and the masked hero "Blue Scarab"), along with her friends, ends up having adventures that rival those of her parents.

Asterix. `GR. 2-8`

Originally begun in France in 1959, Asterix has long been a popular character in European culture. Though not as well known here in America, the series is kid-friendly, with minor adult-themed mischief occasionally interspersed throughout the stories.

The series is set in a fictional province of Gaul (what became modern France) in the year 50 BC. The Roman Empire has conquered the majority of Gaul except for one little holdout costal village. The reason for this is that the Gauls who live in that village can temporarily gain superhuman strength by drinking a magic potion manufactured by the village druid.

The series focuses on the title character, Asterix, and his friends Obelix, the permanently superhuman, and Asterix's dog, Dogmatix, and the adventures they have thwarting the Roman Empire. The total series has close to thirty-five titles, as well as several movies, and video games (most have only been released in Europe).

Asterix and the Golden Sickle. Written by Rene Goscinny. Illustrated by Albert Uderzo. Orion, 2004. 48pp. ISBN-10: 0-7528661-3-3. ISBN-13: 978-07528661-3-0.

After Getafix breaks his golden sickle, Asterix and Obelix offer to get the druid a new one. However, the sicklesmith, a cousin of Obelix, has vanished. Can Asterix find the smith and get Getafix a new sickle?

Asterix the Gaul. Written by Rene Goscinny. Illustrated by Albert Uderzo. Orion, 2004. 48pp. ISBN-10: 0-7528660-5-2. ISBN-13: 978-07528660-5-5.

When Getafix, the village druid, is kidnapped by the Roman Centurion, Crismus Bonus, Asterix must figure out a way to free his friend.

Avatar: The Last Airbender.

Started as a cartoon series on Nickelodeon in 2005, *Avatar* took youth viewing audiences by storm. In a world where clans are divided by fighting styles that emulate the elements, only Aang, the last airbender, can become The Avatar—the only person who can master all four elements. Aang is saved by a brother and sister duo of waterbenders, Katara and Sokka. Now, with the entire Fire Nation bearing down on them, can the waterbenders help Aang learn the three other nations' fighting styles to prevent the Fire Nation from conquering the world? In amazing Cine-manga!

Though the television series has earned many awards and nominations, the book series has not been nominated for any awards.

Avatar Vol. 1. Written by Bryan Kanietzko and Michael Dante Dimartino. TokyoPop, 2006. 96pp. ISBN-10: 1-5954289-1-2. ISBN-13: 978-15953289-1-5. **GR. 3-7**

> Katara and Sokka have found a kid around their age who bears the mark of the Airbender tribe, who haven't been seen for close to 100 years. Could Aang be the Avatar?

Avatar Vol. 2. Written by Bryan Kanietzko and Michael Dante Dimartino. TokyoPop, 2006. 96pp. ISBN-10: 1-5053289-2-0. ISBN-13: 978-15953289-2-2. **GR. 3-7**

> Aang finally comes to terms with the fact that he is the Avatar and sets out with Katara, Sokka, and his flying bison Appa to find a master waterbender. Meanwhile, Zuko of the Fire Nation continues to dog Aang's steps.

Avatar Vol. 3. Written by Bryan Kanietzko and Michael Dante Dimartino. TokyoPop, 2006. 96pp. ISBN-10: 1-5981675-7-X. ISBN-13: 978-15981675-7-3. **GR. 3-7**

> Aang takes Sokka and Katara to the Air Temple where he was raised, but everyone he knew is either dead or 100 years old! Even though his old life is over, the temple reveals some secrets to being the Avatar, and Aang's purpose is redoubled.

Avatar Vol. 4. Written by Bryan Kanietzko and Michael Dante Dimartino. TokyoPop, 2007. 96pp. ISBN-10: 1-5981692-8-9. ISBN-13: 978-15981602-8-7. **GR. 3-7**

> Aang becomes a celebrity when he lands on the island of Kyoshi. While Katara and Sokka try and get Aang's head out of the clouds, Zuko and the Fire Nation attack. Will a new warrior woman be the answer?

Avatar Vol. 5. Written by Bryan Kanietzko and Michael Dante Dimartino. TokyoPop, 2007. 104pp. ISBN-10: 1-59811692-9-7. ISBN-13: 978-15981692-9-4. **GR. 3-7**

> Aang, Sokka, and Katara arrive in the city of Omashu, but soon end up on the wrong side of the law. In return for their freedom, the insane king subjects Aang to a grueling series of tests, and in the process, Aang remembers an old Earthbending friend.

Avatar Vol. 6. Written by Bryan Kanietzko and Michael Dante Dimartino. TokyoPop, 2007. 96pp. ISBN-10: 1-5981693-0-0. ISBN-13: 978-15981693-0-0. **GR. 3-7**

> Infiltrating an Earth Kingdom mining town, Aang discovers it is controlled by the Fire Nation. Meeting a young boy with a powerful secret, Aang and Haru join forces, only to be captured and imprisoned. Will Aang be able to save the world?

Avatar Vol. 7. Written by Bryan Kanietzko and Michael Dante Dimartino. TokyoPop, 2008. 96pp. ISBN-10: 1-4278114-3-1. ISBN-13: 978-14278114-3-1. **GR. 3-7**

> After a village is attacked by a monster from the spirit world, Aang's skills are put to the test. When Aang fails to defeat the monster, Sokka is pulled

into the spirit world. Can Sokka figure out how to bring peace to the village and get back to the real world?

Avatar Vol. 8. Written by Bryan Kanietzko and Michael Dante Dimartino. TokyoPop, 2008. 96pp. ISBN-10: 1-4278114-4-X. ISBN-13: 978-14278114-4-8. **GR. 2-7**

Aang must find the last Avatar who has something to tell him, but Roku is in the temple of the Fire Nation. With Prince Zuko and Admiral Zhao closing in, will Aang succeed?

Buzz Beaker.

Buzz Beaker is the smartest kid in his school, possibly even the world! He constantly invents silly new gadgets to solve problems (sometimes problems that he created himself).

Each book in the <u>Buzz Beaker</u> series has a glossary of terms, writing prompts, and discussion points. A great title series for reading groups and classrooms, and can also be used as teaching aids.

Attack of the Mutant Lunch Lady: A Buzz Beaker Brainstorm. Written by Scott Nickel. Illustrated by Andy J. Smith. Stone Arch Books, 2008. 20pp. ISBN-10: 1-4342050-1-0. ISBN-13: 978-14342050-1-8. **GR. 2-4**

What's the only thing grosser than cafeteria food? How about a mutated lunch lady? Can Buzz and his buddy Larry stop the Cafeteria Creature?

Backyard Bug Battle: A Buzz Beaker Brainstorm. Written by Scott Nickel. Illustrated by Andy J. Smith. Stone Arch Books, 2006. 40pp. ISBN-10: 1-5988922-4-X. ISBN-13: 978-15988922-4-6. **GR. 2-4**

Buzz was playing with his Dad's super fast grow juice, and now he has to deal with gigantic insects and flowers!

Billions of Bats: A Buzz Beaker Brainstorm. Written by Scott Nickel. Illustrated by Andy J. Smith. Stone Arch Books, 2007. 40pp. ISBN-10: 1-5988940-8-0. ISBN-13: 978-15988940-8-0. **GR. 2-4**

Sarah Bellum's invention, the "cosmic copier," has backfired and made thousands of copies of her pet bat, Bobo. Now Buzz and Sarah have to work together to save the day.

Buzz Beaker vs. Dracula: A Buzz Beaker Brainstorm. Written by Scott Nickel. Illustrated by Andy J. Smith. Stone Arch Books, 2009. 40pp. ISBN-10: 1-4342119-1-6. ISBN-13: 978-14342119-1-0. **GR. 1-5**

Dracula has lived for ages, but what he really wants to do is hit the beach. To catch some waves, he captures the wiz kid, Buzz Beaker, and it's up to Buzz to turn this Vampire King into the King of the Beach. If he fails, he's Dracula's lunch!

Robot Rampage: A Buzz Beaker Brainstorm. Written by Scott Nickel. Illustrated by Andy J. Smith. Stone Arch Books, 2007. 40pp. ISBN-10: 1-5988905-5-7. ISBN-13: 978-15988905-5-6. **GR. 1-5**

> When the weird transfer student Elron's science fair robot goes crazy, Buzz has to figure out a way to prevent the robotic menace from destroying the town.

Crogan's Vengeance. **Written and illustrated by Chris Schweizer. Oni Press, 2008. 189pp. ISBN-10: 1-9349640-6-9. ISBN-13: 978-193-49640-6-4. GR. 6-8**

> *Crogan's Vengeance,* the first book in a series that promises to run approximately sixteen books, travels down the Crogan family tree. It focuses on "Catfoot" Crogan, an honest seafarer on a ship captained by a man who has it in for "Catfoot." When their ship is captured by pirates, "Catfoot" falls in easily with his new shipmates.
>
> **Parental Advisory:** violence

Cupcakes of Doom! A Collection of **YARG!** *Piratey Comics.* **Written and illustrated by Ray Friessen. Dont Eat Any Bugs Productions, 2009. 100pp. ISBN-10: 0-98023114-1-8. ISBN-13: 978-09802314-1-0. GR. 3-8**

> Those Heroic-ish pirates from *Yarg! and Other Stories* are back, in their own book. This time the pirates face off against some Lousy Vikings to decide the fate of a kingdom. Only one group can be the bearded, giant-hat-wearing masters of the sea. To top it all off, the battle, in this extremely silly story, is decided through . . . BAKED GOODS!

Into the Volcano. **Written and illustrated by Don Wood. Blue Sky Press, 2008. 176pp. ISBN-10: 0-4397267-1-9. ISBN-13: 978-04397267-1-9. GR. 5-8**

> Annotated in chapter 6.

Lost: A Tale of Survival. **Written by Chris Kreie. Illustrated by Marcus Smith. Stone Arch Books, 2008. 88pp. ISBN-10: 1-5988982-8-0. ISBN-13: 978-15988982-8-6. GR. 3-8**

> Annotated in chapter 6.

Mail Order Ninja. **Written by Joshua Elder and Erich Owen. Illustrated by Joshua Elder. TokyoPop, 2006. 96pp. ISBN-10: 1-5981672-8-6. ISBN-13: 978-15981672-8-3. GR. 1-8**

> Poor Timothy, he's having a difficult time with bullies at his school. Not only is he constantly getting hassled by these bullies, he also has to deal with Felicity Dominique Huffington, the local "stuck-up rich girl." However, things quickly change after Timothy enters "the greatest ninja warrior gunshyo giveaway" and wins his own personal ninja. After his parents agree to Timothy keeping the ninja, even though they say that it's a "bad idea," things really get interesting.

Meridian. `GR. 4-8`

One of the flagship titles of the now defunct CrossGen Comics, <u>Meridian</u> is the tale of an innocent young girl, the daughter of the Minister of the floating land of Meridian, who is suddenly thrown into the harsh realities of life after her father is murdered. Imbued with a strange sigil (a ying-yang type of symbol that was used extensively throughout the CrossGen Universe to mark heroes and villains) and a supernatural ability to create, she is kidnapped; now she must journey home to face her evil uncle, who has a similar sigil and the power and hunger to destroy and dominate.

Note: CrossGen Comics filed for bankruptcy in 2003 and was officially declared defunct in 2004. As of this printing, <u>Meridian</u> remains unfinished.

Meridian Vol. 1: Flying Solo. Written by Barbara Kesel. Illustrated by Steve McNiven and Joshua Middleton. CrossGen Comics, 2002. 192pp. ISBN-10: 1-9314840-3-1. ISBN-13: 978-19314840-3-9.

> Sephie, the only child of the Minister of Meridian, is on the run from her evil Uncle Ilahn, who has killed his brother and looks to take over the floating island. Will Sephie and her mysterious new powers be able to combat her wicked uncle, who just so happens to have amazing new powers as well?

Meridian Vol. 2: Going to Ground. Written by Barbara Kesel. Illustrated by Steve McNiven. CrossGen Comics, 2002. 208pp. ISBN-10: 1-9314840-9-0. ISBN-13: 978-19314840-9-1.

> Sephie has been kidnapped and taken to the world of Calador, and now she has to try to find her way home to confront her uncle. Joined by friends who will fight with her to the end, Sephie learns that love is not the only thing in the world.

Meridian Vol. 3: Taking the Skies. Written by Barbara Kesel. Illustrated by Steve McNiven. CrossGen, 2002. 260pp. ISBN-10: 1-9314842-1-X. ISBN-13: 978-19314842-1-3.

> Sephie and her crew take up arms against Ilahn as pirates, intent on plundering his ships in an effort to break his control of the trade routes and to find a way back onto Meridian.

Recon Academy. `GR. 3-8`

Four teens witnessed terror strike their town when they were young kids. Growing up, they developed unique abilities: forensics, martial arts, computers, and gadgetry. In high school, they meet and form the youngest secret security team on Earth. They are known as the Recon Academy!

Recon Academy: Nuclear Distraction. Written by Chris Everheart. Illustrated by Arcana Studio. Stone Arch Books, 2009. 64pp. ISBN-10: 1-4342116-7-3. ISBN-13: 978-143442116-7-5.

> Hazmat, the team's forensics expert, loses his match at a karate tournament, but wins his first date. However, his date may be permanently interrupted if the team can't stop Shadow Cell from creating a nuclear meltdown!

Recon Academy: Prep Squadron. Written by Chris Everheart. Illustrated by Arcana Studio. Stone Arch Books, 2009. 64pp. ISBN-10: 1-4342116-8-1. ISBN-13: 978-14342116-8-2.

> Jay is getting tired of constantly drilling with the team; the same thing over and over again is getting old. But when Shadow Cell infiltrates the City's naval base, he must make a decision: work with the team, or leave Recon Academy?

Recon Academy: Shadow Cell Scam. Written by Chris Everheart. Illustrated by Arcana Studio. Stone Arch Books, 2009. 64pp. ISBN-10: 1-4342116-6-5. ISBN-13: 978-14342116-6-8.

> The navy needs help with security while they launch a new satellite, but the Recon Academy is too distracted by their new laptops, which they received for free. But when something is too good to be true, the consequences can be disastrous!

Recon Academy: The Hidden Face of Fren-Z. Written by Chris Everheart. Illustrated by Arcana Studio. Stone Arch Books, 2009. 64pp. ISBN-10: 1-4342116-5-7. ISBN-13: 978-14342116-5-1.

> The Federal Reserve Bank has been hacked, and it's up to the Recon Academy to stop the thief. It's up to Ryker, the computer whiz, and the rest of the gang to bust the bad guy and discover who Fren-Z really is.

Tintin.

Originally debuting in a Belgian newspaper in 1929, *The Adventures of Tintin* quickly became a favorite of both children and adults for more than eighty years. The main character, Tintin, is a young Belgian reporter, and he and his fox terrier, Snowy, are constantly getting involved in all sorts of mysteries and adventures. Quite often they are joined by Tintin's closest friend, Captain Archibald, who, though depicted as an alcoholic, has a true heart of gold and slowly becomes respectable in later stories.

Even though the series was originally created in the 1920s, the painstakingly detailed backgrounds and locations, along with the writing, give the series a timeless feel that transcends the ages. The alcoholic Captain Haddock is generally played for comedic relief (usually with the Captain suffering some traumatic impact that either spills his alcohol or injures him).

Parental Advisory: action sequences; alcohol consumption; racial stereotypes

Tintin Adventures Vol. 1. Written and illustrated by Hergé. Methuen, 1993. 196pp. ISBN-10: 0-4161485-2-2. ISBN-13: 978-04161485-2-7. **GR. 3-8**

> Three full-length stories in one book: *Tintin in America, Cigars of the Pharaoh,* and *The Blue Lotus.* In *Tintin in America,* Tintin and Snowy travel to America during the Capone era, meet cowboys and Indians, and manage to solve another mystery. In *Cigars of the Pharaoh,* Tintin and Snowy clash with a gang of smugglers while trying to find the lost tomb of the Pharaoh Kih-Oskh. Drawing on actual historical events (current events at the time), Tintin and Snowy travel to Shanghai amid the Japanese incursion of 1931 in *The Blue Lotus.*

Tintin Adventures Vol. 2. Written and illustrated by Hergé. Little, Brown Young Readers, 1994. 192pp. ISBN-10: 0-3163594-2-4. ISBN-13: 978-03163594-2-9. **GR. 2-8**

> The second collection of full-color adventures includes the stories "The Broken Ear," "The Black Island," and "King Ottokar's Sceptre." In "The Broken Ear," after an Indian fetish is stolen, Tintin must go to South America amid revolution. In "The Black Island," Tintin, Snowy, and the Thomsons must figure out the secret of a cursed castle that no one has ever returned from. Finally, in "King Ottokar's Sceptre," Tintin, Snowy, and Professor Alembick travel to Syldavia to witness the coronation of the king. After the scepter is stolen, it's up to Tintin to recover it and keep the king on his throne.

Tintin Adventures Vol. 3. Written and illustrated by Hergé. Little, Brown Young Readers, 2007. 192pp. ISBN-10: 0-3163594-4-0. ISBN-13: 978-03163594-4-3. **GR. 2-8**

> Collects the stories "The Crab with the Golden Claws" (first appearance of Captain Haddock), "The Shooting Star," and "The Secret of the *Unicorn.*" In the first story, Tintin and Snowy end up on the trail of opium smugglers, but when Tintin is kidnapped, a friendly captain assists in his escape. "The Shooting Star" finds Tintin, Snowy, and Captain Haddock traveling to the arctic in an attempt to recover a meteorite that came to Earth. In "The Secret of the *Unicorn,*" Tintin and Captain Haddock try to discover the secret of a pirate ship, the *Unicorn,* and its lost treasure. "The Secret of the Unicorn" is being made into a movie that will be out in 2011.

Boxed Sets

The Adventures of Tintin: Collector's Gift Set. **Written and illustrated by Hergé. Little, Brown Young Readers, 2008. n.p. ISBN-10: 0-3160066-8-8. ISBN-13: 978-03160066-8-2.** GR. 2-8

> Tintin, his faithful dog Snowy, Captain Haddock, and all the others are collected in this gift set detailing many of their most famous adventures. Longtime fans as well as those new to the series readers will enjoy this collection.

Usagi Yojimbo. GR. 4-8

Originally intended as a semibiographical story of the Edo Age swordsman Miyamoto Musashi, Usagi Yojimbo tells the tale of Miyamoto Usagi, an anthropomorphic rabbit ronin (Japanese swordsman) on a warrior's pilgrimage. Occasionally Usagi sells his services as a bodyguard. Started in 1984, the series has been through three different publishers and (as a creator-owned title) Usagi has been included in many different books. Although Sakai sets his stories in Japan, I hesitate to call it manga because it is written and illustrated in Western-style formats. The stories draw heavily on Japanese history, folklore, and mythical creatures, as well as highlighting elements of Japanese arts and crafts. Due to the incredible efforts with these features, the series was awarded a "Parents' Choice Award" in 1990 for its educational value. (Harvey Award)

Though the art may seem cartoonish, the stories often are serious in tone, so younger readers may get bored.

Usagi Yojimbo Vol. 1: The Ronin. Written and illustrated by Stan Sakai. Fantagraphics Books, 1987. 144pp. ISBN-10: 0-9301933-5-0. ISBN-13: 978-09301933-5-5.

> Miyamoto Usagi, a wandering samurai in seventeenth-century Japan, chooses to travel across a land ravaged by civil war. During his travels he meets cats, snakes, ninja moles, and other anthropomorphic creatures.

Usagi Yojimbo Vol. 2: Samurai. Written and illustrated by Stan Sakai. Fantagraphics Books, 2002. 152pp. ISBN-10: 0-9301938-8-1. ISBN-13: 978-09301938-8-1.

> This book fills in much of Usagi's backstory, on how he first became a samurai and eventually fell to the status of ronin (a swordsman without a master).

Usagi Yojimbo Vol. 3: The Wander's Road. Written and illustrated by Stan Sakai. Fantagraphics Books, 1989. 152pp. ISBN-10: 1-5609700-9-X. ISBN-13: 978-15609700-9-5.

> More tales of the ronin rabbit, making friends with a small dinosaur, pairing up with a sometime adversary, and facing off against Leonardo from *Teenage Mutant Ninja Turtles*!

Usagi Yojimbo Vol. 4: the Dragon Bellow Conspiracy. Written and illustrated by Stan Sakai. Fantagraphics Books, 1998. 180pp. ISBN-10: 1-5609706-3-4. ISBN-13: 978-15609706-3-7.

> The first time Sakai runs a massive story arc covering an entire book (up till this point, it has been short stories and vignettes).

Yikes, It's a Yeti! **Written by Karen Wallace. Illustrated by Mick Reid. Stone Arch Books, 2008. 72pp. ISBN-10: 1-4342045-9-6. ISBN-13: 978-14342045-9-2.** `GR. 2-6`

> Annotated in chapter 6.

Nate's Picks

- <u>Magic Pickle</u> by Scott Morse. This series is an absolute hoot, extremely well written with horribly bad puns that come nonstop. Morse has written more books in this series, but as far as I know they are all straight prose.

- <u>Teen Titans</u> by Various. A good introduction to the superhero series, without getting too dark or high and mighty.

- <u>Buzz Beaker Series</u> by Scott Nickel and Andy J. Smith. Short, quick books that explore basic science principles in a way that most kids won't realize they learn from. In addition, like most Stone Arch Books, it has writing prompts, discussion questions, and glossaries of words used in the book.

- <u>Usagi Yojimbo</u> by Stan Sakai. A historically accurate book that has morphed into a series of excellent and entertaining books. Also listed as a Parent's Choice Award winner.

Chapter 2

Manga

Over the past fifteen years or so, a foreign invasion has taken the American reading populace by storm. Japanese comics (manga) have been around since the mid 1950s, but they did not take off as a trend in America until the late 1980s. With its use of overexaggerated facial features, strange plot devices, and Japanese cultural conventions, manga has attracted a huge audience in America, especially among young readers.

Manga dominates publishing in Japan; thousands of books are published each month, and the animated form (anime) accounts for approximately three out of every four shows on television. In fact, manga is so predominant that in 2009 its market share in Japan was approximately $2.12 billion U.S., while American manga consumption sat at $140 million U.S.[1] At first blush, that may not seem like a whole lot, until you take into consideration that *total* comic book sales for 2009 were $310 million U.S., accounting for a good 35 percent of all graphic novel sales that year.[2] Manga has also taken root here in America, a logical offshoot of the animated cartoons of Japan (anime). Though still not as popular as conventional comic books, manga has a dedicated and vociferous following of readers. And although many Japanese story lines can be a little difficult to comprehend, most kids quickly and eagerly adapt to the situations presented. In addition, a large percentage of these stories have been adapted from anime series and/or have been adapted into video games, further increasing their popularity.

Several of the most popular series in the world are listed first in this section, so be sure to acquaint yourself with these titles. Not only are the stories engaging, but kids can usually tell immediately if you know what you're talking about. One of the most noticeable features that differentiates Japanese comics from American comics is the format of the book. Where Western-style comics read left to right, Japanese books read from right to left. In the early days of manga translation, publishers would reverse (flip) the book to read in a more traditional Western format. Many purists claim that flipping the image runs counter to the writer's or artist's original intention. (For example, if a character's shirt has writing or an asymmetrical image on it, when it gets flipped, the image is mirrored and looks incorrect.) Flipping can also cause a reader to lose interest in a book, by distracting from the story and causing the reader to focus on the incorrect image instead of the story.

Manga does not limit itself to traditional Western themes. Whereas superheroes, biography, and humor tend to reign supreme with Western audiences, every facet of life is fair game for Japanese audiences, and manga readership is not limited to children or socially awkward teenagers. People from all walks of life read manga, and series are often collected into phonebook-sized "dailies" that are read as avidly as newspapers.

The genres of kodomo, shōnen, and shōjo are the most common forms for children. Kodomo is usually a nonepisodic story that serves as a sort of moral or ethical guide to proper behavior. Shōnen and shōjo manga; boy and girl comics, respectively, are some of the most popular styles in the world.

As a final word of warning, manga is not usually created by authors and illustrators who are familiar with Western societal norms. Therefore, it is prudent to review manga titles before suggesting them to readers, because violence, sexuality, and nudity are more prevalent than in Western-style graphic novels.

Shōnen

By far one of the most popular genres of manga in the world, shōnen (literally translated as "few years") is aimed at boys. Generally focused around action/fighting, shōnen manga often contains a sense of humor and strong growing friendship bonds between the characters. Rarely, if ever, is the main character a female, and team setups or tight-knit gangs are prevalent; female characters may play bit parts, and their features may be exaggerated (especially for attractive characters), but this is not a requirement for shōnen.

The titles listed below are some of the most popular currently in circulation, but no book can cover every title out there. Also, there are some titles in other chapters that use manga, but fit more into that specific genre. Where applicable, I have listed the location of the full annotation.

Angelic Layer.

Misaki Suzuhara just moved in with her aunt in Tokyo. Starting the seventh grade, Misaki becomes enamored of a game called "Angelic Layer," in which the "Deus" (players) battle custom-made fighting dolls called "angels." Although Misaki has never played "Angelic Layer," she discovers that she's a natural and quickly climbs up through the ranks of fighters.

Fully annotated in chapter 3.

Astro Boy.

Meet the Japanese equivalent of America's Mickey Mouse: a jet-powered, super-strong, evil-robot-bashing, alien-invasion-smashing robot child called Astro Boy. Osamu Tezuka, said to be the Walt Disney of Japan and the creator of this series, is often credited as the "Father of Manga."

Astro Boy is a robotic boy who battles robots and aliens and tries to understand what it means to be human. All the books listed in chapter 3 are reprints from the traditional Japanese manga books.

Fully annotated in chapter 3.

Blazin' Barrels. GR. 4-8

The West was never this wild! For wannabe bounty hunter Sting, capturing the gang "Gold Romany" is his ticket to fame and fortune. The only things standing in his way? Everyone thinks he's harmless and naïve, and the gang is all girls. The reader has a really exciting adventure ahead.

Blazin' Barrels Vol. 1. Written and illustrated by Min-seo Park. TokyoPop, 2005. 176pp. ISBN-10: 1-5953255-8-1. ISBN-13: 978-15953255-8-7.

Sting may look harmless and naïve, but he's out to make a name for himself. It also helps that he's no slouch with a shotgun and can handle himself in a fight!

Blazin' Barrels Vol 2. Written and illustrated by Min-seo Park. TokyoPop, 2005. 192pp. ISBN-10: 1-5953255-9-X. ISBN-13: 978-15953255-9-4.

Sting faces off against the Lovely Scorpions, a trio of beautiful women.

DRAGON BALL

One of the most influential manga series, Dragon Ball has been a perennial favorite of young readers since it debuted in America in 1993. The series originally started in 1984 in Japan, and was completed in 1995. Dragon Ball has spawned two sequel series (Dragon Ball Z and Dragon Ball GT), and a complete anime series serializing all forty-two books has been released, as well as four animated specials, sixteen films, and a whole arsenal of video games, from the Nintendo Entertainment System through the Playstation 3 and Xbox 360. Plans are currently underway for a MMORPG (Massive Multiplayer Online Role-Playing Game). Two live-action movies have also been released (one in China, one in the United States), along with soundtracks, art books, and a slew of toys.

Dragon Ball and its sequels have been released on video and in books in both edited and uncut versions. Every attempt has been made to include the edited versions in this list.

Parental Advisory: character deaths; crude humor; general naughtiness and mayhem; intense fighting sequences (Most of this is absent from the edited versions.)

Dragon Ball. GR. 4-8

An old martial arts expert finds a monkey tailed boy and decides to raise the young boy as his own grandson. Naming the child "Goku," the old man begins to train the boy in martial arts. Soon, Goku meets Bulma, a lady in search of seven Dragon Balls; mystical spheres that when combined will summon a dragon that will grant one wish to the summoner.

During their escapades, Goku and Bulma meet many friends, fight many enemies, and get into and out of many scrapes with super human fighters. The original series ends with Goku discovering that he is not human, but is a Saiyan–extraterrestrials that destroy planets.

Dragon Ball Vol. 1. Written and illustrated by Akira Toriyama. VIZ Media LLC, 2000. 192pp. ISBN-10: 1-5693149-5-0. ISBN-13: 978-15693149-5-1.

> The book that started it all! Son Goku is a silly little monkey boy who is conned into giving up his magical dragon ball to Bulma, a pretty girl who wants to find all seven. Once all seven of the dragon balls have been found, the owner gets one wish. Lots of action and silliness ensue.

Dragon Ball Vol. 2. Written and illustrated by Akira Toriyama. VIZ Media LLC, 2003. 192pp. ISBN-10: 1-5693192-1-9. ISBN-13: 978-1563192-1-5.

> Goku and Bulma have managed to get six of the seven dragon balls, and they know who has the seventh. The only problem is that dictator Pilaf has it, and he plans on ruling the world! Find out why it's a big, hairy problem when Goku is exposed to moonlight!

Dragon Ball Vol. 3. Written and illustrated by Akira Toriyama. VIZ Media LLC, 2003. 192pp. 1-5693192-2-7. ISBN-13: 978-15693192-2-2.

> Goku decides to do some training in the martial arts with the Turtle Hermit. While undergoing a brutal training regimen, can he survive the preliminaries of the world's biggest martial arts tournament?

Dragon Ball Vol. 4. Written and illustrated by Akira Toriyama. VIZ Media LLC, 2003. 192pp. ISBN-10: 1-5693192-3-5. ISBN-13: 978-15693192-3-9.

> Goku and Kuririn manage to make it to the final eight, but how will they fare when Kuririn can't stand the smell of his opponent Bacterian, and Goku's opponent is right out of a monster movie?

Other Editions

Dragon Ball: The Complete Set. **Written and illustrated by Akira Toriyama. VIZ Media LLC, 2009. n.p. ISBN-10: 1-4215261-4-X. ISBN-13: 978-14215261-4-0.**

> Collects all sixteen books in the original <u>Dragon Ball</u> series in a handy slipcase. Follow Goku's journey from quiet little monkey boy to premiere martial arts fighter. Marvel at Goku's naiveté, be amazed at the horrible food puns, and shudder at the fearsome power that is Goku when the moon is full! This edition is highly recommended for any new manga or graphic novel collection.

Dragon Ball Vol. 1: Collector's Edition. **Written and illustrated by Akira Toriyama. VIZ Media LLC, 2008. 208pp. ISBN-10: 1-4215261-3-1. ISBN-13: 978-14215261-3-3.** `GR. 6-8`

Collects the first book in a nice hardback edition. Goku, a monkey-tailed boy, is living a quiet life until he meets a girl named Bulma, who is on a quest to collect the mystical dragon balls, magical orbs that if collected together, will summon the Great Dragon to grant the user one wish. Will Bulma be able to talk Goku into helping her find them all?

Dragon Ball Vol. 1: VIZBIG Edition. **Written and illustrated by Akira Toriyama. VIZ Media LLC, 2008. 560pp. ISBN-10: 1-4215205-9-1. ISBN-13: 978-14215205-9-9.** `GR. 4-8`

Collects the first three books of the Dragon Ball series into one volume. Meet Goku, a small boy with a monkey tale, a strange grandfather, and no memory of who he is. Big trouble ensues when he teams up with Bulma and goes off in search of the Dragon Balls–mystical spheres that will grant the user one wish if all seven are gathered together.

Dragon Ball Vol. 2: VIZBIG Edition. **Written and illustrated by Akira Toriyama. VIZ Media LLC, 2008. 531pp. ISBN-10: 1-4215206-0-5. ISBN-13: 978-14215206-0-5.** `GR. 6-8`

Collects volumes 4 through 7 of the original Dragon Ball series. Goku and Bulma continue their quest to gather the dragon balls in between battles at the World Martial Arts Tournament.

Dragon Ball Vol. 3: VIZBIG Edition. **Written and illustrated by Akira Toriyama. VIZ Media LLC, 2009. 210pp. ISBN-10: 1-4215206-1-3. ISBN-13: 978-14215206-1-2.** `GR. 6-8`

The only thing standing between the dragon balls and the Red Ribbon Army is Goku, Bulma, and Kuririn. Can the three of them find the next dragon ball when they've got gun-toting bad guys on their tails?

Dragon Ball Vol. 4: VIZBIG Edition. **Written and illustrated by Akira Toriyama. VIZ Media LLC, 2009. 568pp. ISBN-10: 1-4215206-2-1. ISBN-13: 978-14215206-2-9.** `GR. 6-8`

The next Tenka'ichi Budakai martial arts tournament is coming up, and Goku can't wait to face new opponents. Neither can Tsuru-Sen'nin, the rival of Goku's teacher. Tsuru-Sen'nin wants his disciples to kill all of his rival's disciples, and Goku is the main target!

Dragon Ball Z. `GR. 6-8`

The "sequel" to the original <u>Dragon Ball</u> series takes the series from Earth to the broader universe, after revealing that Goku is not actually a human, but a Saiyan, a mystical creature bred for combat, which turns into a giant ape monster under the light of the moon. Introducing new villains as well as locales, <u>DBZ</u> expanded fight sequences to ludicrous lengths, but firmly entrenched the series in pop culture.

Dragon Ball Z Vol. 1. Written and illustrated by Akira Toriyama. VIZ Media LLC, 2000. 184pp. ISBN-10: 1-5693149-7-7. ISBN-13: 978-15693149-7-5.

> The continuing saga of Goku. Now a bit older, he has lost the tail he had as a child. Goku's past is finally revealed when his evil brother Raditz comes to Earth and explains Goku's purpose: to destroy Earth!

Dragon Ball Z Vol. 2. Written and illustrated by Akira Toriyama. VIZ Media LLC, 2000. 184pp. ISBN-10: 1-5693149-8-5. ISBN-13: 978-15693149-8-2.

> Gohan (Goku's son) must go to the wilderness to learn to harness his alter ego. Goku, currently spending some time in the afterlife, meets the strongest martial artist ever. Will he be resurrected in time to face off against Vegeta and Nappa, two Saiyans sent to Earth to finish what Raditz started?

Dragon Ball Z Vol. 3. Written and illustrated by Akira Toriyama. VIZ Media LLC, 2001. 184pp. ISBN-10: 1-5693153-1-0. ISBN-13: 978-15693153-1-6.

> Piccolo has sacrificed himself, Kuririn is dying, and Earth's last hope is the recently resurrected Goku. Will he be strong enough to defeat two Saiyans?

Dragon Ball Z Vol. 4. Written and illustrated by Akira Toriyama. VIZ Media LLC, 2003. 192pp. ISBN-10: 1-5693193-3-2. ISBN-13: 978-15693193-3-8.

> The battle between Goku and Vegeta continues. (This book illustrates a feature that has become the major complaint about the <u>DBZ</u> series: ridiculously long fight sequences.)

Dragon Ball Z Vol. 5. Written and illustrated by Akira Toriyama. VIZ Media LLC, 2003. 192pp. ISBN-10: 1-5693193-4-0. ISBN-13: 978-15693193-4-5.

> Bulma, Gohan and Kuririn take a spaceship to the planet Namek (Piccolo's home planet) to try to find the dragon balls. Unfortunately Vegeta shows up shortly after the gang arrives, and they all have to deal with Emperor Frieza, who has already invaded.

Other Editions

Dragon Ball Z Boxed Set. **Written and illustrated by Akira Toriyama. Viz Media LLC, 2009. n.p. ISBN-10: 1-4215261-5-8. ISBN-13: 978-14215261-5-7.** `GR. 6-8`

Collects books 1–26 (17–42 of the entire series) of the Dragon Ball Z series in a handy (and large) slipcase.

Dragon Ball Z Vol. 1: Collector's Edition. **Written and illustrated by Akira Toriyama. Viz Media LLC. 176pp. ISBN-10: 1-4215261-1-5. ISBN-13: 978-14215261-1-9.** `GR. 6-8`

Hardcover reprint of the first book of Dragon Ball Z. It's been five years since Gohan defeated Piccolo, gotten married, and had a kid. Unfortunately for Gohan, his long-lost brother, Raditz, appears and reveals that Gohan is a Saiyan, and his mission is to destroy the Earth. Will Gohan join his brother, or will he join forces with his former adversary to save the world?

Dragon Ball Z Vol. 1: VIZBIG Edition. **Written and illustrated by Akira Toriyama. Viz Media LLC, 2008. 528pp. ISBN-10: 1-4215206-4-8. ISBN-13: 978-14215206-4-3.** `GR. 6-8`

In the same vein as the *Dragon Ball VIZBIG* editions, this collects the first three books of Dragon Ball Z.

Dragon Ball Z Vol. 2: VIZBIG Edition. **Written and illustrated by Akira Toriyama. Viz Media LLC, 2008. 559pp. ISBN-10: 1-4215206-5-6. ISBN-13: 978-14215206-5-0.** `GR. 6-8`

Goku faces off against Vegeta in a desperate battle to save the world. Unfortunately Vegeta is even stronger than Goku's newest battle techniques. Can Gohan, Kuririn, Yajirobe, and the power of the Genki-dama, or "spirit ball," be enough to defeat Vegeta? It better be, because Vegeta has sworn to destroy not only the human race, but the planet Earth itself!

Dragon Ball Z Vol. 3: VIZBIG Edition. **Written and illustrated by Akira Toriyama. Viz Media LLC, 2008. 210pp. ISBN-10: 1-4215206-6-4. ISBN-13: 978-14215206-6-7.** `GR. 6-8`

Gohan and Kuririn must prevent Frieza and Vegeta from getting the last dragon ball, but first they have to face off against the Ginyu Force, five of the strongest fighters in outer space, personally selected by Frieza himself.

Gon. `GR. 2-7`

This wordless series of stories revolves around a small dinosaur with a short fuse and a large heart. Gon, who appears to be a carnivorous dinosaur but is in fact omnivorous, travels around and helps protect the friendly and furry from the mean and hungry. The series was an instant hit when it debuted in Japan in the early 1990s. The volumes listed here are from the Paradox Press release, which transposed the pages to the Western style left-to-right paging. (Harvey Award)

Gon Again. Written and illustrated by Masashi Tanaka. Paradox Press, 1996. 148pp. ISBN-10: 1-5638929-7-9. ISBN-13: 978-15638929-7-4.

> The continuing adventures of the breadbox-sized dinosaur. Gon rides a shark (from the inside), is tormented by a tick, shakes up a forest, and marches with the penguins.

Gon on Safari. Written and illustrated by Masashi Tanaka. Paradox Press, 2000. 176pp. ISBN-10: 1-5638966-9-9. ISBN-13: 978-15638966-9-9.

> Gon travels to Africa, where the tiny dinosaur joins a trio of outlaw animals, braves the elements while climbing a mountain, and protects an aged elephant from predators.

Gon Swimmin. Written and illustrated by Masashi Tanaka. Paradox Press, 1997. 156pp. ISBN-10: 1-5638938-0-0. ISBN-13: 978-15638938-0-3.

> Little dinosaur Gon dons a turtle shell and learns how to swim among other adventures in this book.

Gon Vol. 1. Written and illustrated by Masashi Tanaka. Paradox Press, 1996. 148pp. ISBN-10: 1-5638929-6-0. ISBN-13: 978-15638929-6-7.

> Gon is a tiny carnosaur, a T. rex-type of dinosaur, who has managed to survive the mass extinction of the dinosaurs. Gon captures and rides a lion, builds his own house, and attempts to learn how to fly, while protecting his nestmate from a hungry bobcat. Winner of the 1997 Harvey Award for Best American Edition of Foreign Material.

Gundam Wing.

A popular genre of Japanese manga is the Giant Robot battlers, where the focus isn't so much on the technology as on the operators of the machinery. A print sequel to the popular television series by the same name, Gundam Wing follows the trials of five younger boys who pilot huge Gundam fighting machines in their battles against corrupt Earth governments.

This series gets rather dark at times, as the characters wax poetic about how horrible it is that they have to fight each other and then proceed to blow up massive ships with thousands of people on board. Manga titles tend to be rather hit or miss with American audiences, so keep that in mind when advising and don't take offense if your reader passes on this one.

Fully annotated in chapter 3.

Hikaru No Go.

Hikaru Shindo was a normal twelve-year-old until the day he decided to rummage through his grandfather's things in an attempt to find something to sell. Coming across an old "Go" board (a Chinese game akin to "Othello" or "Reversi," except the piece has to be blocked on all sides to be captured, then is removed from the play area), Hikaru is surprised when a ghostly apparition appears out of the board. The ghost, Sai Fujiwara, was a "Go" instructor to the Emperor of Japan, but was wrongly accused of cheating. In his shame he committed suicide, but somehow he became linked to the "Go" board. Now, with Hikaru's help, Sai hopes to play the perfect game of "Go," which will release him from the board forever. The only problem? Hikaru's not interested.

Fully annotated in chapter 4.

Kingdom Hearts. GR. 4-7

Based on the smash hit for the Playstation 2 gaming system, <u>Kingdom Hearts</u> follows the story of fourteen-year-old Sora and his adventures in a strange new land. After a bizarre storm hits his island home, Sora is swept into the centralized Traverse Town, where Court Wizard Donald Duck and Captain Goofy are getting ready to quest for their King, Mickey Mouse. Along the way the three friends battle strange shadow creatures called Heartless, who feed on the darkness in the hearts of others. Sora, Donald, and Goofy travel to various lands (that all conveniently resemble Disney locales), joining forces with the heroes of those lands and fighting the villains. Fans of the <u>Final Fantasy</u> franchise will recognize Sora and his friends from the island in *Final Fantasy 9*.

Kingdom Hearts Vol. 1. Written and illustrated by Shiro Amano. TokyoPop, 2005. 135pp. ISBN-10: 1-5981621-7-9. ISBN-13: 978-15981621-7-2.

This first book retells the story of the video game on which it's based. Sora meets Donald and Goofy, Sora gets his Keyblade, and they end up assisting Alice with her adventure in Wonderland.

Kingdom Hearts Vol. 2. Written and illustrated by Shiro Amano. TokyoPop, 2006. 144pp. ISBN-10: 1-5981621-8-7. ISBN-13: 978-15981621-8-9.

Sora and company continue their adventures through Disney properties, discovering more clues to Maleficent's plans to conquer all the Disney worlds.

Kingdom Hearts Vol. 3. Written and illustrated by Shiro Amano. TokyoPop, 2006. 176pp. ISBN-10: 1-5981621-9-5. ISBN-13: 978-15981621-9-6.

Sora and the crew meet Pinocchio and Geppetto, face off against Ursula the Sea Witch, hook up with Riku, and together have to save their friend Kairi from Captain Hook. All in a day's work for a boy with a keysword (literally a sword that is a key) and the power of heart.

Kingdom Hearts Vol. 4. Written and illustrated by Shiro Amano. TokyoPop, 2006. 136pp. ISBN-10: 1-5981622-0-9. ISBN-13: 978-15981622-0-2.

Sora, Goofy, and Donald are forced to make a difficult decision: duty or friendship. If they're going to defeat the Heartless menace, they're going to have to follow their hearts. Will Sora and his friends be able to rescue King Mickey, Riku, and Kairi, or will Maleficent and the other villains win?

Kingdom Hearts: Chain of Memories. GR. 4-7

Following on the heels of the first Kingdom Hearts series, Chain of Memories picks up where the first Kingdom Hearts leaves off. Follows the same basic story line as the video game of the same name.

Kingdom Hearts: Chain of Memories Vol. 1. Written and illustrated by Shiro Amano. TokyoPop, 2006. 208pp. ISBN-10: 1-5981663-7-9. ISBN-13: 978-15981663-7-8.

Sora, Goofy, and Donald join forces with Jiminy Cricket to finish what they started in Kingdom Hearts. Now the group has to rescue King Mickey and Riku from the Kingdom of Hearts.

Kingdom Hearts: Chain of Memories Vol. 2. Written and illustrated by Shiro Amano. TokyoPop, 2007. 240pp. ISBN-10: 1-5981663-8-7. ISBN-13: 978-15981663-8-5.

In the second book of this series, the gang continues its quest to save Mickey and Riku. Running out of time, Sora sees someone that looks like Kairi. Is she another lost soul, or is she part of the "Organization?"

Boxed Sets

Kingdom Hearts: Chain of Memories. **Written and illustrated by Shiro Amano. 448pp. TokyoPop, 2007. ISBN-10: 1-4278062-9-2. ISBN-13: 978-14278062-9-1.** GR. 4-7

Collects volumes 1 and 2 of the Kingdom Hearts: Chain of Memories series in an illustrated slipcase.

Kingdom Hearts II. GR. 4-7

Kingdom Hearts II picks up where Chain of Memories leaves off, except now the main character is a young boy by the name of Roxas who is trying to enjoy the last days of his summer break while experiencing mysterious dreams about a boy named Sora and strange monsters who look eerily familiar to the Heartless. As of this writing, the series is still in active production.

Kingdom Hearts II Vol. 1. Written and illustrated by Shiro Amano. TokyoPop, 2007. 208pp. ISBN-10: 1-4278005-8-8. ISBN-13: 978-14278005-8-9.

> Roxas and his friends must figure out why they're being blamed for crimes in the city of Twilight Town, and then they are attacked by strange creatures. To top it all off, they have to solve the puzzle of a strange girl named Naminé and her connection to Roxas's dreams of a boy named Sora.

Kingdom Hearts II Vol. 2. Written and illustrated by Shiro Amano. TokyoPop, 2008. 192pp. ISBN-10: 1-4278005-9-6. ISBN-13: 978-14278005-9-6.

> Naminé reveals a big surprise to Roxas, and now he must try to figure out what the true connection to Sora, his dream-self, is.

Naruto. `GR. 5-8`

Though the <u>Dragon Ball</u> series was the first major series to gain widespread attention in America, <u>Naruto</u> has taken the torch and run with it. Begun in 1999 in the pages of the Japanese magazine *Weekly Shonen Jump*, <u>Naruto</u> has become *the* biggest shonen manga in the world.

The <u>Naruto</u> franchise has produced forty-six books in Japan, thirty-five of which have been released in America, along with a successful trading card game, a television series that is still in production, several music CDs, four original video animations (kind of like the old cartoon shorts shown at the beginning of movies), five feature-length films, as well as an ongoing chapter book series using video frames from the television show.

Since the franchise shows no signs of slowing down, expect the numbers above to change quickly as more books, movies, and franchise materials are produced.

The protagonist of this series is Naruto Uzamaki. Mischievous, unruly, and constantly drawing attention to himself, Naruto is a ninja-in-training who can't pass even the most simple of tests. However, Naruto plans on becoming Hokage (defender/leader) of the hidden leaf village, even if it kills him. With the mysterious power buried within him, it just might do that.

Naruto Vol. 1. Written and illustrated by Masashi Kishimoto. Viz Media LLC, 2003. 192pp. ISBN-10: 1-5693190-0-6. ISBN-13: 978-15693190-0-0.

> Naruto Uzamaki, an orphan of the Hidden Leaf Village, must pass the incredibly difficult Ninja Academy test to become a ninja. In addition, he has to deal with his rival, Konohamaru, learn to cooperate with his new classmates, and then survive a test with his two teammates against their instructor.

Naruto Vol. 2. Written and illustrated by Masashi Kishimoto. Viz Media LLC, 2003. 216pp. ISBN-10: 1-5911617-8-9. ISBN-13: 978-15911617-8-3.

> Naruto and his teammates have passed their final tests and are now junior ninja. Now they want tougher assignments than having to babysit the Hokage's grandson. The assignment they get *is* tougher—it may even be their last!

Naruto Vol. 3. Written and illustrated by Masashi Kishimoto. VIZ Media LLC, 2004. 208pp. ISBN-10: 1-5911618-7-8. ISBN-13: 978-15911618-7-5.

> Naruto and crew spend time recovering from their injuries, and Kakashi puts them on a strict training program so they can prepare for the next attack. Finally they have to make the decision they've all been dreading: to protect their assignment, are they willing to kill—or even die?

Naruto Vol. 4. Written and illustrated by Masashi Kishimoto. VIZ Media LLC, 2004, 200pp. ISBN-10: 1-5911635-8-7. ISBN-13: 978-15911635-8-9.

> In all ninjas' lives there comes a time when they realize that no matter how noble they are, no matter what they believe, when all is said and done, it all boils down to being killers. As Naruto comes to terms with this, he awakens the nine-tail fox spirit that gives him enough power to defeat his enemy— but will it consume him in the process?

Naruto Vol. 5. Written and illustrated by Masashi Kishimoto. VIZ Media LLC, 2004. 200pp. ISBN-10: 1-5911635-9-5. ISBN-13: 978-15911635-9-6.

> Team 7 now faces their toughest challenge yet: exams! Sakura, Sasuke, and Naruto must pass the Journeyman Ninja Selection Exams if they ever want to become full-fledged Shinobi. If the tests don't kill them, their fellow junior ninjas will!

Other Editions

Naruto 2008 Boxed Set: Vols. 1–27. **Written and illustrated by Masashi Kishimoto. VIZ Media LLC, 2008. n.p. ISBN-10: 1-4215258-2-8. ISBN-13: 978-14215258-2-2.** `GR. 5-8`

> Collects the twenty-seven books of the first story arc of <u>Naruto</u> in one box. Follow Naruto and the rest of Team 7 (Sasuke, Sakura and Kakashi, their Sensei) as they experience ninja training, secret plots, and schisms in their team.

Whistle!

A popular soccer-based manga from Japan, translated for English audiences, tells the story of Shō Kazamatsuri, a young man who wants to play soccer, so he transfers to Sakura Josui Junior High in an attempt to join the team. Shō's problem is that he is a small kid and didn't get much field time at his old school, Musashinomori, home of the famed soccer team. Can Shō improve his game and prove that even though he's small, he can dominate?

Fully annotated in chapter 6.

Yu-Gi-Oh!

Yet another manga turned parental bankrupting machine. Yu-Gi-Oh! is the story of a young man by the name of Yugi Moto who is given a strange device called the "Millennium Puzzle." After completing the puzzle, Yugi is possessed by a 3,000-year-old entity alternately known as "Nameless Pharaoh" or "Dark Yugi." Now Yugi and his friends Joey Wheeler, Téa Gardener, and Tristan Taylor must face off against Yugi's main rival, Seto Kaiba, among other villains. The main field of battle is a game called "Duel Monsters," virtual creatures that appear over the battlefield and fight for the players.

The first series spans thirty-eight books. The first seven were originally released as Yu-Gi-Oh! and then re-released as Yu-Gi-Oh! Duelist to prevent confusion.

Yu-Gi-Oh! has spawned two sequels, an extremely popular trading card game, a not-so-successful dice game, numerous video games, and several movies. The first seven books in the original series did not focus on "Duel Monsters," and as such are a bit more violent in nature than the rest of the series.

Yu-Gi-Oh! Duelist Vol. 1. Written and illustrated by Kazuki Takahashi. VIZ Media LLC, 2005. 216pp. ISBN-10: 1-5911661-4-4. ISBN-13: 978-15911661-4-6. **GR. 5-8**

> The Duelist books follows Yugi and his gang as he faces off against the mysterious Maximillian Pegasus, the American creator of "Duel Monsters," in a battle; the winner gets to reclaim the soul of someone close to him.

Yu-Gi-Oh! Millennium World Vol. 1. Written and illustrated by Kazuki Takahashi. VIZ Media LLC, 2005. 192pp. ISBN-10: 1-5911687-8-3. ISBN-13: 978-15911687-8-2. **GR. 5-8**

> The final story arc of the original Yu-Gi-Oh! series finds Yugi and crew gathering all of the Egyptian God Cards, the keys to unlocking the memories of Pharaoh's life in Egypt. In the process, Yugi's mind is sent back 3,000 years to explore and face an enemy who has been waiting for three millennia.

Yu-Gi-Oh! Millennium World Vol. 2. Written and illustrated by Kazuki Takahashi. VIZ Media LLC, 2005. 192pp. ISBN-10: 1-4215015-1-1. ISBN-13: 978-14215915-1-2. **GR. 5-8**

> Yugi's mind is 3,000 years in the past, but his Pharaoh-self is the target of Diabound. Can physical Yugi and his friends make the leap back to

help out Pharaoh-Yugi and prevent the wholesale destruction of the "world of memory?"

Yu-Gi-Oh! Millennium World Vol. 3. Written and illustrated by Kazuki Takahashi. VIZ Media LLC, 2006. 208pp. ISBN-10: 1-4215040-9-X. ISBN-13: 978-14215040-9-X. `GR. 5-8`

The spirits of Yugi and his friends have traveled to ancient Egypt, when the monsters were real and Yugi's alter ego was king! But the mad tomb robber Bakura has sworn to destroy the kingdom and take the Millennium Items . . . from the Pharaoh's dead body! As Bakura's monstrous spirit Diabound rains death upon the city, Yu-Gi-Oh must resort to his trump cards, the Three Egyptian Gods. If the heroes have really traveled to the past, can they change the course of history, or are they caught in the hands of time?

Yu-Gi-Oh! Millennium World Vol. 4. Written and illustrated by Kazuki Takahashi. VIZ Media LLC, 2006. 208pp. ISBN-10: 1-4215069-3-9. ISBN-13: 978-14215069-3-7. `GR. 5-8`

Zorc Necrophades rewinds time, forcing Yu-Gi-Oh to fight Bakura all over again, except this time, he doesn't have the Egyptian Gods! High Priest Seto awakens the powerful Blue-Eyes White Dragon, but is it going to be enough?

Yu-Gi-Oh! Vol. 1. Written and illustrated by Kazuki Takahashi. VIZ Media LLC, 2003. 200pp. ISBN-10: 1-5693190-3-0. ISBN-13: 978-15693190-3-1. `GR. 5-8`

Tenth grader Yugi Moto has always had his head in some game or another, until his grandfather gave him a strange device called the Millennium Puzzle. Now, with the Puzzle solved, Yugi has released the spirit of a master gambler, who has possessed Yugi. With the stakes being dangerously high, can Yugi survive this new spirit who seems hell bent on playing with his life?

Yu-Gi-Oh! Vol. 2: The Cards with Teeth. Written and illustrated by Kazuki Takahashi. VIZ Media LLC, 2003. 200pp. ISBN-10: 1-5911608-1-2. ISBN-13: 978-15911608-1-6. `GR. 5-8`

The crazy games continue in this series, including a bizarre game called "One Digit" and the most insane game of "Air Hockey with Explosives All over a Hot Stove" ever played.

Yu-Gi-Oh! Vol. 3. Written and illustrated by Kazuki Takahashi. VIZ Media LLC, 2003. 216pp. ISBN-10: 1-5911617-9-7. ISBN-13: 978-15911617-9-0. `GR. 5-8`

Yugi has to fight deadly illusions that will kill his friends if he can't defeat them. In another adventure, Yugi and his friends discover hidden characters in digital keychain pets that lead into a high-stakes game of chess with the father of Yugi's nemesis.

Yu-Gi-Oh! Vol. 4. Written and illustrated by Kazuki Takahashi. VIZ Media LLC, 2004. 208pp. ISBN-10: 1-5911618-5-1. ISBN-13: 978-15911618-5-1. **GR. 5-8**

> Yugi beats his nemesis, Kaiba, at a card game, and Kaiba shows what a sore loser he is by making Yugi take a trip through his "Death T," a theme park of death, while Kaiba sends out a series of evil spells against Yugi's family.

Yu-Gi-Oh! Vol. 5. Written and illustrated by Kazuki Takahashi. VIZ Media LLC, 2004. 208pp. ISBN-10: 1-5911632-4-2. ISBN-13: 978-15911632-4-4. **GR. 4-8**

> Yugi and the gang have survived Kaiba's killer park, but now they have to face off against Seto and his brother. Whereas Seto has dropped millions of dollars and years to create the best "Duel Monsters" deck, Yugi only has his grandfather's old deck. Will Yugi be able to defeat Kaiba again?

Yu-Gi-Oh! GX. **GR. 5-8**

Ten years after the end of events in the original <u>Yu-Gi-Oh!</u>, readers are introduced to Jaden Yuki, a duelist who plans on enrolling in the Duel Academy to become a champion. Scoring poorly on the entrance exams, Jaden is placed in Slifer Red Dorm (the worst dorm possible), where he makes friends with Syrus Truesdale, the Pro League Duelist Zane Truesdale (Syrus's older brother), and Alexis Rhodes, among others. At the academy, Jaden and his friends continually face threats from a group called the Shadow Riders, who want to revive monsters called the Sacred Beasts to prolong their leader's life. The group also has to prevent the Society of Light from enslaving humanity with a mind-control satellite.

This series is currently ongoing, and to date five books have been released in Japan. Only three have been translated into English.

Yu-Gi-Oh! GX Vol. 1. Written and illustrated by Naoyuki Kageyama. VIZ Media LLC, 2007. 224pp. ISBN-10: 1-4215137-8-1. ISBN-13: 978-14215137-8-2.

> Perceived slacker Jaden has to face off against teachers and students alike to carve out a place for himself in the Duel World. Will he be able to bring honor to his dorm, or is his new dorm going to be the big joke on campus?

Yu-Gi-Oh! GX Vol. 2. Written and illustrated by Naoyuki Kageyama. VIZ Media LLC, 2007. 224pp. ISBN-10: 1-4215147-8-1. ISBN-13: 978-14215137-8-2.

> Having proven his dueling skills, Jaden settles into life at Duel Academy. After revealing what drove Jaden to become a Duel Champion, two mysterious American duelists arrive at the Duel Academy. What is their purpose?

Yu-Gi-Oh! GX Vol. 3. Written and illustrated by Naoyuki Kageyama. VIZ Media LLC, 2009. 200pp. ISBN-10: 1-4215267-7-8. ISBN-13: 978-14215267-7-5.

> The dueling tests reach a fevered pitch as Jaden and crew battle to see who gets to face off against the legendary Zane "Kaiser" Truesdale, master duelist and Syrus's older brother. Meanwhile, the American duelists have designs on Jaden's Winged Kuriboh.

Shōjo

Probably the second most popular form of manga, shōjo (literally "young girl") manga does not comprise a specific style or genre as much as it indicates a target demographic. Shōjo manga covers a variety of subjects as well as narratives and graphic styles, from historical drama to science fiction, often with the focus being on human and romantic relationships and emotions. For the most part, shōjo titles are safe for younger readers, although it is recommended that librarians or teachers read the books before suggesting them.

Cardcaptor Sakura.

> After Sakura Kinomoto discovers a weird book in her father's study, she unleashes the cards hidden inside. Now with the help of Cerberus, the guardian beast of the Clow Cards, Sakura must retrieve the missing cards; the only problem is that to get the cards back, she has to fight the magical personification of each card.
>
> One of the flagship titles for the Japanese group CLAMP, <u>Cardcaptor Sakura</u> is one of the eponymous titles in the Western-style shōjo-ai (girl's love) realm of comics. Unlike most shōjo-ai, <u>Cardcaptor Sakura</u> focuses more on puppy love. It is an excellent title to introduce younger readers, especially girls, to graphic novels. Be aware that this series carries an extremely mild shōnen-ai (boy love) undertone. (Lulu Award)

Cardcaptor Sakura Vol. 1. Written and illustrated by CLAMP. TokyoPop, 2004. 200pp. ISBN-10: 1-5918287-8-3. ISBN-13: 978-15918287-8-5. **GR. 4-8**

> Sakura finds a magical book called *The Clow* in her father's library. It once contained magical cards; however, they escaped as the guardian of the book slept. Now that he's awake, he has charged Sakura with reclaiming all of the Clow cards.

Cardcaptor Sakura Vol. 2. Written and illustrated by CLAMP. TokyoPop, 2004. 192pp. ISBN-10: 1-5918287-9-1. ISBN-13: 978-15918287-9-1. **GR. 4-6**

> Sakura meets a rival who is after the Clow cards, who just happens to be a direct descendant of Clow himself! Will Sakura be able to finish the job she started?

Cardcaptor Sakura Vol. 3. Written and illustrated by CLAMP. TokyoPop, 2004. 200pp. ISBN-10: 1-5918288-0-5. ISBN-13: 978-15918288-0-8. **GR. 4-8**

> When missing Clow cards begin turning up alarmingly close to Sakura's home, catching the cards isn't just a matter of responsibility; it's a matter of protecting the ones she loves.

Cardcaptor Sakura Vol. 4. Written and illustrated by CLAMP. TokyoPop, 2005. 200pp. ISBN-10: 1-5918288-1-3. ISBN-13: 978-15918288-1-5. **GR. 4-6**

> A field trip to the beach provides a nice break for Sakura—until students start disappearing. Can Sakura defeat this new Clow card that has trapped everyone?

Cardcaptor Sakura Vol. 5. Written and illustrated by CLAMP. TokyoPop, 2005. 192pp. ISBN-10: 1-5918288-2-1. ISBN-13: 978015918288-2-2. **GR. 4-6**

> Sakura's class is putting on a production of *Sleeping Beauty*, and Sakura has been cast as the prince. The performance is going well until a Clow card shows up. Can Sakura wake Sleeping Beauty and capture the card?

Cardcaptor Sakura Vol. 6. Written and illustrated by CLAMP. TokyoPop, 2005. 192pp. ISBN-10: 1-5918299-3-X. ISBN-13: 978-15918288-3-9. **GR. 4-6**

> In the final book of the series, Sakura faces off against her greatest challenge yet. If she cannot pass the final trial, the cards will unleash a terrible curse.

Cardcaptor Sakura: Master of the Clow. **GR. 4-6**

After Sakura passes her final test, she is deemed "Master of the Clow" and continues her adventures with new cards, new friends and enemies, and more powerful moves.

Cardcaptor Sakura: Master of the Clow Vol. 1. Written and illustrated by CLAMP. TokyoPop, 2002. 184pp. ISBN-10: 1-8922137-5-3. ISBN-13: 978-18922137-5-4.

> Now that Sakura Kinomoto has collected all the Clow cards and has been named the Master of the Clow, she now has a new job. Now she has to transform all of the Clow cards into star cards. To top it off, strange new things have been happening at school in the wake of a mysterious new student by the name of Eroil enrolling.

Cardcaptor Sakura: Master of the Clow Vol. 2. Written and illustrated by CLAMP. TokyoPop, 2002. 184pp. ISBN-10: 1-8922137-6-1. ISBN-13: 978-18922137-6-1.

> Sakura has a crush on Yukito, an older student, and has been creating a handmade teddy bear for him. Li Syaoran has also been busy making one of his own, but who is he going to give it to, Sakura or Yukito? On top of this odd love triangle, Eroil shows up to test Sakura again Perhaps this crisis will help Sakura figure out where her true feelings lie.

Cardcaptor Sakura: Master of the Clow Vol. 3. Written and illustrated by CLAMP. TokyoPop, 2003. 192pp. ISBN-10: 1-8922137-7-X. ISBN-13: 978-18922137-7-8.

> Clow Reed continues to test Sakura, to the point that she can't provide energy to Yue, the Guardian of the Moon, and now he might

disappear forever. Since Yue spends most of his time as the human Yukito, he is now deathly ill, and if Sakura can't help him, he'll have to find new power somewhere else.

Cardcaptor Sakura: Master of the Clow Vol. 4. Written and illustrated by CLAMP. TokyoPop, 2003. 192pp. ISBN-10: 1-8922137-8-8. ISBN-13: 978-18922137-8-5. **GR. 4-6**

> After taking Yukito to the school fair, Sakura confesses her feelings to him. Can love overcome their age difference, not to mention the fact that he's not even human? What's worse is that Clow Reed is back and testing Sakura again, trying to find out if Sakura is really worthy of his enchantments.

Nausicaä.

A thousand years after the "Seven Days of Fire," a horrific war that almost destroyed the human civilization, the earth is covered in a "Sea of Corruption," a vast forest of fungi that secretes poisonous miasma and invasive spores. Living in this deadly growth are large, killer insects that pose a serious threat to anything that comes near. Nausicaä, a princess of a small city-state, had previously pledged her alliance with Torumekia, the Kingdom that houses her land. Now Torumekia is at war with the Dorok Empire, and Nausicaä's life and the fate of the entire human race will be changed forever.

Fully annotated in Chapter 4.

Nui.

Kaya loves her stuffed animals. In fact, she loves them so much, they can come to life and turn into people, especially when she is in trouble. However, not all of her toy animals wish her well; in fact there are some who may try to harm her. Can her stuffed animals protect her from those who wish her harm?

Fully annotated in chapter 4.

Sailor Moon.

One of the most ubiquitous shōjo titles, <u>Sailor Moon</u> is often the first title girls are introduced to when they start reading manga. Although it was not the first series to use the concept of magical girls (girls who are imbued with powers), it was the first to portray these girls using their powers to fight evil. Subsequently, this format is now considered a standard archetype for shōjo manga.

The series follows the story of Usagi Tsukino (in the English version, for some reason, called "Bunny"), an ordinary, if ditzy, middle school girl. She day finds a talking cat by the name of Luna, who reveals to Tsukino that she is actually the reincarnated warrior "Sailor Moon." Tsukino's destiny is to save the planet Earth from bad guys. As the series progresses, more "Sailor Senshi" (sailor scouts) join forces with Tsukino, often taking the title of a planet in the solar system. This manga was also turned into a television series that ran on the Cartoon Network, NBC, and USA Network. A multitude of video games spanning several systems have been released in Japan, with few titles making it to America, and a handful of movies have been released from the series, including a live-action version. Between 1993 and 2005, twenty-five stage shows based on the franchise were released in Japan.

Sailor Moon Vol. 1. Written and illustrated by Naoko Takeuchi. TokyoPop, 1998. 200pp. ISBN-10: 1-8922130-1-X. ISBN-13: 978-18922130-1-3. `GR. 4-8`

> In between trying to maintain a social life and dating, Bunny has to protect Earth from otherworldly villains.

Sailor Moon Vol. 2. Written and illustrated by Naoko Takeuchi. TokyoPop, 1999. 184pp. ISBN-10: 1-8922130-5-2. ISBN-13: 978-18922130-5-1. `GR. 4-7`

> Many discoveries are made: who the princess, Sailor V, and Tuxedo Mask are, and the real identities of Darien and Bunny. Intermixed in all of this, more bad guys attack!

Sailor Moon Vol. 3. Written and illustrated by Naoko Takeuchi. TokyoPop, 1999. 171pp. ISBN-10: 1-8922130-6-0. ISBN-13: 978-18922130-6-8. `GR. 4-7`

> Bunny, Mina, Amy, Raye, and Lita continue to battle the bad guys from the last two books, but this time the monsters have brought Darien back to life and instructed him to kill Sailor Moon. Will the Sailor Scouts be able to dissuade Darien from performing his deadly task?

Sea Princess Azuri.

Queen Onyxis of the Kingdom of Orca's only daughter, the princess Azuri, is next in line for the matriarchal throne. She's also subject to something that hasn't been heard of since the olden days: an arranged marriage. She is betrothed from a young age to the Prince Unagi from the Eel kingdom of Gillenok. As her wedding day approaches, Azuri begins to freak out and confides in her best friend, a young Orcan boy by the name of Thalo, who is now a member of the Royal Guard. Everyone around the two young Orcans can tell they are falling in love, but Azuri and Thalo are completely oblivious. Will Azuri or Thalo realize before Unagi arrives and is made aware of what is going on? Will Azuri be able to save the two kingdoms and prevent an all-out war?

Fully annotated in chapter 6.

Tokyo Mew Mew. `GR. 3-7`

One day, while out with a boy she likes, Ichigo Momomiya attends an exhibit about endangered species at the local zoo. An earthquake strikes, and subsequently, Ichigo and four other girls are enveloped in a strange light. While in this light, Ichigo sees a cat that then merges with her. The following day, Ichigo begins to act like a cat and ultimately discovers that the strange light has infused her body with feline DNA. With her new powers, she can change into a powerful cat girl. Now Ichigo, along with the other four girls, must protect Earth from chimera animas (animals that have been infected with alien parasites that turn them into monsters).

Tokyo Mew Mew a la Mode. Written by Reiko Yoshida. Illustrated by Mia Ikumi. TokyoPop, 2005. 208pp. ISBN-10: 1-5953278-9-4. ISBN-13: 978-15953278-9-5.

> Following in the footsteps of *Tokyo Mew Mew*, a new Mew Mew is introduced, who temporarily takes over the team.

Tokyo Mew Mew Vol. 1: Mew Mew to the Rescue. Written by Reiko Yoshida. Illustrated by Mia Ikumi. TokyoPop, 2003. 184pp. ISBN-10: 1-5918223-6-X. ISBN-13: 978-15918223-6-3.

> What would you do if you went to a museum and were endowed with the ability to turn into a catgirl, asked to join a secret group and to help protect Earth from alien invaders? That's what eleven-year-old Momomiya has to deal with.

Ultra Maniac.

Ayu Tateishi is junior high's "Queen of Cool," a tennis star, and a friend to Nina Sakura, a new girl in school who is more than she seems: Nina is a witch.

Unfortunately Nina is still learning how to use her powers. After Ayu helps Nina out with a small problem, Nina feels compelled to help Ayu magically, with hilarious results. As a modern witch, Nina can download spells through her "portable magic PC" when she needs them.

Fully annotated in chapter 4.

Kodomo

Kodomos (literally "manga directed toward children") are usually self-contained, episodic stories that appeal to younger children. Often used to teach children how to behave as considerate people, kodomo tends to be rather moralistic. Quite often, kodomo readers will graduate to shōnen or shōjo as they get older.

Beyblade. GR. 4-8

The familiar story of a young boy starting a quest to become the best of the best in his chosen field of gaming. This type of theme is also prevalent in Yu-Gi-Oh! and Pokémon, among others. Beyblades are special battle tops that contain sacred spirits. The main character, Tyson Granger, becomes the leader of the Bladebreakers, a group of like-minded kids who are fighting to win the World Beyblading Championships.

Beyblade Vol. 1. Written and illustrated by Takao Aoki. Viz Media, 2004. 200pp. ISBN-10: 1-5911662-1-7. ISBN-13: 978-15911662-1-4.

> After Tyson Granger receives a Beyblade that represents the blue dragon, Seiryu, he and former rival Kai Hiwatari join forces with Tyson's best friend, Max Tate, and Ray Kon, another beyblader, to fight in the beyblade championships.

Beyblade Vol. 2. Written and illustrated by Takao Aoki. Viz Media, 2004. 192pp. ISBN-10: 1-5911669-7-7. ISBN-13: 978-15911669-7-9.

> Tyson has developed a super shooting style called the Vanishing Attack in preparation for the big beyblade tournament coming up. Will his Dragoon be strong enough to defeat all comers?

Beyblade Vol. 3. Written and illustrated by Takao Aoki. Viz Media, 2005. 192pp. ISBN-10: 1-5911670-5-1. ISBN-13: 978-15911670-5-1.

> Having made it to the beyblade finals, Tyson must now use his Dragoon S Beyblade to defeat the mighty Ray and his Dreyger Beyblade.

Beyblade Vol. 4. Written and illustrated by Takao Aoki. Viz Media, 2005. 192pp. ISBN-10: 1-5911670-5-1. ISBN-13: 978-15911670-5-1.

> Tyson and his friends return from Japan, only to discover a new Russian beyblade group called the Demolition Boys waiting for Tyson. Not content to just win, the Demolition Boys play to destroy their opponent's beyblades.

Beyblade Vol. 5. Written and illustrated by Takao Aoki. Viz Media, 2005. 192pp. ISBN-10: 1-5911679-3-0. ISBN-13: 978-15911679-3-8.

> Having made it to the Beyblade World Championships, Tyson and crew must battle the toughest beybladers in the world. Everything is going great until the Russian team hijacks the competition and challenges everyone to a competition on the Russians' own remote island!

Beyblade Vol. 6. Written and illustrated by Takao Aoki. Viz Media, 2005. 192pp. ISBN-10: 1-5911685-7-0. ISBN-13: 978-15911685-7-7.

> After their win at the World Championship, the Bladebreakers are challenged by the Demolition Boys. Will Tyson be able to beat their leader, Tala?

Beyblade Vol. 7. Written and illustrated by Takao Aoki. Viz Media, 2005. 192pp. ISBN-10: 1-4215001-9-1. ISBN-13: 978-14215001-9-5.

> After upgrading his beyblade, Tyson faces off against new opponents by the name of The Saintshields. When Ray and Max join the fight, Ray's bitbeast, the White Tiger, is sucked away and could be lost forever. Will Tyson and the boys be able to get the White Tiger back?

Cowa! **Written and illustrated by Akira Toriyama. Viz Media, 2008. 208pp. ISBN-10: 1-4215180-5-8. ISBN-13: 978-14215180-5-3.** `GR. 4-8`

All the monsters in town are getting sick, and if Paifu, the half-vampire, half-werekoala, can't get the medicine within a month, everyone is going to die! The only problem is that Paifu is the town troublemaker and has never been able to finish anything.

Pokémon

Who's not familiar with this venerable juggernaut of Japanese ingenuity? Started in the mid-1990s as a video game by Nintendo, *Pokémon* quickly gained a following of near epic proportions. The franchise has spawned close to forty video game titles over nine different game systems, twelve theatrical movies, and a super-successful trading card game series, and has come close to bankrupting the parents of almost every parent of young boys for the past fourteen years.

Parental Advisory: perceived occult themes; violence occasionally resulting in Pokémon death

Pokémon: The Original Series. `GR. 2-6`

These books were based on the hit videogame series about the main character, Ash Ketchum, who wants to be the best Pokémon trainer in the world. Some books have him listed as Ash; others have him listed as "Red." It was from these books that the television series was created.

Pokémon Vol. 1: The Electric Tale of Pikachu! Written and illustrated by Toshihiro Ono. Viz Media LLC, 1999. 166pp. ISBN-10: 1-5693137-8-4. ISBN-13: 978-15693137-8-7.

Ash Ketchum discovers a strange creature gnawing on the wiring in his house. Discovering a small electric-based mouse creature named Pikachu, Ash decides to become the world's greatest Pokémon trainer. Based (very) loosely on the television series created by Nintendo.

Pokémon Vol. 2: Pikachu Shocks Back. Written and illustrated by Toshihiro Ono. Viz Media LLC, 1999. 168pp. ISBN-10: 1-5693141-1-X. ISBN-13: 978-15693141-1-1.

Ash is joined by his friends Misty and Brock on his journey to become the World's Best Trainer. Along the way, they cross paths with other trainers as well as Jesse and James, two bumbling agents of the evil Team Rocket.

Pokémon Vol. 3: Electric Pikachu Boogaloo. Written and illustrated by Toshihiro Ono. VIZ Media LLC, 2000. 168pp. ISBN-10: 1-5693143-6-5. ISBN-13: 978-15693143-6-4.

The third installment in this series includes several side stories, culminating in Ash's biggest battle to date, the Great Pokémon Tournament.

Pokémon Vol. 4: Surf's Up, Pikachu. Written and illustrated by Toshihiro Ono. VIZ Media LLC, 2000. 167pp. ISBN-10: 1-5693149-4-2. ISBN-13: 978-15693149-4-4.

> Pikachu and Ash travel to the Orange Islands for new adventures and new challenges.

Pokémon: Diamond and Pearl Adventures. GR. 2-6

A new series starring new characters as well as old favorites, Pokémon: Diamond and Pearl Adventures follows Ash and other characters as they travel to new locations, hunt new Pokémon, and have new adventures. The fourth incarnation of the Pokémon franchise, this is the most popular version outside of the original.

Pokémon: Diamond and Pearl Adventure Vol. 1. Written and illustrated by Ihara Shigekatsu. VIZ Media LLC, 2008. 192pp. ISBN-10: 1-4215228-6-9. ISBN-13: 978-14215228-6-9.

> This series introduces a new protagonist, Hareta. Raised in the wild, Hareta is recruited by Professor Rowan to become a Pokémon trainer. Joined by the professor's assistant, Mitsumi, Hareta sets out to find the Legendary Dialga, a Pokémon rumored to control time. Along the way Hareta and Mitsumi must face off against Cyrus and Team Galactic.

Pokémon: Diamond and Pearl Adventure! Vol. 2. Written and illustrated by Ihara Shigekatsu. VIZ Media LLC, 2008. 192pp. ISBN-10: 1-4215228-7-X. ISBN-13: 978-14215228-7-6.

> Hareta faces off against other trainers and meets new people on his adventure to find the legendary Dialga.

Pokémon: Diamond and Pearl Adventure! Vol. 3. Written and illustrated by Ihara Shigekatsu. VIZ Media LLC, 2009. 200pp. ISBN-10: 1-4215257-4-7. ISBN-13: 978-14215257-4-7.

> Team Galactic's plans to capture Dialga are going forward, and now it is up to Hareta and his friends, along with several Sinnoh Gym Leaders, to prevent Cyrus and Team Galactic from succeeding.

Pokémon: Diamond and Pearl Adventure! Vol. 4. Written and illustrated by Ihara Shigekatsu. VIZ Media LLC, 2009. 192pp. ISBN-10: 1-4215267-4-3. ISBN-13: 978-14215267-4-4.

> Hareta and several of the Sinnoh Gym Leaders launch an attack on Team Galactic's headquarters. Unfortunately, things go wrong, and Hareta's friends end up getting captured. Now he has to face off against Mitsumi, who has joined Team Galactic. Will Hareta succeed, and more important, will Hareta and Mitsumi still be friends afterward?

Pokémon Adventures. `GR. 2-6`

A collection of stories and adventures set in the early years of the franchise. Originally based on two video games released for the Nintendo Gameboy, the series took off, resulting in these stories.

Pokémon: Best of Pokémon Adventures: Red. Written by Hidenori Kusaka. Illustrated by Mato. VIZ Media LLC, 2006. 184pp. ISBN-10: 1-4215092-8-8. ISBN-13: 978-14215092-8-0.

Graphic novel version of *Pokémon Red, Blue & Green* for the original Nintendo Game Boy.

Pokémon: Best of Pokémon Adventures: Yellow. Written by Hidenori Kusaka. Illustrated by Mato. VIZ Media LLC, 2006. 194pp. ISBN-10: 1-4215092-9-6. ISBN-13: 978-14215092-9-7.

This graphic novel is very loosely based on the Game Boy game *Pokémon Yellow*.

Pokémon Adventures Vol. 1: Mysterious Mew. Written by Hidenori Kusaka. Illustrated by Mato. VIZ Media LLC, 1999. 45pp.ISBN-10: 1-5693138-7-3. ISBN-13: 978-15693138-7-9.

Mew, a "new species" of Pokémon that looks like an innocent catlike character, just happens to be the super-rare 151st Pokémon. Join the Trainer (later to become Ash Ketchum), Professor Oak and his nephew, and a slew of other characters all attempting to catch all of the Pokémon to complete the Pokémon collection. This book became the basis for *Pokémon: The Movie*.

Pokémon Adventures Vol. 2: Wanted Pikachu. Written by Hidenori Kusaka. Illustrated by Mato. VIZ Media LLC, 1999. 48pp. ISBN-10: 1-5693138-8-1. ISBN-13: 978-15693138-8-6.

A Trainer travels to Pewter City to try to catch a Pikachu, who is wanted for vandalism.

Pokémon Adventures Vol. 3: Starmie Surprise. Written by Hidenori Kusaka. Illustrated by Mato. VIZ Media LLC, 1999. 200pp. ISBN-10: 1-5693138-9-X. ISBN-13: 978-15693138-9-3.

The Pokémon Starmie gets a turn in the limelight in the third installment of this series.

Pokémon Adventures Vol. 4: The Snorlax Stop. Written by Hidenori Kusaka. Illustrated by Mato. VIZ Media LLC, 1999. 48pp. ISBN-10: 1-5693140-8-X. ISBN-13: 978-15693140-8-1.

Red, the main character of this series, travels by sea and runs into Lt. Surge, a gym leader whose Pokémon are all electric type. Is Red in for a shocking time? Ultimately, Red enters a bicycle race with a huge obstacle: Snorlax.

Pokémon Adventures Vol. 5: The Ghastly Ghosts. Written by Hidenori Kusaka and Toshihiro Ono. Illustrated by Mato. VIZ Media LLC, 2000. 48pp. ISBN-10: 1-5693140-9-8. ISBN-13: 978-15693140-9-8.

> Red follows his nemesis Blue to a graveyard of undead Pokémon in Lavender Town. However, Koga, a Ninja-inspired trainer with ghostly Pokémon, has designs on Red. Will Blue help Red fight Koga, or will he help Koga bury Red?

Pokémon Adventures Vol. 6: Yellow Caballero: The Cave Campaign. Written by Hidenori Kusaka. Illustrated by Mato. VIZ Media LLC, 2002. 200pp. ISBN-10: 1-5911602-8-6. ISBN-13: 978-15911602-8-1.

> Red and Blue join forces with several gym leaders as well as Team Rocket to fight an even tougher foe, the Elite Four.

Pokémon Adventures Vol. 7: The Yellow Caballero: The Pokémon Elite. Written by Hidenori Kusaka. Illustrated by Mato. VIZ Media LLC, 2003. 208pp. ISBN-10: 1-5693185-1-4. ISBN-13: 978-15693185-1-5.

> The battle against the Elite Four reaches its crescendo as both sides start pulling out their biggest and baddest Pokémon for a final showdown.

Yotsuba&! Written and illustrated by Azuma Kiyohiko. 232pp. ADV Manga, 2005. ISBN-10: 1-4139031-7-7. ISBN-13: 978-14139031-7-1. `GR. 4-8`

The Koiwai family, little Yotsuba and her father, have just moved to a new town. As their new neighbors get to know them, it becomes obvious that Yotsuba is one very weird little girl. (ALA Great Graphic Novel)

> Fully annotated in chapter 6.

Nate's Picks

- <u>Naruto</u> by Masashi Kishimoto. Styled the "Greatest Manga of All Time." Engaging story lines and believable characters make this title a must have for any collection.

- *Cowa!* by Akira Toriyama. A fun and safe title for younger readers from the man who created <u>Dragon Ball</u> and <u>Dragon Ball Z</u>.

- <u>Cardcaptor Sakura</u> by CLAMP. Great for younger (especially female) audiences. Strong female protagonist who perseveres against difficult odds.

- <u>Pokémon</u> by Various. For younger readers, the title alone should get them hooked. Just be aware that in some titles, when a Pokémon is defeated, it dies.

Notes

1. Publishers Weekly, http://www.publishersweekly.com/pw/print/ 20100419/42976-u-s-graphic-novel-sales-down-6-.html.

2. Anime News Network, http://www.animenewsnetwork.com/news/ 2010-04-16/icv2/u.s-manga-sales-down-20-percent-in-2009.

Chapter 3

Science Fiction

For many readers, nothing stirs the imagination like science fiction. In text-driven novels, movies, and video games, science fiction happens to be one of the most popular genres today. From such instant classics as <u>Star Wars</u> and <u>Avatar</u> to Orson Scott Card's <u>Ender's Game</u> and Asimov's <u>Foundation</u> series, as well as an abundance of other movies, books, and video games (*Halo* anyone?), it is obvious that science fiction is alive and well. From stories grounded in scientific theory to complete flights of fancy, science fiction is one of the most flexible genres.

Using such elements as space/time travel, robots, cyborgs, and futuristic weaponry, science fiction makes the impossible believable. Though science fiction can be complex and deal with exceedingly mature themes, the books listed in this chapter try to stay as kid friendly as possible.

Space Opera

Space opera generally deals with normal human characters and traditional science fiction issues. Aliens, cyborgs, laser swords, and the like may make an appearance, but ultimately they take a back seat to the main characters and the problems they face

Agent Boo. `GR. 4-8`

With thousands of parallel universes out there, a regulatory force is needed to make sure that normal folks don't ever see them. That's the job of the Agents. Three new recruits have joined the ranks of the Agents, including tiny fourth grader Boo, the smallest agent to ever graduate. At first, everyone thinks that she's too small to be of any use, but given the chance, she'll prove everyone wrong.

Agent Boo Vol. 1. Written by Alex De Campi. Illustrated by Edo Fuijkschot. TokyoPop, 2006. 96pp. ISBN-10: 1-5981680-2-9. ISBN-13: 978-15981680-2-0.

> Boo is left behind to guard Space City while the rest of the Agents race to prevent Queen Misery from conquering a parallel world. When devious enemies attack, it's up to Boo and her feline companion to thwart their plans.

Agent Boo Vol. 2: The Star Heist. Written by Alex De Campi. Illustrated by Edo Fuijkschot. TokyoPop, 2006. 96pp. ISBN-10: 1-5981680-3-7. ISBN-13: 978-15981680-3-7.

> Celebrating her defeat of Queen Misery, Boo and her team are sent to Jungle City for their first official mission. Unfortunately the jungle is a dangerous place for an Agent, especially the smallest. To top it off, her teammates can't seem to get along! Can Boo complete the mission and bring her team back in one piece?

Agent Boo Vol. 3: The Heart of Iron. Written by Alex De Campi. Illustrated by Edo Fuijkschot. TokyoPop, 2007. 96pp. ISBN-10: 1-5981680-4-5. ISBN-13: 978-15981680-4-4.

> Boo's friend Agent Kira has been kidnapped, and now it's up to Boo and Asano to get her back. All they have to do is infiltrate Iron City, the heart of Queen Misery's empire. Will Boo be able to make some difficult decisions?

Space Cops. Written by Steve Bowkett. Illustrated by Liz McIntosh. Stone Arch Books, 2008. 72pp. ISBN-10: 1-4342045-7-X. ISBN-13: 978-14342047-7-8. `GR. 2-6`

> After detecting something strange on their radar screens, the Space Cops investigate. What they discover threatens the safety of the entire universe.

Star Trek.

Originally created in the 1960s by Gene Roddenberry as a television show, *Star Trek* ran for only three seasons and was cancelled due to poor ratings. After the show was cancelled, a strange thing happened: Fans demanded more. In the late 1970s' Roddenberry delivered a lukewarm theatrical release of the television show. In spite of yet another failure, the series somehow managed to become a cult classic. In the late 1980s' Roddenberry decided to revisit the series, albeit with a new cast. *Star Trek: The Next Generation* was just the shot in the arm the franchise needed, turning it from cult classic into worldwide phenomenon.

Star Trek and its various spin-offs are a great series for kids to get into. The ideals of equality, exploration, and goodwill fully infuse the series, with occasional detours into personal vendettas and revenge. However, these are the exceptions to the rule.

Star Trek: Countdown. Written by J. J. Abrams, Robert Orci, Alex Kurtzman, Tim Jones, Mike Johnson, and David Messin. Illustrated by Tim Jones, Mike Johnson, and David Messina. IDW Publishing, 2009. 104pp. ISBN-10: 1-6001042-0-7. ISBN-13: 978-16001042-0-6. `GR. 5-8`

> Set before the new *Star Trek* movie, this stand-alone story explains the origin of Nero, the Romulan villain whom Captain Kirk and the crew of the Enterprise must defeat.

Star Trek: The Key Collection Vol. 1. Written by Len Wein and George Kashden. Illustrated by Nevio Zaccara and Alberto Giolitti. Checker Book Publishing Group, 2004. 228pp. ISBN-10: 0-9741664-4-8. ISBN-13: 978-09741664-4-5. `GR. 4-8`

> Collects the original comic book series from the 1960s' while the television show was still on the air. All the stories are original to the book and bear little resemblance to the television series. Diehard fans may be offended, but it's still entertaining in a kitschy way.

Star Trek: The Key Collection Vol. 2. Written by Len Wein and George Kashden. Illustrated by Nevio Zaccara and Alberto Giolitti. Checker Book Publishing Group, 2004. 228pp. ISBN-10: 0-9710249-8-7. ISBN-13: 978-09710249-8-4. `GR. 4-8`

> The second book from the original comic book series, which ran longer than the television show, continues to use the characters from the show in nonseries stories in a sort of ham-fisted, lurching way.

Star Trek: The Next Generation—The Space Between. Written by David Tischman. Illustrated by Casey Maloney. IDW Publishing, 2007. 144pp. ISBN-10: 1-6001011-6-X. ISBN-13: 978-16001011-6-8. `GR. 5-8`

> Twenty years after the television show *Star Trek: TNG* debuted, the comic book series came out. This is a collection of stories involving Captain Picard and the crew of the new Starship *Enterprise.*

Star Trek Ultimate Edition. Written by Bettina Kurkoski. Illustrated by Chris Dows. TokyoPop, 2009. 342pp. ISBN-10: 1-4278135-2-3. ISBN-13: 978-14278135-2-7. `GR. 5-8`

> A collection of stories from the successful <u>Star Trek</u> manga trilogy, along with bonus features. Every story included in this edition was selected by fans from the TokyoPop Web site, plus a sneak peak of a story from <u>Star Trek: The Next Generation</u> manga.

Star Trek: The Next Generation.

A sequel of sorts to the original *Star Trek* television series, *Star Trek: the Next Generation* (often abbreviated as ST: tNG) is set approximately seventy years after the original series. Whereas the original series only lasted three and a half seasons, ST: tNG went a full seven years, winning not only eighteen Emmy Awards and two Hugo Awards, but also a Peabody Award for excellence in television programming. As Mr. Spock from the original series might say, "It's only logical that they would make a graphic novel series out of the broadcast."

Star Trek: The Next Generation Vol. 1. Written by Christine Boylan. Illustrated by Diane Duane. TokyoPop, 2009. 192pp. ISBN-10: 1-4278127-2-1. ISBN-13: 978-14278127-2-8. **GR. 5-8**

> The first book in what is currently an ongoing series of stories written with the characters of the television series *Star Trek: The Next Generation*. The characters are much truer to their original television characters, and the stories draw on events from the show.

Star Trek Movie Omnibus. Illustrated by Various. IDW Publishing, 2009. 380pp. ISBN-10: 1-6001055-5-6. ISBN-13: 978-16001055-5-5. GR. 5-8

> Collects the graphic adaptations of the six *Star Trek* movies: *Star Trek: The Motion Picture*, *Star Trek: The Wrath of Khan*, *Star Trek: The Search for Spock*, *Star Trek: The Voyage Home*, *Star Trek: The Final Frontier*, and *Star Trek: The Undiscovered Country*.

System Shock. Illustrated by Janek Matysiak. Stone Arch Books, 2007. 88pp. ISBN-10: 1-5988908-3-2. ISBN-13: 978-15988908-3-9. GR. 3-8

> Several kids get trapped in a virtual reality world, and as in most stories of this type, they run the risk of being erased if they can't escape soon.

Time Blasters.

David and Ben are perennial slackers who always find a way to get themselves into trouble. After David's brother Darren builds a time machine, the amount of trouble the two get into becomes legendary.

Time Blasters: Back to the Ice Age. Written by Scott Nickel. Illustrated by Enrique Corts. Stone Arch Books, 2008. 40pp. ISBN-10: 1-4342045-0-9. ISBN-13: 1-4342045-0-2. **GR. 1-5**

> Stuck with the world's worst babysitter, David wishes something would happen. When she accidentally zaps herself back in time, David and his friend Ben must go back in time to save her.

Time Blasters: Blast to the Past. Written by Scott Nickel. Illustrated by Steve Harpster. Stone Arch Books, 2006. 40pp. ISBN-10: 1-5988916-7-7. ISBN-13: 978-15988916-7-6. **GR. 3-6**

> Those perennial slackers David and Ben borrow a time machine to go back in time to retake a test they failed. Unfortunately, they go back too far and face off against dinosaurs!

Time Blasters: T. Rex vs. Robo-Dog 3000. Written by Scott Nickel. Illustrated by Enrique Corts. Stone Arch Books, 2009. 40pp. ISBN-10: 1-4342076-1-7. ISBN-13: 978-14342076-1-6. **GR. 1-5**

> After Darrin invents a radio-controlled dog, Ben uses the time machine to bring back a T. rex from the distant past. Now Robo-Dog 3000 has transformed into a giant robot intent on battling the dinosaur. The smack down of the century is brewing, and David and Ben are stuck in the middle!

The Time Machine. **Written by H.G. Wells. Illustrated by Tod Smith. Stone Arch Books, 2008. 72pp. ISBN-10: 1-5988983-3-7. ISBN-13: 978-15988983-3-0.** `GR. 2-8`

> A scientist creates a machine that can travel through time, going to the far future. While there, he meets a race of gentle, innocent humans, as well as a monstrous race of creatures called morlocks.

Zapt!

> Armand Jones thinks he's having a bad day. Unfortunately for him, it's going to get much worse. Inducted into the ranks of P.O.O.P. (Pan-galactic Order Of Police) against his will, he now has to help protect the universe from alien outlaws and rogue P.O.O.P. agents while still juggling school and making it home in time for dinner.

> *Zapt! Vol. 1.* Written by Shannon Denton and Keith Giffen. Illustrated by Armand Villavert Jr. TokyoPop, 2006. 96pp. ISBN-10: 1-5981658-8-7. ISBN-13: 978-15981658-8-3. `GR. 3-8`
>
> > Armand Jones just got inducted into P.O.O.P., and now he not only has to worry about bullies at school, he also has to try to thwart the plans of a former agent gone rogue—all before dinner!

> *Zapt! Vol. 2.* Written by Shannon Denton and Keith Giffen. Illustrated by Armand Villavert Jr. TokyoPop, 2007. 96pp. ISBN-10: 1-5981658-9-5. ISBN-13: 978-15981658-9-0. `GR. 4-8`
>
> > Armand is getting used to being an agent of P.O.O.P., but he's having major difficulties avoiding getting detention at school. Now he has to try to stop Gongar the Peeved from enslaving the entire known universe.

Space Fantasy

A lot of science fiction could be described as a shiny, futuristic shell that is filled with a gooey, tasty, fantasy nougat center. The books here may have robots, space ships, and burp guns, but at the heart of the matter, the theme is still good vs. evil in a never-ending cycle.

The best known example of space fantasy is George Lucas's most famous contribution to the genre, *Star Wars*. A small time country boy travels to the stars, only to find out that his destiny is bigger than anything he could ever imagine. Ultimately he must face the full embodiment of evil, his fallen father, Darth Vader.

Falls from grace, redemptions, and fantastic elements are all hallmarks of this genre, and the following books involve these ideals in some form or another, in varying intensities. Science fiction always seems to be a popular genre, equally so with both male and female audiences.

Bionicle.

What started as a toy line for LEGO has become a worldwide phenomenon that has captivated the hearts and minds of countless boys and a fair number of girls between ages seven and twelve. Spawning more than fifteen toy lines, three movies, a video game, and a print series from Scholastic, this series is a must have to draw in reluctant readers.

When Bionicle first stormed onto the scene, no one could have imagined that these strange mechanical humanoid creatures would go anywhere, but they have firmly ensconced themselves in the canon of modern science fiction.

Bionicle Vol. 1: Rise of the Toa Nuva. Written by Greg Farshtey. Illustrated by Carlos D'Anda, Richard Bennett, and Randy Elliott. Papercutz, 2008. 112pp. ISBN-10: 1-5970710-9-9. ISBN-13: 978-15970710-9-3. `GR. 3-7`

> The Toa must save the Great Spirit Mata Nui from the Evil Makuta. Now the Toa must not only protect the Matorans from the Makuta, they must also learn to combine their skills, elemental powers, and mask powers.

Bionicle Vol. 2: Challenge of the Rahkshi. Written by Greg Farshtey. Illustrated by Randy Elliott. Papercutz, 2008. 112pp. ISBN-10: 1-5970711-1-0. ISBN-13: 978-15970511-1-6. `GR. 3-7`

> The Toa Nuva have lost their powers, and only the mask of time can help them out. At the same time, Takua and his friend Jaller have discovered the legendary Mask of Light. When Takua puts the mask on, he becomes the Toa of Light, Takanuva, and discovers the long-lost city of Metru Nui.

Bionicle Vol. 3: City of Legend. Written by Greg Farshtey. Illustrated by Randy Elliott. Papercutz, 2008. 112pp. ISBN-10: 1-5970712-1-8. ISBN-13: 978-15970712-1-5. `GR. 2-5`

> The Matoran have rediscovered their original homeland, Metru Nui, and are preparing to return there for the first time in 1,000 years. The six Turaga who rule the island of Mata Nui reveal that they too were once Toa, and guardians of Metru Nui, but were too late to stop Makuta from plunging both the Matoran and the Great Spirit into unending sleep.

Bionicle Vol. 4: Trial by Fire. Written by Greg Farshtey. Illustrated by Randy Elliott. Papercutz, 2009. 112pp. ISBN-10: 1-5970713-2-3. ISBN-13: 978-15970713-2-1. `GR. 2-5`

> The Toa are in search of the Disks of Power, devices that will grant them enough power to defeat the Morbuzak attacking the city of Metru Nui. The Matoran say they'll help, but are they really going to, or do they have their own ulterior motives?

Bionicle Vol. 5: The Battle of Voya Nui. Written by Greg Farshtey. Illustrated by Stuart Sayger. Papercutz, 2009. 96pp. ISBN-10: 1-5970714-5-5. ISBN-13: 978-15970714-5-1. `GR. 2-5`

> In a brand new chapter in the Bionicle universe, Voya Nui is an island with a dangerous treasure. Ruthless Piraka have enslaved the matoran inhabitants

of the island and are searching for the treasure. Can six Toa transform into Toa Inika and stop the Piraka from finding the Mask of Life?

Bionicle Vol. 6: The Underwater City. Written by Greg Farshtey. Illustrated by Stuart Sayger. Papercutz, 2009. 96pp. ISBN-10: 1-5960615-7-9. ISBN-13: 978-15970715-7-4. **GR. 2-7**

The Mask of Life has sunk to the bottom of the sea, where it turns up in Mahri Nui, a city that must constantly protect itself from vicious underwater predators. Defilak, a matoran inventor, finds the mask and discovers its deadly secret. The Mask of Light or "Ignika" brings great power, as well as paranoia, jealousy, and madness.

Bionicle Vol. 7: Realm of Fear. Written by Greg Farshtey. Illustrated by Leigh Gallaghe. Papercutz, 2009. 96pp. ISBN-10: 1-5970716-8-4. ISBN-13: 978-15970716-8-0. **GR. 2-7**

Mahri Matora has sacrificed himself to save the spirit Mata Nui, and the remaining Toa are squabbling among themselves now. With the Makuta closing in, the Toa struggle to find some way to awaken Mata Nui. Meanwhile, the Mask of Life has become an entity itself and decides to guard itself. Can the Mask of Life be just the thing the Toa need to awaken Mata Nui and repel the Makuta once and for all?

Boxed Sets

Bionicle Boxed Set: Vols. 1-4. Written by Greg Farshtey. Illustrated by Carlos D'Anda, Richard Bennett, and Randy Elliott. Papercutz, 2009. 400pp. ISBN-10: 1-5970717-6-5. ISBN-13: 978-15970717-6-5.

The first four books of the Bionicle series, slip-cased for easy storage. Contains the stories "Rise of the Toa Nuva," "Challenge of the Rahkshi," "City of Legends," and "Trial by Fire," detailing the trials and dangers of an alien race called the Toa, their efforts to protect their way of life, and the enemies they face.

Sardine in Outer Space. **GR. 3-8**

Join that adorable little scallywag Sardine, her pirate uncle, Captain Yellow Shoulder, and her cousin Little Louie as they fight the evil forces of good manners.

Sardine in Outer Space I. Written by Emmanuel Guibert. Illustrated by Joann Sfar. First Second, 2006. 128pp. ISBN-10: 1-5964312-6-1. ISBN-13: 978-15964312-6-3.

Sardine, her cousin, Little Louie, and their uncle, Captain Yellow Shoulder, travel through the universe, opposing Supermuscleman (a costumed villain who runs an orphanage designed to teach children proper manners) and his henchman, Doc Krok. Join them in their battles for freedom, children's rights, and disobedience.

Sardine in Outer Space II. Written by Emmanuel Guibert. Illustrated by Joann Sfar. First Second, 2006. 128pp. ISBN-10: 1-5964312-7-X. ISBN-13: 978-15964312-7-0.

> Sardine and her uncle, Captain Yellow Shoulder, are back along with Little Louie for more madcap mayhem. This time, the evil Supermuscleman has developed a child-controlling device that brainwashes children into doing what they're supposed to! Sardine and her crew also have to face off against pesky flies, intergalactic yogurt thieves, and a little monster carpet salesman.

Sardine in Outer Space III. Written by Emmanuel Guibert. Illustrated by Joann Sfar. First Second, 2007. 112pp. ISBN-10: 1-5964312-8-8. ISBN-13: 978-15964312-8-7.

> Supermuscleman and Doc Krok are up to their naughtiness again, except this time, they want to ruin not only the universe, but their adversaries, Sardine and Little Louie. Will a shrunken Supermuscleman and a Space Boxing Championship spell doom for the space-faring cousins?

Sardine in Outer Space IV. Written by Emmanuel Guibert. Illustrated by Joann Sfar. First Second, 2007. 112pp. ISBN-10: 1-5964312-8-8. ISBN-13: 978-15964312-8-7.

> Chronicles yet another day in the life of the famous space pirate, Sardine. In this installment, Sardine faces off against monsters under the bed, flesh-eating tattoos, time machines, and worst of all . . . boredom. As if that wasn't enough, Supermuscleman is constantly lurking in the background, waiting to destroy her.

STAR WARS

No other title exemplifies science fiction fantasy the way *Star Wars* does. Originally a throw-away film on a shoestring budget in the 1970s, this movie by a young, little-known director not only changed the face of the industry, but also spawned an entire generation of young fans.

The director, George Lucas, went on to make a career out of the *Star Wars* franchise, from movies to prose novels, television shows, and video games to graphic novels. At current count, more than fifty graphic novels have been published featuring the Star Wars universe.

For the most part, the Star Wars universe is split into seven time periods:

- The Old Republic Era (starting approximately 5,000 years before the first *Star Wars* movie)

- The <u>Rise of the Republic Era</u> (starting approximately 1,000 years before the first *Star Wars* movie)

- The <u>Rebellion Era</u> (the first *Star Wars* trilogy occurs during this time)

- The <u>New Republic Era</u> (starting approximately five years after the first trilogy)

- The <u>New Jedi Order Era</u> (approximately twenty-five years after the first trilogy)

- The <u>Legacy Era</u> (approximately 130 years after the first trilogy)

- <u>Infinities</u> (covers anything that is not dated, or works that are "alternate reality" from the traditional canon)

Old Republic Era. GR. 4-8

Star Wars Omnibus: Tales of the Jedi Vol. 1. Written and illustrated by Various. Dark Horse Comics, 2007. 395pp. ISBN-10: 1-5930783-0-7. ISBN-13: 978-15930783-0-0.

> Set 5,000 years before Luke Skywalker's successful destruction of the Death Star, these stories describe the Old Republic, when the Sith were prevalent and the Jedi were forced to fight them for their very lives. The first omnibus collects the individual books *The Golden Age of the Sith*, *The Fall of the Sith Empire*, and *Knights of the Old Republic*, detailing the rise and fall of the Sith and the eventual founding of the Empire.

Star Wars Omnibus: Tales of the Jedi Vol. 2. Written and illustrated by Various. Dark Horse Comics, 2008. 464pp. ISBN-10: 1-5930791-1-7. ISBN-13: 978-15930791-1-7.

> The Sith Empire is nothing more than a bitter memory, but an ancient evil has risen and corrupted one of the greatest Jedi, igniting a world-ravaging war. The Sith have been reborn, and the universe will never be the same again.

Rise of the Empire. GR. 4-8

Star Wars: Episode 1: The Phantom Menace. Adapted by Henry Gilroy. Illustrated by Rodolfo Damaggio and Al Williamson. Dark Horse Comics, 1999. 112pp. ISBN-10: 1-5697135-9-6. ISBN-13: 978-15697135-9-4.

> Details the history and events leading up to the foundation of the Rebel Alliance and their battle against the corrupt Empire. Adapted from the motion picture of the same name.

Star Wars: Episode 2: Attack of the Clones. Adapted by Henry Gilroy. Illustrated by Jan Duursema and Ray Kryssing. Dark Horse Comics, 2002. 44pp. ISBN-10: 1-5697160-9-9. ISBN-13: 978-15697160-9-0.

> Adapts the second movie of the second trilogy, Anakin has become a full-fledged padawan under the tutelage of Obi-Wan. Count Dooku and General Grevious are leading the separatist movement, Anakin and Padme have fallen in love; and the Emperor is one step closer to absolute power.

Star Wars: Clone Wars Adventures. **GR. 4-8**

> Before Anakin Skywalker became Darth Vader, Obi-Wan took Anakin under his wing, and they fought in the Clone Wars, the universe-spanning battle that brought the Chancellor to Emperor status. Clone Wars Adventures covers those battles, big and small, that precipitated the fall and near total termination of all Jedi.

Clone Wars Adventures Vol. 1. Written by Haden Blackman and Ben Caldwell. Illustrated by Matt Fillbach and Shawn Fillbach. Dark Horse Comics, 2004. 96pp. ISBN-10: 1-5930724-3-0. ISBN-13: 978-15930724-3-8.

> Obi-Wan and Anakin must learn to fight in the dark, while Jedi Masters Mace Windu and Saesee Tiin discover new ways to fight battledroids. Elsewhere, Kit Fisto and his troops face off against separatist forces on Mon Calamari.

Clone Wars Adventures Vol. 2. Written by Haden Blackman and Welles Hartley. Illustrated by Matt Fillbach and Shawn Fillbach. Dark Horse Comics, 2004. 96pp. ISBN-10: 1-5930727-1-6. ISBN-13: 978-15930727-1-1.

> Anakin and Obi-Wan fight a daring space battle with droids and human pilots supporting Count Dooku. Meanwhile, Luminara Unuli and Barriss Offee must evacuate a village before General Grevious rolls into town. More excitement from the war!

Star Wars: Episode 3: Revenge of the Sith. Adapted by Miles Lane. Illustrated by Doug Wheatley. Dark Horse Comics, 2005. 96pp. ISBN-10: 1-5697160-9-9. ISBN-13: 978-15697160-9-0.

> The fall of the Jedi, the Republic, and even Anakin Skywalker is detailed in the final chapter of the second trilogy. The clone wars rage on, and Chancellor Palpatine has orchestrated the fall of the Republic, the slaughter of the Jedi, and the seduction of Anakin to the dark side.

The Rebellion.

Star Wars: Episode 4: A New Hope—Special Edition. Written by Bruce Jones and Eduardo Barreto. Illustrated by Al Williamson. Dark Horse, 1995. 104pp. ISBN-10: 1-5697121-3-1. ISBN-13: 978-15697121-3-9. **GR. 5-8**

> Adapted from the 1978 blockbuster that not only started a franchise, but also altered the face of pop culture. Luke Skywalker is a boy who dreams of one day escaping from the moisture farms of his aunt and uncle on Tatooine, but

he can't figure out how. One day Luke's uncle purchases two droids who are more than they appear, and Luke is drawn into a battle for the freedom of the entire universe.

Star Wars: Episode V: The Empire Strikes Back. Written by Archie Goodwin and Al Williamson. Illustrated by Carlos Garzon. Dark Horse, 2009. 104pp. ISBN-10: 1-5697123-4-4. ISBN-13: 978-15697123-4-4. **GR. 5-8**

The Death Star has been destroyed, and the Emperor has declared martial law throughout the galaxy. Luke, Leia, and Han now fight for their survival as both the Emperor and Darth Vader tighten their grip on the throat of the rebel alliance. Luke begins his training with the Jedi master Yoda, while Han joins up with an old friend who may or may not have ulterior plans for Han and Leia.

Star Wars: Return of the Jedi—The Special Edition. Written and illustrated by Various. Dark Horse, 2005. 104pp. ISBN-10: 1-5697123-5-2. ISBN-13: 978-15697123-5-1. **GR. 4-8**

The graphic novel adaptation of the third movie of the same title in the original trilogy finds Luke Skywalker, now a Jedi Knight, facing down gangsters, dying Jedi, and his own father in an epic finale, while Han, Leia, and Lando scheme with the rebel alliance to take down the Empire once and for all.

The New Republic. **GR. 4-8**

Star Wars: Heir to the Empire. Written by Timothy Zahn. Adapted by Mike Baron. Illustrated by Olivier Vatine and Fred Blanchard. Dark Horse, 1996. 160pp. ISBN-10: 1-5697120-2-6. ISBN-13: 978-15697120-2-3.

The Empire has fallen, Han and Leia have married and are expecting twins, and Luke has begun the task of reviving the Jedi. In the furthest reaches of space, the last of the Emperor's warlords has taken command of the remnants of the Imperial Fleet, has readied it for war, and plans on taking out the fragile heart of the new Republic. Will two devastating secrets that Grand Admiral Thrawn has discovered spell doom for the galaxy?

Star Wars: Union. Written by Michael A Stackpole. Illustrated by Various. Dark Horse, 2000. 96pp. ISBN-10: 1-5697146-4-9. ISBN-13: 978-15697146-4-5.

In the aftermath of Grand Admiral Thrawn's defeat, Luke Skywalker and Mara Jade, an ex-assassin groomed by the Emperor to kill Skywalker, decide to get married. Neither the new Republic nor the remnants of the old Empire will stop until their union is destroyed.

The New Jedi Order.

Star Wars: Chewbacca. Written and illustrated by Various. Dark Horse, 2001. 96pp. ISBN-10: 1-5697151-5-7. ISBN-13: 978-15697151-5-4. `GR. 4-8`

At the end of *Vector Prime*, the beloved wookie, Chewbacca, met his heroic end. This book collects tales about Chewbacca from the people who knew him best: Lando Calrissian, Princess Leia, Han Solo, and Luke Skywalker. This book also reveals the culture of Wookies in general and discusses their home world, Kashyyyk.

Aliens

Standard fare in science fiction, aliens have long been a big part of the genre. From the tripods of H. G. Wells's *War of the Worlds*, to James Cameron's *Na'vi*, aliens tend to play an integral part in science fiction. Sometimes benevolent, often hostile, aliens work quite often as metaphors for dealing with people who are different from us. In the books in this section, aliens run the spectrum from friendly to hostile.

Aargh, It's an Alien! **Written by K. Wallace. Illustrated by Michael Reid. Stone Arch Books, 2006. 72pp. ISBN-10: 1-5988902-3-9. ISBN-13: 978-15988902-3-5.** `GR. 2-6`

Albert's parents give him everything he wants, except time together. When aliens from outer space visit Albert, they make him an amazing offer. Will he decide to stay home with his family, or will Albert fly away with his new friends?

Ed's Terrestrials. **Written by Scott Sava. Illustrated by Diego Jourdan. Idea & Design Works LLC, 2008. 88pp. ISBN-10: 1-6001031-0-3. ISBN-13: 978-16001031-0-0.** `GR. 3-8`

Three aliens escape from their boring life working in the Intergalactic Food Court and hijack a space ship to Earth. Hot on their tails is the mall security officer, Maximus Obliterus, who plans on dragging these wayward aliens back to their jobs. The escapees crash land in Ed's tree house and quickly befriend Ed, who agrees to help them blend in and become more human. Unfortunately, Obliterus manages to find human help as well: Ed's nemesis, the bratty Natalie.

Eek and Ack.

What happens to the seminal alien idea of conquering Earth when you put in the tentacles of two bumbling extraterrestrials who have no idea what they are doing? If you add in kid-friendly dialogue and silly pictures, you get these two goofballs!

Eek and Ack: Beyond the Black Hole. Written by Blake A. Hoena. Illustrated by Steve Harpster. Stone Arch Books, 2009. 40pp. ISBN-10: 1-4342075-9-5. ISBN-13: 978-14342075-9-3. **GR. 1-5**

> Getting pulled through a black hole, Eek and Ack find another Earth, but it's a weird pink color. Regardless of the color, Eek and Ack will try to conquer it.

Eek and Ack: Invaders from the Great Goo Galaxy. Written by Blake A. Hoena. Illustrated by Steve Harpster. Stone Arch Books, 2007. 40pp. ISBN-10: 1-5988905-2-2. ISBN-13: 98-15988905-2-5. **GR. 1-5**

> Eek and Ack, two aliens, get bored one day, so they decide to conquer that weird planet, Earth!

Eek and Ack: The Puzzling Pluto Plot. Written by Blake A. Hoena. Illustrated by Steve Harpster. Stone Arch Books, 2008. 40pp. ISBN-10: 1-4342045-2-9. ISBN-13: 978-14342045-2-3. **GR. 1-5**

> In their latest attempt to conquer Earth, those bumbling aliens, Eek and Ack, take a wrong turn. Pluto will never be the same!

Eek and Ack, Ooze Slingers from Outer Space. Written by Blake A. Hoena. Illustrated by Steve Harpster. Stone Arch Books, 2007. 40pp. ISBN-10: 1-5988941-0-2. ISBN-13: 978-15988941-0-3. **GR. 2-4**

> Coming from the Great Goo Galaxy, the terrible two are up to their old tricks again; making new plans to conquer Earth. Unfortunately, something sticky with eyes and feet is gumming up their plans.

Eek and Ack vs. the Wolfman. Written by Blake A. Hoena. Illustrated by Steve Harpster. Stone Arch Books, 2009. 40pp. ISBN-10: 1-4342118-9-4. ISBN-13: 978-14342118-9-7. **GR. 1-5**

> Those goofball aliens decide to try to take over Earth on Halloween. After dressing up in costumes to hide themselves, they land on Earth, only to find that an actual werewolf has dressed up to hang out with Earthlings as well. Unfortunately, he thinks Eek and Ack look quite tasty, and he has built up a terrible hunger.

The War of the Worlds. **Written by H. G. Wells. Retold by Davis Worth Miller and Katherine Mclean Brevard. Illustrated by Tod Smith. Stone Arch Books, 2009. 72pp. ISBN-10: 1-4342075-7-9. ISBN-13: 1-4342075-7-9.** **GR. 2-8**

> Here is Wells's classic tale of intergalactic invasion in a kid-friendly format. The invaders are completely impervious to all of Earth's weapons, but George must find the one thing that can stop them.

When Vegetables Attack. **Written by Mark Burgess. Illustrated by Bridget MacKeith. Stone Arch Books, 2008. 72pp. ISBN-10: 1-4342045-8-8. ISBN-13: 978-14342035-8-5.** **GR. 2-6**

> In the aftermath of an experiment gone wrong, mutant veggies threaten to conquer the world. Can Agent Spike of the Secret Service defeat this vegetative menace?

Robots, Androids, and Cyborgs

Yet another staple of science fiction is the artificial being: the robot, the android, and the cyborg. Although on the surface they may seem like the same thing, and they are grouped together here for practical purposes, there are small but major distinctions between them.

Robots are basically mechanical automatons, usually metallic, that sometimes break their programming. Androids are robots designed to look, act, and think like humans. Cyborgs are humans with robotic implants or replacement parts that make them not quite human, but not quite robot.

Angelic Layer. GR. 3-7

Misaki Suzuhara just moved in with her aunt in Tokyo. Starting the seventh grade, Misaki becomes enamored of a game called "Angelic Layer," in which the "Deus" (players) battle custom-made fighting dolls called "angels." Although Misaki has never played "Angelic Layer," she discovers that she's a natural and quickly climbs up through the ranks of fighters.

Angelic Layer Vol. 1. Written and illustrated by CLAMP. TokyoPop, 2002. 200pp. ISBN-10: 1-9315144-7-X. ISBN-13: 978-19315144-7-7.

> Misaki creates her own angel after watching a battle on the vid screens. Encouraged by a mysterious stranger, Misaki plans on taking the game by storm.

Angelic Layer Vol. 2. Written and illustrated by CLAMP. TokyoPop, 2002. 172pp. ISBN-10: 1-5918200-3-0. ISBN-13: 978-15918200-3-1.

> Misaki may be smarting from her first defeat, but that's not going to stop her from taking on Ringo Seto, the Japanese pop star, or the Fujisaki sisters, fierce competitors who will stop at nothing to win. With the help of her friends and her mad scientist mentor, she might just stand a chance.

Angelic Layer Vol. 3. Written and illustrated by CLAMP. TokyoPop, 2002. 172pp. ISBN-10: 1-5918200-4-9. ISBN-13: 978-15918200-4-8.

> The regional finals have come to Kanto, and an all-new area has been unveiled. Now Misaki not only has to contend with Kaede Saitou, a super-experienced Angel fighter, but the new battle layer full of craggy peaks and smoky crevices!

Angelic Layer Vol. 4. Written and illustrated by CLAMP. TokyoPop, 2003. 200pp. ISBN-10: 1-5918208-6-3. ISBN-13: 978-15918208-6-4.

> Against all odds, Misaki managed to win the regional finals. Now she has to face off against her most difficult opponent yet. Will she be able to beat the "Prince of the Layer," Ohjiro Mihara, or is this the end?

Angelic Layer Vol. 5. Written and illustrated by CLAMP. TokyoPop, 2003. 200pp. ISBN-10: 1-5918208-6-3. ISBN-13: 978-15918208-6-4.

> Misaki thought she was done with the Fujisaka sisters, but now she has to face Arisu, the mechanical genius who has Misaki in her crosshairs. Topping it all off, the newest layer is a winter wonderland that can freeze an angel in its tracks. If Misaki can prevail, she'll become the master of the layer.

Astro Boy. GR. 4-8

Meet the Japanese equivalent of America's Mickey Mouse: a jet-powered, super-strong, evil-robot-bashing, alien-invasion-smashing robot child called Astro Boy. Osamu Tezuka, said to be the Walt Disney of Japan and the creator of this series, is often credited as the "Father of Manga." Astro boy is the story of a robotic boy who battles robots and aliens and tries to understand what it means to be human. All the books listed here are reprints from the traditional Japanese manga books.

Astro Boy Vols. 1 & 2. Written and illustrated by Osamu Tezuka. Dark Horse Comics, 2008. 424pp. ISBN-10: 1-5958215-3-8. ISBN-13: 978-15958215-3-9.

> This edition collects the first two books in the Astro Boy series. In the year 2030, a brilliant robotics engineer loses his son in a tragic car accident. In an attempt to re-create his son, the scientist constructs an android in the boy's image. After Dr. Boyton realizes that the android cannot fill the void in his heart, he abandons the android to a carnival where androids are forced to fight each other. Rescued by an Android rights advocate, Astro Boy learns how to use his powers to benefit humankind.

Astro Boy Vol. 3. Written and illustrated by Osamu Tezuka. Dark Horse Books, 2002. 208pp. ISBN-10: 1-5697167-8-1. ISBN-13: 978-15697167-8-6.

> A former sultan has created a powerful robot by the name of Pluto. To prove that his robot is the most powerful in the world, the sultan instructs Pluto to battle and destroy the seven most powerful robots in the world. Astro refuses to fight at first, but when Pluto kidnaps Astro's little sister, Astro has no choice. However, Uran may hold the key to ending the battle before a single punch is thrown.

Astro Boy Vol. 4. Written and illustrated by Osamu Tezuka. Dark Horse Books, 2002. 216pp. ISBN-10: 1-59697167-9-X. ISBN-13: 978-15697167-9-3.

> Another collection of stories involving Astro Boy. First he fights to free abused robots from a theme park that masks a secret weapons factory. Then Astro gets stranded on the moon with other robots, only to discover a valley full of diamonds—and something that guards

them. Later Astro becomes trapped in the twentieth century after a time machine malfunction. Finally, Astro gets involved in a battle to overthrow a dictator who has a machine capable of producing clones.

Gundam Wing. GR. 4-8

A popular genre of Japanese manga is the Giant Robot battlers. Like most of these types of stories, the focus isn't so much on the technology as on the operators of the machinery. A print sequel to the popular television series by the same name, Gundam Wing follows the trials of five younger boys who pilot huge Gundam fighting machines in their battles against corrupt Earth governments. This series gets rather dark at times, as the characters wax poetic about how horrible it is that they have to fight each other and then proceed to blow up massive ships with thousands of people on board. Manga titles tend to be rather hit or miss with American audiences, so keep that in mind when advising; and don't take offense if your reader passes on this one.

Gundam Wing: Battlefield of Pacifists. Written and illustrated by Katsuhiko Chiba. TokyoPop, 2002. 176pp. ISBN-10: 1-9315147-1-2. ISBN-13: 978-19315147-1-2.

In the aftermath of the War between Earth and the Colonies, the Gundam pilots must now maintain the peace. When a weapons factory is discovered near Mars, the Gundams are called in for a final battle to ensure peace.

Gundam Wing: Blind Target. Written by Akemi Omode and Sakura Asagi. Illustrated by Reku Fuyunagi. VIZ Media LLC, 2003. 152pp. ISBN-10: 1-5693195-9-6. ISBN-13: 978-15693195-9-8.

The Gundam pilots have become the targets of a shadowy conspiracy that will resort to anything to get the Gundams.

Gundam Wing: Endless Waltz. Written by Hajime Yatate and Yoshiyuki Tomino. Illustrated by Kouichi Tokita. TokyoPop, 2002. 192pp.ISBN-10: 1-9315147-2-0. ISBN-13: 978-19315147-2-9.

After the war, after the peace, after the realization that the boys must destroy their Gundams to ensure peace, a descendant of their nemesis declares a war of independence against the United Earth Nation. Is it wise to pull the Gundams out for one last battle?

Gundam Wing: Episode Zero. Written and illustrated by Reku Fuyunagi. VIZ Media LLC, 2003. 185pp. ISBN-10: 1-5693199-4-4. ISBN-13: 978-15693199-4-9.

A prequel of sorts about the pilots of the Gundams: Duo, Heero, Trowa, Quatre, and Chang. The stories are split up as individual tales about each character, with the main focus being on both Duo and Quatre, covering their childhoods before they began fighting with the Gundams.

Gundam Wing Vol. 1. Written by Hajime Yatate and Yoshiyuki Tomino. Illustrated by Kouichi Tokita. TokyoPop, 2000. 192pp. ISBN-10: 1-8922134-1-9. ISBN-13: 978-18922134-1-9.

> In the year AC 195, a network of space-based rebels strike back at their opposing force, OZ. Rebel scientists, using a super-strong armor called gundanium, create giant mobile battle suits called Gundams. Five boys from all facets of life pilot the Gundams in an interstellar battle for freedom.

Gundam Wing Vol. 2. Written by Hajime Yatate and Yoshiyuki Tomino. Illustrated by Kouichi Tokita. TokyoPop, 2001. 185pp. ISBN-10: 1-8922135-1-6. ISBN-13: 978-18922135-1-8.

> Heero, Duo, Trowa, Quatre, and Chang continue their battle to fight the powers of OZ. Will they succeed, or will OZ and Zechs, the pilot of the Gundam Epyon, prove too much?

Gundam Wing Vol. 3. Written by Hajime Yatate and Yoshiyuki Tomino. Illustrated by Kouichi Tokita. TokyoPop, 2001. 184pp. ISBN-10: 1-8922136-0-5. ISBN-13: 978-18922136-0-0.

> The finale of the main <u>Gundam Wing</u> series finds the boys fighting not only for their cause, but also for their very lives.

Transformers.

In 1984 two Japanese toy designers came up with a novel idea for a line of toys: robots that could transform into various forms of transportation or electronics. Needing a "hook" to introduce the line to American audiences, they hit upon the idea of a cartoon. The rest, they say, is history.

The <u>Transformer</u> franchise, now more than twenty-five years old, is one of the most popular franchises in the world. With two live-action movies out, a laundry list of toys that could bankrupt Donald Trump if he were to buy every single one, several cartoon series, and comic books, <u>Transformers</u> are not going away anytime soon.

Transformers Vol. 1: Beginnings. Written by Ralph Macchio, Bob Budiansky, and Jim Salicrup. Illustrated by Bob Budiansky and Jim Salicrup. Titan Books, 2003. 152pp. ISBN-10: 1-8402362-3-X. ISBN-13: 978-18402362-3-1. **GR. 3-8**

> This is it! The original comic book series based on the television show, detailing the arrival of the noble Autobots and the nefarious Decepticons on Earth. This is one of those rare adaptations that actually captures the feel of the original cartoon series. (**Note:** The Ralph Macchio who wrote this series is *not* the actor and star of the *Karate Kid* series.)

Transformers Vol. 2: New Order. Written by Bob Budiansky. Illustrated by William Johnson, Ricardo Villamonte, and Herb Trimpe. Titan Books, 2004. 144pp. ISBN-10: 1-8402362-5-6. ISBN-13: 978-18402362-5-5. `GR. 3-8`

> The continuing adventures of Buster Witwicky and his friends, the Autobots. The war is not going well for the Autobots: Optimus has been destroyed, and Megatron is moving in for the kill. Can the mysterious Dinobots be persuaded to help?

Transformers Vol. 3: Cybertron Redux. Written by Bob Budiansky. Illustrated by Don Perlin and Graham Nolan. Titan Books, 2003. 144pp. ISBN-10: 1-8402365-7-4. ISBN-13: 978-18402365-7-6. `GR. 4-8`

> The fight between the Autobots and Decepticons rages on across two fronts: Earth, and the transformer home world, Cybertron. If the Autobots cannot defeat the Decepticon Straxus, Earth will be obliterated!

Transformers Vol. 4: Showdown. Written by Bob Budiansky. Illustrated by Don Perlin, Herb Trimpe, and Nancy Jones. Titan Books, 2004. 300pp. ISBN-10: 1-8402368-7-6. ISBN-13: 978-18402368-7-3. `GR. 4-8`

> Optimus Prime and Megatron face off for the last time. Only one will walk away from the battle. Regardless of who wins, this battle will change the face of the war between the two factions forever.

Nate's Picks

- <u>Bionicle</u> by Various. Any boy worth his Legos® will happily snap these titles up, as they explain much of the history of the characters.

- <u>Zapt!</u> by Shannon Denton, Keith Giffen, and Armand Villavert Jr. Engaging story quickly pulls even the most reluctant reader in.

- <u>Star Wars</u> by Various. The grand master of modern space fantasy. Anything from this series is good, if uneven.

- <u>Transformers</u> by Various. Although conceived in Japan, this brand has been wholly consumed by American culture. The original series is dated, but it is still an excellent read.

Chapter 4

Fantasy

One of the most popular genres today, fantasy can encompass many different subgenres and styles, from high fantasy with swords and sorcery and mythical beasts, to the Victorian era Steampunk, to futuristic vistas with familiar themes.

Fantasy is also one of the first genres kids get into. Growing up with fairy tales and fables tends to lay the groundwork for exploration in this genre, and many kids read and enjoy fantasy.

The fantastic captures our imaginations. Even though something may be impossible, after reading about it in a fantasy novel, the reader feels it is possible. From J. K. Rowling's Harry Potter series (which desperately needs to be translated into a graphic novel) to J. R. R. Tolkien's *The Hobbit* (which has been given the graphic novel treatment), fantasy books have inspired, influenced, and shaped generations of writers and illustrators.

Sword and Sorcery

This category is usually characterized by swashbuckling heroes with elements of romance as well as magic and the supernatural. Unlike more traditional high fantasy tales, sword and sorcery stories concentrate more on personal battles than on world-threatening fights. Examples of traditional sword and sorcery are *Conan the Barbarian* and *The Hobbit*.

Bone.

Follow the adventures of three cousins as they enter a strange, magical, yet dangerous valley full of dragons, Rat Creatures, displaced royalty, and talking bugs. Winner of multiple awards, Bone is a must have series that every librarian should read at least once.

Though not a "traditional" sword and sorcery story, Bone follows the template of this genre: The stories focus mostly on Fone Bone and his attempts to keep his two cousins from getting killed and help his friend Thorn defeat an ancient enemy. (The publication dates listed below are for the collected books; the series started out as single issues in 1991.) (Harvey Award, Eisner Award, Lulu Award)

Parental Advisory: Later books get into some scary-ish situations that may not sit well with younger readers.

Bone Vol. 1: Out from Boneville. Written and illustrated by Jeff Smith. Scholastic, 2005. 144pp. ISBN-10: 0-4397064-0-8. ISBN-13: 978-04397064-0-7. `GR. 3-8`

> The first book in the series introduces Fone Bone and his two cousins, Phoncible (Phoney) Bone, and Smiley Bone, who are on the run from the city of Boneville. Phoney has been run out-of-town by an angry mob, and his cousins Fone and Smiley leave with him to try to keep him out of trouble. Entering a mystical valley, Fone is separated from his cousins and meets new friends and enemies, and begins to realize he's in over his head.

Bone Vol. 2: The Great Cow Race. Written and illustrated by Jeff Smith. Graphix, 2005. 144pp. ISBN-10: 0-4397963-9-4. ISBN-13: 978-04397063-9-1. `GR. 4-8`

> The Bone Cousins begin adjusting to pastoral life (as it were). While Fone Bone tries to find a way to express his feelings for Thorn, Phoney (with some "help" from Smiley) attempts to rig the annual cow race so he can fleece the townspeople. The series takes a darker tone in this book, but is still acceptable for younger readers.

Bone Vol. 3: Eyes of the Storm. Written and illustrated by Jeff Smith. Graphix, 2006. 192pp. ISBN-10: 0-439-7063-8-6. ISBN-13: 978-04397063-8-4. `GR. 4-8`

> Phoney and his cousins have to face the repercussions of the failed attempt to fix the cow race, Thorn's royal past, and the connection between Gran'ma Ben and the Dragons. With this volume, the series moves toward a high fantasy feel.

Bone Vol. 4: The Dragonslayer. Written and illustrated by Jeff Smith. Graphix, 2006. 176pp. ISBN-10: 0-4397063-7-8. ISBN-13: 978-04397063-7-7. `GR. 4-8`

> After the Rat Creatures attack, Fone, Gran'ma Ben, and Thorn flee the farm. While they are in Barrelhaven, rumors of dragons inspire Phoney to present himself as a real dragonslayer, rallying the townsfolk to his banner (and his side of the bar). Possibly inspired by Star Wars, the concept of "The Dreaming" is introduced.
>
> **Parental Advisory:** graphic violence involving fantasy characters

Bone Vol. 5: Rock Jaw: Master of the Eastern Border. Written and illustrated by Jeff Smith. Graphix, 2007. 128pp. ISBN-10: 0-4397063-6-X. ISBN-13: 978-04397063-6-0. `GR. 4-8`

> After Smiley makes a new friend with a Rat Creature cub, Fone explains that they have to return "Bartleby" to his kind. In the process of eluding the two "Stupid Rat Creatures,," Fone and Smiley meet Roque Ja, a giant mountain lion.
>
> **Parental Advisory:** scenes of intense peril and violence

Bone Vol. 6: Old Man's Cave. Written and illustrated by Jeff Smith. Graphix, 2007. 128pp. ISBN-10: 0-4397063-5-1. ISBN-13: 978-04397063-5-3. **GR. 4-8**

> The Bones—Thorn, Gran'ma Ben, and Lucius—make their final stand against the Rat Creatures at "Old Man's Cave.." The history of the Bones is finally revealed, as is why they put up with so much of Phoney's nonsense, and readers finally discover why the Hooded One was so interested in capturing Phoney.
>
> **Parental Advisory:** supernatural suspense and scary images

Bone Vol. 7: Ghost Circles. Written and illustrated by Jeff Smith. Graphix, 2008. 160pp. ISBN-10: 0-4397063-4-3. ISBN-13: 978-04397063-4-6. **GR. 5-8**

> The Lord of the Locusts stirs in its prison, bringing down the mountain everyone is hiding out in. Escaping through the tunnels Fone originally used to escape Roque Ja, the group experiences a *Moby-Dick*–inspired hallucination. A deadly new phenomenon appears as well: Ghost Circles, which are pockets of evil power that nothing can survive in.
>
> **Parental Advisory:** supernatural suspense and scary images

Bone Vol. 8: Treasure Hunters. Written and illustrated by Jeff Smith. Graphix, 2008. 144pp. ISBN-10: 0-4397063-3-5. ISBN-13: 978-04397063-3-9. **GR. 5-8**

> Thorn, Gran'ma Ben, and the Bones finally make it to the Ancestral Homelands of Altheia, only to find that there is no safe sanctuary inside the city walls, either. Thorn finally discovers the one item that can ultimately destroy the Lord of the Locusts, but at what cost?

Bone Vol. 9: Crown of Horns. Written and illustrated by Jeff Smith. Graphix, 2009. 224pp. ISBN-10: 0-4397063-2-7. ISBN-13: 978-04397063-2-2. **GR. 5-8**

> Fone Bone and Thorn must make the dangerous trek to find the Crown of Horns, knowing full well that it will probably kill them and take out the valley as well.

Bone: The Complete Cartoon Epic in One Volume. **Written and illustrated by Jeff Smith. Cartoon Books, 2004. 1,300pp. ISBN-10: 1-8889631-4-X. ISBN-13: 978-18889631-4-4.** **GR. 5-8**

> The complete 1,300-page epic adventure collected into one huge book! Three cousins find themselves in a pretechnological valley. Over the course of one year, events place them in the eye of a maelstrom of events that will change not only a kingdom, but also the very landscape of the world they inhabit. As Gordon Flagg stated in his review for *Booklist:* "Be prepared for overdues: even

the most voracious readers will be hard-pressed to get through this hefty, phone book-like tome before they're supposed to return it."

After Jeff Smith completed the series <u>Bone</u>, Scholastic purchased the rights to reprint the series in full color. What was already an enjoyable read became even more engrossing with the addition of full coloring. As the story was not changed, only basic information is provided.

Bone Vol. 1: Out from Boneville. **Written and illustrated by Jeff Smith. Scholastic, 2005. 144pp. ISBN-10: 0-4397064-0-8. ISBN-13: 978-04397064-0-7.**

Bone Vol. 2: The Great Cow Race. **Written and illustrated by Jeff Smith. Graphix, 2005. 144pp. ISBN-10: 0-4397063-9-4. ISBN-13: 978-03597063-9-1.**

Bone Vol. 3: Eyes of the Storm. **Written and illustrated by Jeff Smith. Graphix, 2006. 192pp. ISBN-10: 0-4397063-8-6. ISBN-13: 978-04397063-8-4.**

Bone Vol. 4: The Dragonslayer. **Written and illustrated by Jeff Smith. Graphix, 2006. 176pp. ISBN-10: 0-4397063-7-8. ISBN-13: 978-04397064-7-7.**

Bone Vol. 5: Rock Jaw Master of the Eastern Border. **Written and illustrated by Jeff Smith. Graphix, 2007. 128pp. ISBN-10: 0-4397063-6-X. ISBN-13: 978-04397063-6-0.**

Bone Vol. 6: Old Man's Cave. **Written and illustrated by Jeff Smith. Graphix, 2007. 128pp. ISBN-10: 0-4397063-5-1. ISBN-13: 978-0439706353-5-3.**

Bone Vol. 7: Ghost Circles. **Written and illustrated by Jeff Smith. Graphix, 2008. 160pp. ISBN-10: 0-4397063-4-3. ISBN-13: 978-04397063-4-6.**

Bone Vol. 8: Treasure Hunters. **Written and illustrated by Jeff Smith. Graphix, 2008. 144pp. ISBN-10: 0-4397063-3-5. ISBN-13: 978-04397063-3-9.**

Bone Vol. 9: Crown of Horns. **Written and illustrated by Jeff Smith. Graphix, 2009. 224pp. ISBN-10: 0-4397063-2-7. ISBN-13: 978-04397063-2-2.**

Castle Waiting. `GR. 4-8`

This classic tale for modern times shows that while rescuing princesses, saving kingdoms, and fighting in epic battles between good and evil are nice, quite often the most powerful fairy tales are those in which being a hero in your own home is the noblest thing to do. (ALA Top 10 Great Graphic Novels, Eisner Award, Lulu Award)

Castle Waiting Vol. 1: Lucky Road. Written and illustrated by Linda Medley. Olio Press, 2002. 184pp. ISBN-10: 0 -9651852-3-0. ISBN-13: 978-09651852-3-3.

After Sleeping Beauty is rescued and leaves her castle, it falls into disrepair. Eventually a group of fairy tale characters with troubled pasts take up residence in the now run-down building.

Parental Advisory: veiled discussions of domestic abuse

Castle Waiting Vol. 2. Written and illustrated by Linda Medley. Olio Press, 2003. 192pp. ISBN-10: 0-9651852-4-9. ISBN-13: 978-09651852-4-0.

> Peaceful Warren, a young woman who resides at the castle, is bound and determined to live an unconventional life, and she's in the perfect place for it.

The Courageous Princess. **Written and illustrated by Rod Espinosa. Dark Horse, 2007. 240pp. ISBN-10: 1-5930771-9-X. ISBN-13: 978-15930771-9-8.** `GR. 4-8`

> Princess Mabelrose may not be the fairest in the land, but what she lacks in stunning beauty, she more than makes up for in bravery and brains. After she frees herself from being a dragon's prisoner, her adventure really begins.

Dreamland Chronicles. `GR. 4-8`

> Originally a Web comic, the <u>Dreamland Chronicles</u> has become an even more popular graphic novel series. Alexander Carter has found a key that opens the way back to the land of dreams from his childhood, a land filled with dragons, fairies, and giants. Rejoining his childhood friends, Alexander must embark on a quest to save Dreamland from an all-consuming war against the nightmare realm.

Dreamland Chronicles: Book One. Written and illustrated by Scott Sava. Blue Dream Studios, 2008. 300pp. ISBN-10: 1-6001030-7-3. ISBN-13: 978-16001030-7-0.

> Once upon a time, Alex used to visit the Dreamland every night. Now Alex is in college and has rediscovered Dreamland. All his friends are still there: Nastajia the elf princess, Paddington the rock giant, and Kiwi the fairy. Highly recommended for all audiences.

Dreamland Chronicles: Book Two. Written and illustrated by Scott Sava. Blue Dream Studios, 2008. 276pp. ISBN-10: 1-6001030-8-1. ISBN-13: 978-16001030-8-7.

> Alex continues to shift between his normal waking life and his life in Dreamland. After a suspicious cat woman joins their group, they battle a kraken and discover that Alex's young cousin can also visit. Will these revelations give Alex an edge in battling the evil Dragon King?

Dreamland Chronicles: Book Three. Written and illustrated by Scott Sava. Blue Dream Studios, 2009. 268pp. ISBN-10: 1-6001030-9-X.

> Alex and crew are closing in on Nastajia's parents, but first they have to get out of Nicodemus's prison. With things heating up between Alex and Nastajia, the stakes are getting higher and higher, while the dangers are getting deadlier.

The Hobbit: An Illustrated Edition of the Fantasy Classic. **Written by J. R. R. Tolkien. Adapted by Chuck Dixon and Sean Deming. Illustrated by David Wenzel. Del Rey, 2001. 144pp. ISBN-10: 0-3454456-0-0. ISBN-13: 978-03454456-0-5. `GR. 5-8`**

> A stunning adaptation of Tolkien's classic of fantasy. Join Bilbo Baggins and a group of dwarves as they seek to reclaim the dwarves' ancient home from the Dragon Smaug. (**Note:** As of this printing, there is no known graphic novel adaptation of the Lord of the Rings trilogy.)

Nausicaä.

> A thousand years after the "Seven Days of Fire,," a horrific war that almost destroyed the human civilization, Earth is covered in a "Sea of Corruption," a vast forest of fungi that secretes poisonous miasma and invasive spores. Living in this deadly growth are large, killer insects that pose just as serious a threat to anything that comes near. Nausicaä, a princess of a small city-state, had previously pledged her alliance with Torumekia, the Kingdom that houses her land. Now Torumekia is at war with the Dorok Empire, and Nausicaä's life and the fate of the entire human race will be changed forever.

Nausicaä of the Valley of the Wind Vol. 1. **Written and illustrated by Hayao Miyazaki. VIZ Media LLC, 2004. 136pp. ISBN-10: 1-5911640-8-7. ISBN-13: 978-15911640-8-1. `GR. 6-8`**

> The story of a gentle, strong-willed princess with the ability to understand and influence the giant insects that evolved from the destruction of the ecosystem. From the author/illustrator of such international hits as *Spirited Away, Princess Mononoke, Howl's Moving Castle, Kiki's Delivery Service, and Poco Rosso.*

Nausicaä of the Valley of the Wind Vol. 2. **Written and illustrated by Hayao Miyazaki. VIZ Media LLC, 2004. 228pp. ISBN-10: 1-5693108-7-4. ISBN-13: 978-15693108-7-8. `GR. 6-8`**

> Nausicaä has been separated from the Torumekian fleet and finds herself facing the mysterious Ohmu, who open their hearts to her. Will she be able to figure out their urgent warnings about the southern forest?

Once in a Blue Moon. **Written by Nunzio Defilippis and Christina Weir. Illustrated by Jennifer Quick. Oni Press, 2004. 120pp. ISBN-10: 1-9299988-3-X. ISBN-13: 978-10200088-3-8. `GR. 5-8`**

> Aeslin has discovered a new book that is the sequel to the book her father used to read to her as a child, but now she's in the book. She has a chance to change the flow of the story and be the hero that she's always admired.

Redwall. **Written by Brian Jacques. Illustrated by Bret Blevins. Philomel, 2007. 148pp. ISBN-10: 0-3992448-1-6. ISBN-13: 978-039924481-0. `GR. 3-8`**

> The classic tale by Brian Jacques is adapted to graphic novel form in this adequate translation. Fans of the original book may be disappointed by

certain omissions, but others will be delighted by the artistry and poetic storytelling. When Cluny the Scourge, a villainous rat, attacks Redwall Abbey, the inhabitants rise up to defend their home; at the same time Matthias, a young mouse, embarks on a quest to recover the legendary sword of Martin the Warrior, one of the founders of Redwall Abbey.

The Tale of Despereaux. **Adapted and Illustrated by Matt Smith and David Tilton. Candlewick, 2008. 128pp. ISBN-10: 0-7636407-5-1. ISBN-13: 978-07636407-5-0.** `GR. 3-8`

An adaptation of the movie by the same name (which itself was an adaptation of the original book), this is actually the story of several unlikely heroes—Despereaux, a brave mouse; Roscuro, a good-hearted rat; Pea, a princess; and Mig, a servant girl—and their intertwining story lines.

Tellos. `GR. 2-7`

A cross between high fantasy and the Dr. Moreau creatures of H. G. Wells stories, Tellos tells the story of a young boy, Jarek, and his crew of half-human, half-animal friends who attempt to figure out the mystery behind Jarek's origin and eventually try to take down a mad boy-wizard who wants to destroy Jarek. The series currently stands uncompleted because the artist, Mike Wieringo, passed away in 2007.

Tellos Colossal Vol. 1. Written and illustrated by Todd Dezago and Mike Wieringo. Image Comics, 2008. 288pp. ISBN-10: 1-5824094-0-4. ISBN-13: 978-15824094-0-5.

> Young Jarek and his companion Koj, the tiger-warrior, join forces with Serra, the pirate princess, in an effort to confront the dreaded Malesur. Written in such a way that it can be read at bedtime without causing nightmares.

Tellos Colossal Vol. 2. Written and illustrated by Various. Image Comics, 2008. 240pp. ISBN-10: 1-5824099-2-7. ISBN-13: 978-15824099-2-4.

> The second book collects all the other Tellos stories that came after the original ten-issue story collected in *Tellos Colossal Vol. 1*. Includes the stories "Maiden Voyage," "The Last Heist," "Sons and Moons" and "Tales of Tellos."

Fairy Tales and Folklore

Most of the books listed in this section are retellings of the stories our parents told us as children, which we may tell our own children at night. Some are more traditional versions; others have been updated or contemporized to help readers understand the story.

Beauty and the Beast: The Graphic Novel. **Retold and illustrated by Luke Feldman. Stone Arch Books, 2009. 40pp. ISBN-10: 1-4342076-5-X. ISBN-13: 978-143243076-5-4.** `GR. 1-8`

> This retelling of the classic French fairy tale is in a format that is not threatening to younger readers. A merchant traveling through a dark forest picks a rose for his daughter, Beauty. Unfortunately the rose bush belongs to a hideous beast. In exchange for his life, the merchant offers up his daughter. Will Beauty be able to overcome her fear of the beast and possibly fall in love?

Calamity Jack. **Written by Shannon Hale and Dean Hale. Illustrated by Nathan Hale. Bloomsbury USA Children's Books, 2010. 144pp. ISBN-10: 1-5999007-6-9. ISBN-13: 978-15999007-6-6.** `GR. 4-8`

> In this semi-sequel to *Rapunzel's Revenge* (see below), we get to meet Jack before he joins forces with Rapunzel. Jack considers himself a master criminal with a touch of bad luck, and an angry giant wants his bones!

Cinderella: The Graphic Novel. **Retold by Beth Bracken. Illustrated by Jeffrey Stewart Timmins. Stone Arch Books, 2008. 40pp. ISBN-10: 1-4342086-0-5. ISBN-13: 978-14342086-0-6.** `GR. 3-6`

> A retelling of the classic fairy tale finds the eponymous Cinderella slaving away under the watchful eye of her wicked stepmother. Will a chance encounter at the ball prove to be the chance for Cinderella to escape her miserable life?

Hansel and Gretel: The Graphic Novel. **Retold by Donald Lemke. Illustrated by Sean Dietrich. Stone Arch Books, 2008. 40pp. ISBN-10: 1-4342086-3-X. ISBN-13: 978-14342086-3-7.** `GR. 3-6`

> After Hansel and Gretel are abandoned in the forest by their parents, they find a new house. Unfortunately for them, it's owned by a wicked old witch who eats children!

Jack and the Beanstalk: The Graphic Novel. **Retold by Blake A. Hoena. Illustrated by Ricardo Tercio. Stone Arch Books, 2008. 40pp. ISBN-10: 1-4342086-2-1. ISBN-13: 978-14342086-2-0.** `GR. 2-6`

> After Jack sells the family cow for some magic beans, his mother becomes very unhappy. However, a giant beanstalk begins to grow, and Jack decides to climb it. What lies above could be the answer to all of his family's problems, if he can get past the giant!

The Legend of Sleepy Hollow. **Written by Washington Irving. Illustrated and adapted by Bo Hampton. Image Comics, 2004. 64pp. ISBN-10: 1 -5824041-1-9. ISBN-13: 978-15824041-1-0.** `GR. 4-8`

> A spooky retelling of the nervous schoolteacher, the jealous suitor, and a mythical horseman. May be a little too intense for younger readers.

Little Lit: Folklore and Fairy Tale Funnies. **Edited by Art Spiegelman and Françoise Mouly. Written and illustrated by Various. Raw Junior, 2000. 64pp. ISBN-10: 0-0602862-4-5. ISBN-13: 978-00602862-4-8.** `GR. 2-8`

Fully annotated in Chapter 8.

Otto's Orange Day. **Written and illustrated by Frank Cammuso and Jay Lynch. Toon Books, 2008. 40pp. ISBN-13: 978-0-9799238-2-1. ISBN-10: 0-9799238-2-4.** `GR. K-3`

In a humorous and easy-to-read style, the tale of King Midas is retold through the world of Otto, a cat that loves the color orange.

The Princess and the Frog. **Retold and illustrated by Will Eisner. Nantier Beall Minoustchine Publishing, 1996. 29pp. ISBN-10: 1-5616324-4-9. ISBN-13: 978-15616324-4-2.** `GR. K-4`

Eisner's take on the frog prince story fleshes out the characters and indulges in some "after story" shenanigans with the prince's revenge on the evil spellcaster.

Rapunzel: The Graphic Novel. **Adapted and illustrated by Jeffery Stewart Timmins. Stone Arch Books, 2009. 40pp. ISBN-10: 1-4342119-4-0. ISBN-13: 978-14342119-4-1.** `GR. 1-8`

Rapunzel is taken by an evil witch and is forced to live in a tall tower. One day a prince finds her: Will he be able to save Rapunzel and spirit her away from the evil witch?

Rapunzel's Revenge. **Written by Shannon Hale and Dean Hale. Illustrated by Nathan Hale. Bloomsbury USA Children's Books, 2008. 144pp. ISBN-10: 1-5999007-0-X. ISBN-13: 978-15999007-0-4.** `GR. 4-8`

The story of Rapunzel is retold with a decidedly Western twist to it. Rapunzel lives within the confines of her mother's royal villa, surrounded by high garden walls. One day she climbs the wall to see that the world outside is a dark and oppressed place, ruled by her cruel mother. As punishment for climbing the wall, Rapunzel is placed in a tower. After eventually escaping, she vows to destroy her wicked mother, utilizing her hair in a unique way. (ALA Great Graphic Novels)

Red Riding Hood: The Graphic Novel. **Retold by Martin Powell. Illustrated by Victor Rivas. Stone Arch Books, 2008. 40pp. ISBN-10: 1-4342086-5-6. ISBN-13: 978-14342086-5-1.** `GR. 3-6`

Young Ruby sets out one day to visit her Grandmother. Even though she wears a red hood to protect her, will it be enough to thwart the plans of the wolf?

Rumpelstiltskin: The Graphic Novel. **Retold by Martin Powell. Illustrated by Erik Valdez y Alanis. Stone Arch Books, 2008. 40pp. ISBN-10: 1-4342086-4-8. ISBN-13: 978-14342986-4-4.** `GR. 2-6`

> A father makes a boast, and his daughter must now pay his debts by spinning straw into gold. Knowing full well she will never succeed, she strikes a bargain with a wicked troll. In return, he wants something far more precious, unless she can guess his name.

Sleeping Beauty: The Graphic Novel. **Adapted and illustrated by Sean Dietrich. Stone Arch Books, 2009. 40pp. ISBN-10: 1-4342119-3-2. ISBN-13: 978-1434219-3-4.** `GR. 1-8`

> Sleeping Beauty lies in perpetual slumber in a castle surrounded by poisonous thorns and deadly creatures. Will the brave prince be able to rescue her?

Snow White: The Graphic Novel. **Adapted and illustrated by Erik Valdez y Alanis. Stone Arch Books, 2009. 40pp. ISBN-10: 1-4342119-2-4. ISBN-13: 978-14342119-2-7.** `GR. 1-8`

> After a wicked queen discovers that she is no longer the fairest in the land, she attempts to destroy the beautiful maiden, Snow White.

The Three Little Pigs: The Graphic Novel. **Adapted and illustrated by Aaron Blecha. Stone Arch Books, 2009. 40pp. ISBN-10: 1-4342119-5-9. ISBN-13: 978-14342119-5-8.** `GR. 1-8`

> The wolf is coming! Will the little pigs build strong enough houses to survive?

Contemporary Fantasy

Another subgenre that is quickly gaining popularity is the contemporary fantasy, also known as "urban fantasy," which has fantastic elements in a contemporary setting. From goblins driving taxis to trolls working for the sanitation department, magical elements infuse everyday life in contemporary fantasy.

Amulet. `GR. 4-8`

> After the tragic death of their father, Emily, Navin, and their mother move into the house of their great-grandfather. However, the house proves to be dangerous, and when their mother is kidnapped by a strange creature, the kids must follow her into a strange underground world populated by demons, robots, and talking animals.

Amulet Vol. 1: The Stonekeeper. Written and illustrated by Kazu Kibuishi. GRAPHIX, 2008. 192pp. ISBN-10: 0-4398468-1-1. ISBN-13: 978-04398468-1-3.

> > After Emily and Navin's mother has been kidnapped, Emily has been designated the Stonekeeper, and is tasked with saving a strange new world, as well as rescuing her mother.

Amulet Book 2: The Stonekeeper's Curse. Written and illustrated by Kazu Kibuishi. GRAPHIX, 2009. 224pp. ISBN-10: 0-4398468-3-8. ISBN-13: 978-04398468-3-7.

> Emily and Navin are now headed to Kanalis to try to find an antidote to the poison coursing through their mother's body. Will Emily be able to thwart the demon Trellis, control the power of the amulet, and get the antidote?

Artemis Fowl.

Adapted by Eoin Colfer from his own books, <u>Artemis Fowl</u> is about a twelve-year-old evil genius. The series, described by Colfer as *"Die Hard with fairies,"* revolves around Artemis Fowl, a mastermind whose main goal is the acquisition of money. This prose series is wildly popular, and talk of a movie has been circulating for quite a while.

Artemis Fowl: The Arctic Incident Graphic Novel. Written by Eoin Colfer. Adapted and illustrated by Andrew Donkin and Giovanni Rigano. Hyperion Book CH, 2009. 128pp. ISBN-10: 1-4231140-7-8. ISBN-13: 978-14231140-7-9. **GR. 3-8**

> Artemis is back, and time has slightly mellowed the criminal mastermind. Now that he has half a horde of fairy gold and his mother's mind is back to full health, he can focus on rescuing his father, a man who has been declared dead for several years. Artemis and his fey police friend/antagonist must face off against the Russian Mafiya.

Artemis Fowl: The Graphic Novel. Written by Eoin Colfer. Adapted and illustrated by Andrew Donkin and Giovanni Rigano. Hyperion Book CH, 2007. 112pp. ISBN-10: 0-7868488-1-2. ISBN-13: 978-07868488-1-2. **GR. 2-7**

> Artemis Fowl is not your average twelve-year-old. For one, he's a world famous criminal mastermind. Now his latest plan is to kidnap a member of the fairyfolk in order to blackmail them into getting their pot of gold. Unfortunately for him, he has a tenacious fey cop and her boss on his trail.

Bumperboy & the Loud, Loud Mountain. **Written and illustrated by Debbie Huey. AdHouse Books, 2006. 128pp. ISBN-10: 0-9766610-1-2. IBSN-13: 978-09766610-1-6. GR. 2-7**

> Bumperboy and his dog Bumperpup have found a lonely, talking mountain by the name of Jumbra. Jumbra is in trouble, because the Grums, little marshmallow-type people, have been disappearing. Without the Grums, Jumbra will die. Can Bumperboy save the Grums and Jumbra?

Herobear and the Kid: The Inheritance. **Written and illustrated by Mike Kunkel. Astonish Factory, 2003. 220pp. ISBN-10: 0-9721259-1-4. ISBN-13: 978-09721259-1-8.** `GR. 5-8`

Tyler has just inherited a broken pocket watch and a stuffed bear. The strange thing is that Tyler's bear comes to life from time to time—as Herobear! (Eisner Award)

Knights of the Lunch Table. `GR. 3-8`

In this delightful series by Frank Cammuso, the legend of King Arthur is presented in a kid-friendly format. An understanding of Arthurian legend lends more weight to the humor, but it is by no means necessary.

Artie King is the new kid at Camelot Middle School. Bullied by his older sister Morgan and hassled by not only the mean principal, Mrs. Dagger, but also Big Mo and the Horde, can Artie survive middle school? He just might, especially considering that he's got a couple of friends to help him out, including his science teacher, Mr. Merlyn.

Knights of the Lunch Table: The Dodgeball Chronicles. Written and illustrated by Frank Cammuso. Graphix, 2008. 144pp. ISBN-10: 0-4399032-2-X. ISBN-13: 978-04399032-2-6.

Artie King was hoping for a quiet, uneventful life at his new school, but unfortunately, his life at Camelot Middle is anything but. His older sister Morgan hates him, his mean principal has it in for him, and Big Mo has challenged him to a dodgeball game. Can Artie, along with his friends Percy and Wayne, as well as his science teacher, Mr. Merlyn, beat Big Mo, and what's with Artie's Locker that no one can open?

Knights of the Lunch Table: The Dragon Players. Written and illustrated by Frank Cammuso. GRAPHIX, 2009. 128p. ISBN-10: 0-4399032-3-8. ISBN-13: 978-04399032-3-3.

Artie, Percy, and Wayne are preparing for the annual Dragon Day at school, but after Wayne's bowling ball ends up in Principal Dagger's windshield, the boys have no choice but to enter the Dragon Duel robot tournament. Can the boys defeat an opponent that is known for cheating, and will Artie stoop to cheating as well?

Korgi. `GR. K-8`

Set in a fantasy setting in which fairy-like "Mollies" have close relationships with their pet Korgis (a type of sausage-shaped dog with short legs). Ivy, a young Mollie, and her Korgi cub, Sprout, have many adventures in their village of Korgi Hollow.

Korgi Vol. 1. Written and illustrated by Christian Slade. Top Shelf Productions, 2007. 80pp. ISBN-13: 978-18918309-0-7. ISBN-10: 1-8918309-0-2.

> Join Ivy and her dog Sprout in their adventures in Korgi Hollow, a fictitious land inhabited by dinosaurs, spiders, and a troll so big, he towers over houses.

Korgi Vol. 2. Written and illustrated by Christian Slade. Top Shelf Productions, 2008. 88pp. ISBN-10: 1-6030901-0-X. ISBN-13: 978-16030901-0-0.

> A mysterious hunter has trapped and clipped the wings of several Mollies, and Ivy and Korgi search for answers in the surrounding wood. Unfortunately, they could be facing something from out of this world!

The Land of Sokmunster. Written and illustrated by Mike Kunkel and Randy Heuser. Astonish Factory, 2004. 55pp. ISBN-10: 0-9721259-2-2. ISBN-13: 978-097212590205. GR. K-3

Journey with Sam to the Land of Sokmunster and meet Spike, the sok with attitude; King Jacque, the leader of Sokmunster; and the villainous Moth King, enemy of the soks.

Nui. GR. 4-8

Kaya loves her stuffed animals. In fact, she loves them so much, they can come to life and turn into people, especially when she is in trouble. However, not all of her toy animals wish her well; in fact, there are some who may try to harm her. Can her stuffed animals protect her from those who wish her harm?

Nui Vol. 1. Written and illustrated by Natsumi Mukai. Broccoli Books, 2008. 224pp. ISBN-10: 1-5974118-4-1. ISBN-13: 978-15974118-4-4.

> Kaya runs into some trouble one day, and instead of a knight in shining armor coming to her rescue, it's her stuffed animals. Everyone thinks she's imagining things, but Kaya loves her stuffed animals so much, they come to life and turn into people! However, as Kaya's about to find out, not all of her plushies want the best for her.

Nui Vol. 2. Written and illustrated by Natsumi Mukai. Broccoli Books, 2008. 224pp. ISBN-10: 1-5974118-4-1. ISBN-13: 978-15974118-4-4.

> Kaya loves her stuffed animals so much that they turn into cute young men! Purple and Gray, Kaya's protectors are getting caught up in all sorts of adventures, but when Shara, Shinri's cousin (Shinri is the boy Kaya likes), tries to interfere in Kaya and Shinri's relationship, a new protector may be required.

Vogelein: Clockwork Faerie. **Written by Jane Irwin and Jeff Berndt. Illustrated by Jane Irwin. Fiery Studios, 2003. 168pp. ISBN-10: 0-9743110-0-6. ISBN-13: 978-09743110-0-6.** `GR. 5-8`

Vogelein, a seventeenth-century mechanical fairy, must be wound every thirty-six hours or she will wind down and lose her memories of the last 300 years. When her guardian of fifty years dies quietly in his sleep, Vogelein must set out to find a new guardian. The only problem is that she only has five hours before she winds down completely. (Lulu Award)

W.I.T.C.H. `GR. 3-7`

This was originally an Italian fantasy/superhero series. Disney purchased the American rights to publish it in 2005. Especially popular with prepubescent (ages six through eleven) girls, the television series ran for two years, and the graphic novel series is still being published.

W.I.T.C.H. stands for Will, Irma, Taranee, Cornelia, and Hay Lin, who are the principal characters in the series. The W.I.T.C.H.es are selected to be the new guardians of Kandrakar, a utopian land at the center of the universe.

Parental Advisory: magic; mild coming-of-age issues

W.I.T.C.H. Vol. 1: The Volume of Friendship. Written and illustrated by Various. Hyperion Book CH, 2005. 128pp. ISBN-10: 0-7868367-4-1. ISBN-13: 978-07868367-4-1.

> Will, the new girl in town, makes friends with several other girls, who all seem to be able to manipulate different aspects of their lives. Before long they discover that they have been chosen to protect the Veil, the boundary between good and evil.

W.I.T.C.H. Vol. 2: Meridian Magic. Written and illustrated by Various. Hyperion Book CH, 2005. 128pp. ISBN-10: 0-7868097-4-4. ISBN-13: 978-07868097-4-5.

> The W.I.T.C.H. girls travel to Metamoor, the land beyond the veil, and learn to harness their powers.

W.I.T.C.H. Vol. 3: The Revealing. Written and illustrated by Various. Hyperion Book CH, 2005. 128pp. ISBN-10: 0-786365-5-5. ISBN-13: 978-07868365-5-0.

> The witch girls are sucked into a weird world inside a painting, where their powers don't work! Will they escape?

W.I.T.C.H. Vol. 4: Between Light and Dark. Written and illustrated by Various. Hyperion Book CH, 2006. 128pp. ISBN-10: 0-7868365-6-3. ISBN-13: 978-07868365-6-7.

> After finding a lantern, Hay Lin and the Guardians travel through a portal to another world where they must save an imprisoned city.

W.I.T.C.H. Vol. 5: Legends Revealed. Written and illustrated by Various. Hyperion Book CH, 2006. 128pp. ISBN-10: 0-7868487-6-6. ISBN-13: 978-07868487-6-8.

> Hay Lin shares a story with her fellow Guardians revealing the origins of their powers, and then Elyon seeks help from her old friends to save Meridian once again.

W.I.T.C.H. Vol. 6: Forces of Change. Written and illustrated by Various. Hyperion Book CH, 2006. 128pp. ISBN-10: 0-7868487-7-4. ISBN-13: 978-07868487-7-5.

> When the W.I.T.C.H. girls discover that Prince Phobos is plotting to take over Metamoor and destroy Elyon, they vow to stop him before it's too late. In the end, a new queen will reign, but one of the Guardians will be changed forever.

W.I.T.C.H. Vol. 7: Under Pressure. Written and illustrated by Various. Hyperion Book CH, 2007. 128pp. ISBN-10: 1-4231061-8-0. ISBN-13: 978-14231061-8-0.

> The evil Prince Phobos has finally been defeated; in the process, the Veil has been destroyed. Now the Guardians are up against new problems: their powers are fading, friendships are being strained, and Will has some devastating news that could tear W.I.T.C.H. apart.

W.I.T.C.H. Vol. 8: An Unexpected Return. Written and illustrated by Various. Hyperion Book CH, 2007. 128pp. ISBN-10: 1-4231090-3-1. ISBN-13: 978-14231090-3-7.

> Their powers are still gone, and the Guardians are struggling to keep the team together. When an ancient enemy unexpectedly returns, the W.I.T.C.H. girls discover the true power of friendship.

Parallel World/Reality Shift

Although the parallel world or reality shift can be found within almost any genre, in this guide it is placed in this chapter because most parallel worlds seem to have fantastic elements to them that under normal circumstances would ground them in fantasy.

The idea of a parallel world appeals to kids because, for the most part, things are usually the same as in the real world, except for some major plot device that reminds them, "We're not in Kansas anymore, Toto!"

Age of Reptiles. GR. 5-8

> Long before humans roamed the earth, the dinosaurs were king. In this wordless series, the eat-or-be-eaten mentality that ruled the day is on display, relating tales of survival of the fittest. Including this title in your

collection may cause controversy, but it comes highly recommended from several advisory boards for reluctant readers.

Age of Reptiles: The Hunt. Written and illustrated by Ricardo Delgado. Dark Horse, 1997. 128pp. ISBN-10: 1-5697119-9-2. ISBN-13: 978-1567119-9-6.

> This story involves a juvenile allosaur who must travel across the sweltering deserts of Jurassic North America after his mother is killed by a pack of ceratosaurs. Told entirely in picture format.
>
> **Parental Advisory:** animal violence; blood

Age of Reptiles: Tribal Warfare. Written and illustrated by Richard Delgado. Dark Horse, 1993. 128pp. ISBN-10: 1-5697110-1-1. ISBN-13: 978-15697110-1-9.

> Tyrannosaurus rex, the most fearsome carnivore that ever lived, is king, but even T. rex isn't safe from the greedy eyes and ravenous appetites of a band of bird-quick Deinonychus.
>
> **Parental Advisory:** graphic animal violence

Coraline. Written and adapted by Neil Gaiman. Illustrated by P. Craig Russell. HarperCollins Books, 2008. 192pp. ISBN-13: 978-0-0608254-3-0. ISBN-10: 0-0608254-3-X. `GR. 3-8`

When Coraline steps through a door in her family's new house, she finds her house, only better. Things are great at first, until Coraline finds another mother and father, who want her to stay forever. Will she ever escape this gilded prison? (Eisner Award)

Parental Advisory: Contains scenes of peril and supernatural events.

Hikaru No Go. `GR. 4-8`

Hikaru Shindo was a normal twelve-year-old until the day he decided to rummage through his grandfather's things in an attempt to find something to sell. Coming across an old "Go" board (a Chinese game akin to "Othello" or "Reversi," except the piece has to be blocked on all sides to be captured; then it is removed from the play area), Hikaru is surprised when a ghostly apparition appears out of the board. The ghost, Sai Fujiwara, was a "Go" instructor to the Emperor of Japan, but was wrongly accused of cheating. In his shame he committed suicide, but somehow he became linked to the "Go" board. Now, with Hikaru's help, Sai hopes to play the perfect game of "Go," which will release him from the board forever. The only problem is that Hikaru's not interested.

Hikaru No Go Vol. 1. Written by Yumi Hotta. VIZ Media LLC, 2004. 192pp. ISBN-10: 1-5911622-2-X. ISBN-13: 978-15911622-2-3.

> After Hikaru Shindo discovers a bloodstained "Go" board in his grandfather's attic, his life becomes more complicated. For starters, he has the spirit of an ancient "Go" master in his head. Can Hikaru, with the help of Fujiwara-no-Sai, not only defeat "Go" players who have dedicated their

entire lives to the game, but also find the "Divine Move" that will allow the "Go" master to move on?

Hikaru No Go Vol. 2. Written by Yumi Hotta. Illustrated by Takeshi Obata. VIZ Media LLC, 2004. 192pp. ISBN-10: 1-5911649-6-6. ISBN-13: 978-15911649-6-8.

> After twice beating the son of the most successful "Go" master alive, Hikaru ends up unwittingly joining a "Go" team. Now he has a team to help him out, but he's drawing a lot of attention to himself, and he's still not sure he wants to play "Go."

Hikaru No Go Vol. 3. Written by Yumi Hotta. Illustrated by Takeshi Obata. VIZ Media LLC, 2004. 192pp. ISBN-10: 1-5911649-6-6. ISBN-13: 978-15911649-6-8.

> Akira (Hikaru's rival) starts a new school year, but quickly discovers that his reputation as Toya Meijin's son has preceded him. With the help of an upperclassman, Akira finds the confidence to continue his hunt in finding a way to beat Hikaru. Meanwhile, Hikaru is having trouble finding another teammate, but will his choice help, or shy away from making money at the game?

Lions, Tigers and Bears. GR. 4-8

Joey Price realizes that what he fears most, the Beasties—monsters that delight in eating children—lurk in his closet, waiting for him to sleep so they can devour him. Fortunately for Joey, his grandmother gave him a set of Night Pride, stuffed animals that come to life at night to protect him. One night Joey is attacked in his bed, and in the ensuing scuffle, he is pulled into the Stuffed Animal Kingdom, where the Beasties and Night Pride live.

Lions, Tigers & Bears I: Fear and Pride. Written by Mike Bullock. Illustrated by Jack Lawrence. Image Comics, 2006. 128pp. ISBN-10: 1-5824065-7-X. ISBN-13: 978-15824065-7-2.

> Joey is afraid of a lot of things, but the monsters in his closet scare him the most. That is, until his grandma gives him the "Night Pride," four stuffed animals that come to life after everyone goes to sleep. An excellent story for younger kids (this series is aimed directly at them) about facing those things that scare you the most.

Lions, Tigers &Bears II: Betrayal. Written by Mike Bullock. Illustrated by Jack Lawrence. Image Comics, 2008. 128pp. ISBN-10: 1-5824093-0-7. ISBN-13: 978-15824093-0-6.

> Winter has fallen in the Stuffed Animal Kingdom, much to the delight of Joey and Courtney. Their fun is ruined when the Big Cats arrive with terrible news. Now it's up to Joey, Courtney, and their imaginations to prevent the Beasties from attacking children everywhere.

Lookit! Comedy & Mayhem Series. `GR. 3-8`

Melville the penguin and his friends face off against various groups of silly villains who are trying to execute nefariously silly plans.

Lookit! Volume 1: A Cheese Related Mishap. Written and illustrated by Ray Friesen. Don't Eat Any Bugs Productions, 2005. 100pp. ISBN-10: 0-9728177-6-X. ISBN-13: 978-09728177-6-9.

> Follow the adventures of Melville the Penguin and a cast of several other characters as they race to save exploding cheese from the vast hordes of chicken ninjas! (Well, not that vast; there are like five of them.)

Lookit! Volume 2: Yang! and Other Stories. Written and illustrated by Ray Friesen. Don't Eat Any Bugs Productions, 2007. 96pp. ISBN-10: 0-9728177-9-4. ISBN-13: 978-09728177-9-0.

> Melville and company must race to be the first to find enough gold to pay the rent on the castle of Pellmellia. In the process, they hope to help the cheese-loving king beat a silly, cookie-obsessed group of pirates.

Owly. `GR. K-5`

A sweet, funny, touching series about a "bird of play" by the name of Owly, who has adventures with his best friend Wormy. Heartwarming, touching, and not the least bit schmaltzy or sugary, this series is along the lines of A. A. Milne's *Winnie the Pooh* or the Frog and Toad series by Arnold Lobel. (Harvey Award)

Owly: A Time to Be Brave. Written and illustrated by Andy Runton. Top Shelf Productions, 2007. 120pp. ISBN-10: 1-8918308-9-9. ISBN-13: 978-18918308-9-1.

> A new visitor is in the forest, and nobody likes him because he looks funny. However, things aren't always what they seem, and everyone soon finds out that the power of friendship can fix just about anything.

Owly: Flying Lessons. Written and illustrated by Andy Runton. Top Shelf Productions, 2005. 128pp. ISBN-10: 1-8918307-6-7. ISBN-13: 978-18918307-6-1.

> Owly tries to make friends with a flying squirrel who is afraid of all owls. Can Owly overcome his new friend's fear and teach him how to fly, especially when he can't fly himself?

Owly: Just a Little Blue. Written and illustrated by Andy Runton. Top Shelf Productions, 2005. 120pp. ISBN-10: 1-8918306-4-3. ISBN-13: 978-18918306-4-8.

> Owly learns that sometimes you have to make sacrifices and work at things that are important, especially friendships. When Owly and Wormy spot a bluebird building a nest, they want to help out, but what can they do to overcome Little Blue's distrust of them?

Owly: The Way Home & The Bittersweet Summer. Written and illustrated by Andy Runton. Top Shelf Productions, 2004. 160pp. ISBN-10: 1-8918306-2-7. ISBN-13: 978-18918396-2-4.

> Owly and his friend Wormy are best friends. They live together in a nonthreatening forest and have grand adventures every day. This series is almost completely dialogue free, so it is an excellent title for very young children as well.

Stone Rabbit. `GR. PK-5`

Stone Rabbit, a quick-tempered, quick-witted little bunny, gets himself into some improbable adventures. Aimed squarely at kids, Stone Rabbit is a fun, fast-paced, silly series that appeals to all sorts of kids.

Stone Rabbit: B.C. Mambo. Written and illustrated by Erik Craddock. Random House Books for Young Readers, 2009. 96pp. ISBN-10: 0-3758436-0-4. ISBN-13: 978-03758436-0-0.

> After opening a deep hole in his bathroom, Stone Rabbit lands in a prehistoric world where he is chased by dinosaurs and proclaimed a god by prehistoric rabbits. Throw into the mix a madman who plans to open a chain of fast-food stores, and Stone Rabbit has a full day ahead of him.

Stone Rabbit: Deep Space Disco. Written and illustrated by Erik Craddock. Random House Books for Young Readers, 2009. ISBN-10: 0-3758587-6-8. ISBN-13: 978-03758587-6-5.

> In this third installment of the series, Stone Rabbit is beamed into space and imprisoned by intergalactic enforcers. Can he prove it's a case of mistaken identity, or will an alien invader destroy Earth?

Stone Rabbit: Pirate Palooza. Written and illustrated by Erik Craddock. Random House Books for Young Readers, 2009. 96pp. ISBN-10: 0-3758566-0-9. ISBN-13: 978-03758566-0-0.

> Stone Rabbit is back for another adventure. This time, after Stone Rabbit's table leg breaks, he replaces it with the cursed peg-leg of a long-dead pirate. Now Stone Rabbit has to face off with the ghost of Captain Barnacle Bob.

Ultra Maniac. `GR. 5-8`

Ayu Tateishi is junior high's "Queen of Cool," a tennis star, and a friend to Nina Sakura, a new girl in school who is more than she seems: Nina is a witch.

Unfortunately Nina is still learning how to use her powers. After Ayu helps Nina out with a small problem, Nina feels compelled to help Ayu magically, with hilarious results. As a modern witch, Nina can download spells through her "portable magic PC" when she needs them.

Ultra Maniac Vol. 1. Written and illustrated by Wataru Yoshizumi. VIZ Media LLC, 2005. 184pp. ISBN-10: 1-5911691-7-8. ISBN-13: 978-15911691-7-8.

> This volume introduces Ayu and Nina. One day Ayu Tateishi finds a sad girl sitting outside her school. Striking up a conversation, Ayu discovers that the girl, named Nina Sakura, has lost something very dear to her. Nina refuses to explain what she lost, but eventually decides that Ayu can be trusted. The only problem is, does Ayu really want to know Nina's secret?

Ultra Maniac Vol. 2. Written and illustrated by Wataru Yoshizumi. VIZ Media LLC, 2005. 184pp. ISBN-10: 1-5911697-4-7. ISBN-13: 978-15911697-4-1.

> A boy from Nina's home dimension has enrolled in the same school as Nina and Ayu. Why is he here, and what is with the camera that he secretly gives to Ayu?

Ultra Maniac Vol. 3. Written and illustrated by Wataru Yoshizumi. VIZ Media LLC, 2005. 184pp. ISBN-10: 1-4215005-6-6. ISBN-13: 978-14215005-6-0.

> Nina realizes that learning how to be a witch isn't nearly as fun or easy as she had thought. Fortunately one of her teachers comes from the Magic Kingdom. Two are better than one, right? Maybe not this time.

Ultra Maniac Vol. 4. Written and illustrated by Wataru Yoshizumi. VIZ Media LLC, 2006. 184pp. ISBN-10: 1-4215020-4-6. ISBN-13: 978-14215020-4-5.

> Nina is beginning to realize that not everyone is happy to have her on campus. A half-witch named Sayaka is jealous of Nina's spotlight-stealing ways (real or not). As they say in the Magic Kingdom, "There's no fury like that of a teenage witch ignored!"

Ultra Maniac Vol. 5. Written and illustrated by Wataru Yoshizumi. VIZ Media LLC, 2006. 184pp. ISBN-10: 1-4215033-0-1. ISBN-13: 978-14215033-0-1.

> The final installment in the series finds Nina having to make some very difficult decisions about what she's going to do with the rest of her life. Will she stay on Earth and pursue Hiroki, or will she go back to the Magic Kingdom to attend the prestigious Eltora Imperial University of Magic?

Wizard of Oz.

One of the most beloved children's book series of all times, The Wizard of Oz has been reproduced countless times, on stage, on screen, and in books. Much has been made of Baum's books, and this is just a small sampling of the graphic novels out there based on the series.

Adventures in Oz. Written by L. Frank Baum. Adapted and Illustrated by Eric Shanower. IDW Publishing, 2006. 272pp. ISBN-10: 1-9332396-1-1. ISBN-13: 978-19332396-1-3. `GR. 5-8`

> Tells new stories about the Land of Oz, using both established characters and new characters. Collects Shanower's individual stories originally published by First Comics and Dark Horse.

Wizard of Oz. Written by L. Frank Baum. Adapted and illustrated by Michael Cavallaro. Puffin, 2005. 176pp. ISBN-10: 0-1424047-1-3. ISBN-13: 978-01424047-1-3. **GR. 3-6**

> An updated version of Baum's classic tale finds Dorothy and Toto traveling to Oz. This time Dorothy wears jeans, the Wicked Witch of the West is both evil and funny, and the Tin Man has a buzz saw.

Mythology

From the beginnings of civilization there have been stories to explain how and why the world is the way it is. When you think about it, mythology is really nothing more than fantasy; however, it is used to explain why certain things are or are not. Each culture had its own rich tapestry of legends and stories, and following is a selected list of books on cultures that have received graphic novel treatment.

Ancient Greece

Some of the most famous adventures of all time come from Greek mythology. From heroes who battled fantastic creatures to powerful gods who walked among men, it's not hard to see why Greek (and later, Roman) mythology continues to be so fascinating.

Atalanta. **Written by Ron Fontes and Justine Fontes. Illustrated by Thomas Yeates. Graphic Universe, 2008. 48pp. ISBN-10: 0-8225656-9-2. ISBN-13: 978-08225656-9-7. GR. 4-7**

> Atalanta is the most desirable woman in ancient Greece, with a horrible secret: If she ever marries, doom and misfortune will befall her and her family. When her father begins to insist that she marry, Atalanta must come up with a way to maintain her freedom without defying her father.

Demeter & Persephone: Spring Held Hostage. **Written by Justine Fontes and Ron Fontes. Illustrated by Steve Kurth. Graphic Universe, 2008. 48pp. ISBN-10: 0-8225657-0-6. ISBN-13: 978-08225657-0-3. GR. 4-7**

> Demeter is the Greek goddess of the harvest, ruling over a perpetual summer on Earth, where crops, trees, and flowers grow in abundance. Persephone, her daughter, unknowingly attracts the attention of Hades, the lonely god of the Underworld. Hades kidnaps Persephone, causing Demeter to go into mourning, the crops to die, and the ground to freeze. Can anything be done to bring spring back to the earth?

Hercules.

The Roman name for the Greek Demigod Heracles, Hercules is probably one of the most popular mythological characters to survive to the modern era. Hercules is most famous for the twelve tasks that were set before him by the goddess Hera (his stepmother, who hated him because her husband had dallied with a mortal woman, Hercules's mother), as well as his superhuman strength.

The Adventures of Hercules. Written by Martin Powell. Illustrated by Tod Smith. Stone Arch Books, 2009. 72pp. ISBN-10: 1-4342116-9-X. ISBN-13: 978-14342116-9-9. **GR. 2-8**

> To pay for a mistake in his past, Hercules, the son of a mortal woman and the god Zeus, must undertake twelve impossible tasks. What start out as simple labors soon become a struggle for his very life that will challenge not only his strength, but his mind as well.

Hercules: The Twelve Labors. Written by Paul D. Storrie. Illustrated by Steve Kurth. Graphic Universe, 2007. 48pp. ISBN-10: 0-8225648-5-8. ISBN-13: 978-08225648-5-0. **GR. 4-7**

> Famous for his superhuman strength, Hercules is tricked into performing a series of twelve seemingly impossible labors, each a test of his strength, courage, cunning, and fighting skills. Is Hercules strong enough to complete the tasks and thwart Hera's schemes?

The Iliad.

One of the two most famous epic poems by Homer, *The Iliad* tells the story of the ten-year siege of Illium. The story centers on a few weeks in the last year of the war and a quarrel between King Agamemnon and the warrior Achilles.

The Iliad. Written by Homer. Adapted by Roy Thomas. Illustrated by Miguel Angel Sepulveda. Marvel Comics, 2008, 200pp. ISBN-10: 0-7851238-3-0. ISBN-13: 978-07851238-3-5. **GR. 5-8**

> The ancient world is embroiled in a mighty clash of armies, Greek vs. Trojan. Helen, the most beautiful woman in the world, has betrayed her husband, Menelaus, and fled to Troy with the Trojan prince, Paris. The Greeks have sailed to Troy to bring her back—and crush all who stand in their way!

The Trojan Horse: The Fall of Troy. Written by Justine Fontes and Ron Fontes. Illustrated by Gordon Purcell and Barbara Jo Shulz. Graphic Universe, 2007. 48pp. ISBN-10: 0-8225648-4-X. ISBN-13: 978-08225648-4-3. **GR. 4-7**

> For ten years, thousands of ancient Greek warriors battled their enemies, the Trojans, in a desperate attempt to win back King Menelaus's beautiful wife, Helen. After a decade of fighting and thousands dead, the Greek forces retreated, leaving a giant wooden horse behind. What's going to happen if the Trojans accept the peace offering?

Jason and the Argonauts.

Jason was a Greek hero, famous for leading the Argonauts (literally Argo sailors) on the ship the *Argos* in a bid to find the mythical Golden Fleece, in order to place Jason rightfully on the throne of Iolcus in Thessaly (near the modern city of Volos). His adventures seem to echo those of Odysseus.

Jason: Quest for the Golden Fleece. Written by Jeff Limke. Illustrated by Tim Seeley. Graphic Universe, 2008. 48pp. ISBN-10: 0-8225657-1-4. ISBN-13: 978-08225657-1-0. **GR. 4-7**

> Jason was born a prince of the Kingdom of Argos. But his uncle Pelias steals the throne while Jason is still a child. As Jason matures, he returns to claim his birthright; in order to do so, he must first retrieve the priceless, magical Golden Fleece.

Jason and the Golden Fleece. Written and illustrated by Gerardo Sandoval. Stone Arch Books, 2009. 72pp. ISBN-10: 1-4342117-2-X. ISBN-13: 978-14342117-2-9. **GR. 2-8**

> Brave Jason comes to claim his throne, but the old king will not give up his rule so easily. To prove his worth, Jason must find the greatest treasure in the world, the Golden Fleece.

The Odyssey.

Homer's epic tale of Odysseus (one of the heroes of the Trojan War) and his extended trip returning to his home after the war. Essentially the first template for every "road trip" story to be created, Odysseus faces all manner of problems on his way home, from angry gods to hungry monsters, even angry suitors for the hand of his wife!

Odysseus: Escaping Poseidon's Curse. Written by Dan Jolley. Illustrated by Thomas Yeates. Graphic Universe, 2008. 48pp. ISBN-10: 0-8225851-5-4. ISBN-13: 978-08225851-5-2. **GR. 4-7**

> After winning a decade-long war, Odysseus, captain of the Greek army, only has to guide men back home across the sea. Yet the journey will prove more perilous than any battle.

The Odyssey. Written by Homer. Adapted by Tim Mucci. Illustrated by Ben Caldwell and Emanuel Tenderini. Sterling, 2010. 128pp. ISBN-10: 1-4027315-5-8. ISBN-13: 978-14027315-5-6. **GR. 4-8**

> After helping with the Trojan War, Odysseus and his crew face a long, arduous journey home, facing witches, monsters, and angry suitors competing for his wife's hand! What is Odysseus to do?

The Odyssey. Written by Homer. Adapted by Roy Thomas. Illustrated by Greg Tocchini. Marvel Comics, 2009. 192pp. ISBN-10: 0-7851190-8-6. ISBN-13: 978-07851190-8-1. `GR. 5-8`

> Odysseus, one of the great Greek warriors, is blown off course on his way home from the Trojan War. His travails over many years pit him against some of the worst characters from Greek mythology. Will he make it home to his wife?

Perseus.

The only child of the human Danaë and the god Zeus, Perseus was foretold to be one of the favorites of the gods, who would claim the princess Andromeda as his wife and kill the gorgon Medusa.

Perseus: The Hunt for Medusa's Head. Written by Paul D. Storrie. Illustrated by Thomas Yeates. Graphic Universe, 2009. 48pp. ISBN-10: 1-5801388-8-8. ISBN-13: 978-15801388-8-8. `GR. 4-7`

> Could a monster whose very look turns men to stone be a challenge too perilous even for the son of Zeus? King Polydectes has set forth an impossible task: to remove Perseus from the picture in order to take Perseus's mother and slay the snake-haired monster Medusa, whose very look turns men to stone.

Perseus and Medusa. Written and illustrated by Daniel Perez. Stone Arch Books, 2009. 72pp. ISBN-10: 1-4342117-0-3. ISBN-13: 978-14342117-0-5. `GR. 2-8`

> In this reinterpretation of the Greek myth, Perseus must slay a hideous monster by the name of Medusa in order to claim his throne. But will he be able to do that when Medusa can turn men to stone just by looking at them?

Psyche & Eros: The Lady and the Monster. **Written by Marie P. Croall. Illustrated by Ron Randall. Lerner Publishing Group, 2009. 48pp. ISBN-10: 1-5801382-7-6. ISBN-13: 978-15801382-7-7.** `GR. 4-7`

> Psyche, a beautiful mortal, draws the ire of the goddess Aphrodite. Fearing for her safety, she is moved to an isolated mountain to live in hiding, but she must marry a monster in order to stay there. Will Psyche ever be able to find love with her mysterious new husband, or will Aphrodite get her revenge?

Theseus and the Minotaur. **Retold by Nel Yotov. Illustrated by Tod Smith. Stone Arch Books, 2009. 72pp. ISBN-10: 1-4342117-1-1. ISBN-13: 978-14342117-1-2.** `GR. 2-8`

> In ancient Crete the evil king demands a tribute of fourteen young Athenians every year to face the labyrinth and the monster at its center. Can Prince Theseus defeat the monstrous Minotaur?

Theseus Battling the Minotaur. **Written by Jeff Limke. Illustrated by John McCrea. Graphic Universe, 2008. 48pp. ISBN-10: 0-8225851-7-0. ISBN-13: 978-08225851-7-6.** `GR. 4-7`

> Theseus sets out to claim his birthright as ruler of Athens and faces his greatest challenge, defeating the Minotaur, a savage beast who is half-man, half-bull, who has been eating his fellow Athenians.

Medieval Europe

The tales we normally associate with knights and dragons, of chivalry and magic, are usually associated with these tales of western might. The underlying theme of these stories is one of noble causes, and that good always triumphs over evil.

Beowulf: Monster Slayer. **Written by Paul D. Storrie. Illustrated by Ron Randall. Graphic Universe, 2008. 48pp. ISBN-10: 0-8225851-2-X. ISBN-13: 978-08225851-2-1.** `GR. 4-7`

A vicious monster is killing the Danes as they sleep. When the warrior Beowulf is called in, will he be able to destroy the vicious creature known as Grendel?

King Arthur.

King Arthur was a legendary British leader who allegedly led the defense of Britain against the Saxon invaders in the early sixth century. The legends of King Arthur actually come from many different areas, and there is no text that one can point to as definitive. On the whole, however, most people are willing to look past apparent conflicts in the stories. The Arthurian legends have provided potent fodder for books, movies, video games, and even role-playing games.

Arthur & Lancelot: The Fight for Camelot. Written by Jeff Limke. Illustrated by Thomas Yeates. Graphic Universe, 2008. 48pp. ISBN-10: 0-8225851-3-8. ISBN-13: 978-08225851-3-8. `GR. 4-7`

King Arthur rules his realm from the shining castle of Camelot, where he relies on the wisdom of his wife, Guinevere, and the bravery of his Knights of the Round Table. However, dark forces are at work in Camelot. Enemies in Arthur's midst seek to take his throne, and rumors abound regarding Guinevere and Lancelot, King Arthur's closest friend. Will Arthur fight to restore the peace, or is this the end of Camelot?

King Arthur: Excalibur Unsheathed. Written by Jeff Limke. Illustrated by Thomas Yeates. Graphic Universe, 2007. 48pp. ISBN-10: 0-8225648-3-1. ISBN-13: 978-08225648-3-6. `GR. 4-7`

Young Arthur spends his days toiling as a squire for his older brother. England is in turmoil with no king to lead it, but that all changes one day when Arthur pulls the sword from the stone. Taken under the magician Merlin's wing, Arthur becomes the rightful king of England, but will he be able to win peace and freedom for his country?

King Arthur and the Knights of the Round Table. Retold by M. C. Hall. Illustrated by C. E. Richards. Stone Arch Books, 2007. 72pp. ISBN-10: 1-5988904-8-4. ISBN-13: 978-15988904-8-8. **GR. 2-8**

> King Arthur and his knights are the only defense against the forces of evil that threaten the Kingdom of Camelot. Are they up to the challenge?

Robin Hood.

Known for "robbing from the rich and giving to the poor," Robin Hood, assisted by a group of fellow outlaws known as the "Merry Men," allegedly ran wild through Sherwood Forest during the late twelfth century. Popular culture describes Robin as a fallen aristocrat who was falsely accused of wrongdoing against the evil Prince John (brother of King Richard, who was battling in the Third Crusade). In response to being branded an outlaw, Robin turned to banditry to support Richard, while disrupting John's plans.

Many songs, stories, movies, and even stage plays have been written about Robin Hood, with another major film released by Ridley Scott in 2010. Though not very accurate, Disney's 1973 version is the most popular (and well known) animated version.

Robin Hood. Retold by Aaron Shepard and Anne L. Watson. Illustrated by Jennifer Tanner. Stone Arch Books, 2007. 72pp. ISBN-10: 1-5988904-9-2. ISBN-13: 978-15988904-9-5. **GR. 2-8**

> Fighting for the poor and downtrodden, Robin Hood and his Merry Men fight the evil Sheriff of Nottingham by stealing from the rich and giving to the poor. Will Robin and his men be able to survive long enough for King Richard to return and restore order to medieval England?

Robin Hood: Outlaw of Sherwood Forest. Written by Paul D. Storrie. Illustrated by Thomas Yeates. Graphic Universe, 2008. 48pp. ISBN-10: 0-8225657-2-2. ISBN-13: 978-08225657-2-7. **GR. 4-7**

> Fooled into committing a crime by the king's foresters, young Robin Hood finds himself branded an outlaw. Taking refuge in Sherwood Forest, he discovers others who have also found themselves unjustly on the wrong side of the law. Under Robin's leadership, the outlaws form a band of "merry men" who exact justice against the unfair laws of the land by stealing from the rich and giving their spoils to the poor. The sheriff of Nottingham vows to capture Robin at any cost, but will he succeed?

Other Ancient Cultures

The titles collected below are from various cultures, from Japanese and Egyptian to the ancient Mayan.

Amaterasu: Return of the Sun. **Written by Paul D. Storrie. Illustrated by Ron Randall. Graphic Universe, 2008. 48pp. ISBN-10: 0-8225657-3-0. ISBN-13: 978-08225657-3-4.** `GR. 4-7`

Japanese Shinto goddess Amaterasu is placed in charge of the sun after her parents create the first eight islands of Japan. Susano, Amaterasu's brother and god of the sea and storms, becomes jealous of his sister's position. Fearing her brother's temper, she hides herself away in a cave, plunging the world into perpetual darkness. Now the other gods and goddesses must come up with a plan to lure her out and restore order to the world.

Egyptian Myths. **Written by Gary Jeffrey. Illustrated by Romano Felmang. Rosen Publishing Group, 2006. 48pp. ISBN-10: 1-4042081-2-7. ISBN-13: 978-14042081-2-4.** `GR. 4-7`

For centuries Egyptian mythology has fascinated countless people. The most popular myths are collected in this book suitable for younger audiences. The tales included discuss Isis and Osiris; Ra, the sun god; and the myth of how Horus fought with his uncle Seth.

Guan Yu: Blood Brothers to the End. **Written by Dan Jolley. Illustrated by Ron Randall. Graphic Universe, 2009. 48pp. ISBN-10: 1-5801389-0-X. ISBN-13: 978-15801389-0-1.** `GR. 4-8`

During the reign of the Han dynasty, an ancient Chinese warrior named Guan Yu faced off against the Yellow Scarves, a dangerous peasant uprising that threatened to destroy his country. Teaming up with other warriors, Guan Yu travels across China, facing difficult opponents in his battle to prevent the collapse of Chinese civilization.

The Hero Twins: Against the Lords of Death: A Mayan Myth. **Written by Dan Jolley. Illustrated by David Witt. Graphic Universe, 2009. 48pp. ISBN-10: 1-5801389-2-6. ISBN-13: 978-15801389-2-5.** `GR. 4-7`

Huanphu and Xbalanque are twin brothers who excel at the Mayan ball game "Pok-ta-Pok." Unfortunately for them, the rulers of the underworld are not impressed and challenge the brothers to a game, if they don't get wiped out just getting to the playing field!

Isis & Osiris: To the Ends of the Earth. **Written by Jeff Limke. Illustrated by David Witt. Graphic Universe, 2007. 48pp. ISBN-10: 0-8225648-2-3. ISBN-13: 978-08225648-2-9.** `GR. 4-7`

Retells the myth of Osiris and Isis, in which Osiris's brother Seth kills Osiris, and Isis must travel the world to resurrect her husband and bring peace back to ancient Egypt.

Sinbad: Sailing into Peril: An Arabian Tale. **Written by Marie. P. Croall. Illustrated by Clint Hilinski. Lerner Publishing Group, 2008. 48pp. ISBN-10: 0-8225851-6-2. ISBN-13: 978-08225851-6-9.** `GR. 4-7`

> After wasting his fortune, Sinbad becomes a sea-faring merchant, where he comes up against some of the most amazing fantastical creatures ever created. Will Sinbad ever regain his wealth, and more important, will he ever see his beloved Baghdad again?

Thor & Loki: In the Land of Giants. **Written by Jeff Limke. Illustrated by Ron Randall. Graphic Universe, 2007. 48pp. ISBN-10: 0-8225648-1-5. ISBN-13: 978-08225648-1-2.** `GR. 4-7`

> Hailing from Asgard, Thor, powerful god of thunder, and Loki, the trickster, are eager to get to the bottom of an argument: Does strength always win, or do brains beat brawn? To find the answer to this question, the two travel to the land of the Giants, their mortal enemies. There they face a series of challenges that will hopefully prove once and for all who is right. Or will it?

Yu the Great Conquering the Flood. **Written by Paul D. Storrie. Illustrated by Sandy Carruthers. Graphic Universe, 2008. 48pp. ISBN-10: 0-8225656-2-5. ISBN-13: 978-08225656-2-8.** `GR. 4-7`

> Yu the Great, a Chinese hero from the twenty-first century BC, must save China from floods by using magical soil to plug underwater springs with the help of a tortoise, an owl, and a dragon.

Nate's Picks

- <u>Bone</u> by Jeff Smith. Another essential title for every collection, it starts out light and fun, then grows serious, but isengaging the entire way through.

- *Rapunzel's Revenge* by Shannon Hale and Dean Hale. A wickedly smart and funny reinterpretation of the traditional fairy tale.

- *Knights of the Lunch Table* by Frank Cammuso. Probably one of the most original and engaging adaptations of the legend of King Arthur. Too much fun.

- <u>W.I.T.C.H.</u> by Various. Though it's sappy and sugary, the integral theme of friendship and a strong belief in self make this a good series for female readers.

Chapter 5

Mystery and Scary Stories

Kids are naturally inquisitive, and mysteries play into a child's need to discover answers to questions that pop up. Though mysteries and suspense stories can sometimes get scary or intense, the books in this chapter are relatively kid friendly in that they have minimal suspense, or the situations are not very intense. Popular titles in this genre include graphic novel versions of <u>The Hardy Boys</u>, <u>Nancy Drew</u>, and <u>Sherlock Holmes</u>.

Suspense titles, sometimes known as spooky or scary stories, have long been a staple of children's comic books. Scary stories can very easily transition from something entertaining to something too frightening for young audiences; every reader is different. The titles in this chapter have been examined closely, but as a readers' advisor, you need to weigh each title against the prospective reader.

Detectives

Detectives tend to work by themselves, sometimes having a sidekick or contact they keep in touch with, but ultimately they solve the crimes by themselves. They can range from kids who have not had any formal training to investigators who have been doing their jobs for years.

The most well-known detectives for the younger set are probably Nancy Drew and Sherlock Holmes. Younger detectives seem to be popular with younger audiences because they are easier to relate to, and what young reader doesn't enjoy reading about a kid who can outsmart the most accomplished adult sleuths as well as the worst criminals?

Arf. `GR. 2-6`

Arf is a boy who constantly gets into mischief, always managing to find adventure in the process. This series is written with young readers as well as struggling older readers in mind.

Arf and the Greedy Grabber. Written by Philip Wooderson. Illustrated by Bridget MacKeith. Stone Arch Books, 2006. 72pp. ISBN-10: 1-5988902-2-0. ISBN-13: 978-15988902-2-8.

> Uh-oh . . . Arf's practical jokes have gotten him in trouble with the police, even though he and his sister saw who did it. What will he do?

Arf and the Metal Detector. Written by Philip Wooderson. Illustrated by Bridget MacKeith. Stone Arch Books, 2007. 72pp. ISBN-10: 1-5988908-5-9. ISBN-13: 978-15988908-5-3.

> Arf's curiosity gets the best of him when he receives a package for his neighbor. After discovering what's inside, Arf ends up facing off against crooks and buried treasure.

Arf and the Three Dogs. Written by Philip Wooderson. Illustrated by Bridget MacKeith. Stone Arch Books, 2006. 72pp. ISBN-10: 1-5988902-1-2. ISBN-13: 978-15988902-1-1.

> Arf tries his hand at photography by taking pictures of local dogs. After developing the photos, he realizes something's amiss at the local animal shelter.

Claire. GR. 4-8

Claire is a young girl who has just moved to the country with her family and gets caught up in adventures involving her family and friends. Written for a female audience that is right in between elementary school and middle/junior high, it is highly recommended for girls who are starting to feel the tug of growing up, but aren't ready to completely give in.

Claire and the Bakery Thief. Written and illustrated by Janice Poon. Kids Can Press Ltd., 2008. 104pp. ISBN-10: 1-5545324-5-0. ISBN-13: 978-1554324-5-2.

> Claire and her family moved to the country, where they have opened an organic bakery. Claire is not happy with the move, but soon finds a new friend, Jet. After Claire's mom runs off with the artificial flavoring salesman, Claire and Jet follow them back to the city, where the girls discover a plan to conquer the world through artificial baking. This book also includes recipes.

Claire and the Water Wish. Written and illustrated by Janice Poon. Kids Can Press Ltd., 2009. 120pp. ISBN-10: 1-5545338-1-3. ISBN-13: 978-15545338-1-7.

> Claire is starting at her new school with her friends, Jet and Sky. They begin a science project about toxic waste in the local lake; will they be able to set aside their differences long enough to figure out who is poisoning the lake? This book also includes crafts.

Detective Files. **Written by Steve Bowkett. Illustrated by David Burroughs. Stone Arch Books, 2008. 88pp. ISBN-10: 1-5988982-6-4. ISBN-13: 978-15988982-6-2.** GR. 3-8

A priceless diamond has been stolen. The police are stumped, so they call the TV detective, Roy Kane. Kane seeks out the help of the magician Dr. Pretorious, but is Kane playing into the thief's hands?

Guard Dog. **Written by Philip Wooderson. Illustrated by David Burroughs. Stone Arch Books, 2008. 88pp. ISBN-10: 1-5988982-9-9. ISBN-13: 978-15988982-9-3.** `GR. 3-8`

Nothing could be more boring to Ryan than helping his dad sell artwork at the local flea market. However, when the art is stolen, Ryan and his friend take on the case. They quickly learn that detective work is not a game.

Jimmy Sniffles. `GR. 1-5`

Jimmy is not your usual kid detective. For one thing, he has fantastic adventures; for another, his nose is so special that it verges on the level of superpowers. In addition, he has traveled up the president's nose!

(**Note:** Each book in this series contains a glossary of words used in the story, facts about the story, and discussion prompts for classroom use at the end.)

Jimmy Sniffles: A Nose for Danger. Written by Scott Nickel. Illustrated by Steve Harpster. Stone Arch Books, 2006. 40pp. ISBN-10: 1-5988903-6-60. ISBN-13: 978-15988903-6-5.

Jimmy has allergies, but not to normal items. He's allergic to danger! When a bag of diamonds is found to be missing from the jewelry store, Jimmy and his schnozz have to save the day.

Jimmy Sniffles: Dognapped! Written by Scott Nickel. Illustrated by Steve Harpster. Stone Arch Books, 2007. 40pp. ISBN-10: 1-5988905-3-0. ISBN-13: 978-15988905-3-2.

Jimmy, the kid sleuth, and his nose are on the case again. This time they have to figure out who's stealing dogs.

Jimmy Sniffles: Double Trouble! Written by Scott Nickel. Illustrated by Steve Harpster. Stone Arch Books, 2007. 400pp. ISBN-10: 1-5988931-4-9. ISBN-13: 978-15988931-4-4.

Jimmy has faced a lot of difficult challenges, but this is probably the toughest one yet—an evil clone of himself!

Jimmy Sniffles: The Super Powered Sneeze. Written by Scott Nickel. Illustrated by Steve Harpster. Stone Arch Books, 2007. 40pp. ISBN-10: 1-5988931-6-5. ISBN-13: 978-15988931-6-8.

Jimmy's in trouble! His normally superpowered sniffles have been wiped out by a dose of cold medicine. Will he be able to beat the bad guys when he's powerless?

Jimmy Sniffles vs. the Mummy. Written by Scott Nickel. Illustrated by Steve Harpster. Stone Arch Books, 2009. 40pp. ISBN-10: 1-4342119-0-8. ISBN-13: 978-14342119-0-3.

Jimmy and his class take a trip to the local museum, and some of the museum's artifacts go missing. Will Jimmy be able to figure out if the curse of the mummy is real?

Mystery at Manzanar: A WWII Internment Camp Story. **Written by Eric Fein. Illustrated by Kurt Hartman. Stone Arch Books, 2009. 56pp. ISBN-10: 1-4342075-1-X. ISBN-13: 978-14342075-1-7.** `GR. 2-8`

Tommy Yamamoto and his family are forced into the Manzanar internment camp for Japanese Americans during World War II. After one of the internees is attacked and a camp guard is charged with the crime, it's up to Tommy to figure out who did it.

Nancy Drew: Girl Detective.

Based on the venerable series of stories about girl detective Nancy Drew churned out by the Stratemeyer Syndicate over decades starting in the 1930s, the <u>Nancy Drew: Girl Detective</u> series follows yet another revamped series originally started in 2004. Although the technology has been updated to reflect the times, the basic premise remains the same: Nancy discovers a mystery, gets into and out of scrapes, and solves the crime, proving that girls can be just as strong, creative, and resourceful as boys—not to mention adults.

Books in the new series written by Stephan Petrucha have been published monthly since 2005, resulting in dozens of titles for voracious readers. The original series are all still in publication, although they have been re-edited to be less controversial. A live-action movie of the same name was released in 2007, starring Emma Roberts.

Nancy Drew: Vol. 1. The Demon of River Heights. Written by Stefan Petrucha. Illustrated by Vaughn Ross. Papercutz, 2005. 96pp. ISBN-10: 1-5970700-0-9. ISBN-13: 978-15970700-0-3.

Nancy, her boyfriend Ned, and their friends George and Bess try their hands at making a monster movie, but while they're playing with fiction, is there a real monster attacking kids?

Nancy Drew: Vol. 2. Writ in Stone. Written by Stefan Petrucha. Illustrated by Sho Murase. Papercutz, 2005. 96pp. ISBN-10: 1-5970700-2-5. ISBN-13: 978-15970700-2-7.

Owen Zucker, a boy Nancy used to babysit, is missing, as well as an ancient artifact that may prove the Chinese discovered America before Columbus. With all of River Heights watching, will Nancy be able to solve two mysteries at the same time?

Nancy Drew: Vol. 3. The Haunted Dollhouse. Written by Stefan Petrucha. Illustrated by Sho Murase. Papercutz, 2005. 96pp.ISBN-10: 1-5970700-8-4. ISBN-13: 978-15970700-8-9.

It's Nostalgia Week in River Heights, and everyone is dressing up 1930s style. After Emma Blavatsky's dollhouse starts showing crime scenes that come true, Nancy stakes it out, only to see a doll version of herself murdered! Will Nancy be able to solve the mystery before this scene comes true?

Nancy Drew: Vol. 4. The Girl Who Wasn't There. Written by Stefan Petrucha. Illustrated by Sho Murase. Papercutz, 2006. 96pp.ISBN-10: 1-5970701-2-2. ISBN-13: 978-1597071-2-6.

> After the girl she befriends on the phone while getting tech support vanishes mid-conversation, Nancy, her father, George, and Bess must race to India to try and rescue Kalpana from becoming a sacrifice to the Goddess Kali.

Nancy Drew: Vol. 5. The Fake Heir. Written by Stefan Petrucha. Illustrated by Sho Murase. San Val, 2006. 96pp. ISBN-10: 1-4177464-4-0. ISBN-13: 978-14177464-4-6.

> Nancy, Bess, and George find a wrecked yacht with a safe inside it. The owners of the boat willed everything to their cousin, as long as the cousin's wife doesn't get anything. Mr. Druthers has been missing for ten years, and it's widely believed that his wife killed him to get the safe. Then Mr. Druthers shows up, and his wife disappears! Confused yet?

Sherlock Holmes.

The greatest detective of all time, Holmes was the invention of Sir Arthur Conan Doyle. Able to draw large conclusions from the smallest observations, Holmes was an incredibly popular character. The only story of his to be told in graphic novel format so far is *The Hound of the Baskervilles*, a rather dark, spooky mystery. These titles are a little frightening, so caution is suggested.

The Hound of the Baskervilles. Written by Sir Arthur Conan Doyle. Adapted by Martin Powell. Illustrated by Daniel Perez. Stone Arch Books, 2009. 72pp. ISBN-10: 1-4342075-5-2. ISBN-13: 978-14342075-5-5. **GR. 2-8**

> Sir Charles Baskerville is attacked by a spectral dog outside his castle one night. Is it the legendary creature that haunts the moors? Only Sherlock Holmes, the world's greatest detective, can solve the case.

The Hound of the Baskervilles: A Sherlock Holmes Graphic Novel. Written by Sir Arthur Conan Doyle. Adapted by Ian Edginton. Illustrated by I. N. J. Sterling, 2009. 128pp. ISBN-10: 1-4027700-0-6. ISBN-13: 978-140-27700-0-5. **GR. 5-8**

> Another interpretation of Doyle's classic mystery. Holmes and Watson are off on another mystery; this time they have to deal with monstrous spectral dogs and a plot to kill Sir Charles Baskerville.

Detective Teams

Though individual detectives can get a job done, it's always more fun when they have friends or relatives to help them out. Characters in a group detective setting may not be as brilliant as Sherlock Holmes or intuitive as Nancy Drew, but they more than make up for any lack with different approaches to the same problem.

The Boxcar Children. `GR. 2-6`

Originally written in the 1940s, this story of four children surviving on their own raised a lot of eyebrows when it first came out, but was an instant hit with kids. It is now illustrated in graphic novel format for a new generation. Although the series starts out with a group of kids trying to survive on their own, it morphs into a mystery series in subsequent books.

The Boxcar Children. Written by Gertrude Chandler Warner. Adapted and illustrated by Mike Dubisch. Albert Whitman & Company, 2009. 32pp. ISBN-10: 0-8075286-7-6. ISBN-13: 978-08075286-7-9.

> The Alden children are four orphans, and the only way they can stay together is by making it on their own. One night they discover an abandoned boxcar and decide to make it their home.

The Boxcar Children Vol. 2: Surprise Island. Written by Gertrude Chandler Warner. Adapted and illustrated by Mike Dubisch. Albert Whitman & Company, 2009. 32pp. ISBN-10: 0-8075286-8-4. ISBN-13: 978-08075286-8-6.

> The Alden children now live with their grandfather, but they're not done with their adventures. They get to spend their summer on their own island.

The Boxcar Children Vol. 3: The Yellow House Mystery. Written by Gertrude Chandler Warner. Adapted and illustrated by Mike Dubisch. Albert Whitman & Company, 2009. 32pp. ISBN-10: 0-8075286-9-2. ISBN-13: 978008075286-9-3.

> After finding a run-down yellow house on an island called Surprise, the Alden children find clues that might lead them to a man who vanished from the house.

The Boxcar Children Vol. 4: Mystery Ranch. Written by Gertrude Chandler Warner. Adapted and illustrated by Mike Dubisch. Albert Whitman & Company, 2009. 32pp. ISBN-10: 0-8075287-0-6. ISBN-13: 978-08075287-0-9.

> Spending the summer with their Aunt Jane, the Alden girls spy a mystery man who might reveal something about Aunt Jane's ranch that could change everything.

The Boxcar Children Vol. 5: Mike's Mystery. Written by Gertrude Chandler Warner. Adapted and illustrated by Mike Dubisch. Albert Whitman & Company, 2009. 32pp. ISBN-10: 0-8075287-1-4. ISBN-13: 978-08075287-1-6.

> While spending another summer at Aunt Jane's ranch, the Alden children realize that their friend Mike Wood lives in the new town near the ranch. One night a terrible thing happens, and Mike is blamed.

The Boxcar Children Vol. 6: Blue Bay Mystery. Written by Gertrude Chandler Warner. Adapted and illustrated by Mark Bloodworth. Albert Whitman & Company, 2009. 32pp. ISBN-10: 0-8075287-2-2. ISBN-13: 978-08075287-2-3.

> The Alden children travel to a deserted South Seas island for their latest adventure. While exploring the island, they discover it may not be as deserted as they thought.

Hardy Boys. GR. 4-8

One of the flagship titles of the Stratemeyer Syndicate, the <u>Hardy Boys</u> series has been a staple of youth reading since it started the late 1920s. Revised and reimagined over the decades, the Hardy Boys have weathered the storms of changing ideals and have continually sold millions of books yearly. Spun off into five television shows, several computer games, and tons of merchandising deals, it only made sense to also re-create them as a graphic novel series.

The Hardy boys are Joe and Frank Hardy, teenage brothers and amateur detectives. Courteous and thoughtful, Frank and Joe are now tech-savvy crime solvers whose adventures take them all across the world. While the boys face off against murderers, drug dealers, thugs, and other villains, they stay true to their principles.

Hardy Boys Undercover Brothers Vol. 1: The Ocean of Osyria. Written by Scott Lobdell. Illustrated by Daniel Rendon. Papercutz, 2005. 96pp. ISBN-10: 1-5970700-5-X. ISBN-13: 978-15970700-5-8.

> A good friend of the boys has been framed for stealing a priceless artifact. Joe and Frank must travel the world to recover it and clear their friend.

Hardy Boys Undercover Brothers Vol. 2: Identity Theft. Written by Scott Lobdell. Illustrated by Daniel Rendon. Papercutz, 2005. 96pp. ISBN-10: 1-5970700-3-3. ISBN-13: 978-15970700-3-4.

> Frank and Joe are asked to help out a young lady by the name of Joy, who claims that her identity has been stolen—literally! A different girl is living her life, with her parents, in her body; is she telling the truth, or is she completely insane?

Hardy Boys Undercover Brothers Vol. 3: Mad House. Written by Scott Lobdell. Illustrated by Daniel Rendon. Papercutz, 2005. 96pp. ISBN-10: 1-5970701-0-6. ISBN-13: 978-15970701-0-2.

> How far will the producers of a new reality show be willing to go with a contestant's life to boost ratings? Frank and Joe go undercover for the new show *Madhouse* and come dangerously close to hitting epic numbers in the ratings.

Hardy Boys Undercover Brothers Vol. 4: Malled. Written by Scott Lobdell. Illustrated by Daniel Rendon. Papercutz, 2006. 96pp. ISBN-10: 1-5970701-4-9. ISBN-13: 978-15970701-4-0.

> A new mall is opening, and it's up to Frank and Joe to investigate several suspicious accidents that have occurred there. Unfortunately they, along with several other people, are locked in, and now they are slowly being picked off by someone. Add in a few disasters, and this could be the boys' last adventure!

Hardy Boys Undercover Brothers Vol. 5: Sea you, Sea Me. Written by Scott Lobdell. Illustrated by Daniel Rendon. Papercutz, 2006. 96pp. ISBN-10: 1-5970702-2-X. ISBN-13: 978-15970702-2-5.

> Something aboard an old fishing boat is, well, fishy. The boys go undercover to find out why teenage crew members keep disappearing. Things really heat up when one of the crew is discovered dead.

Hardy Boys Undercover Brothers Vol. 6: Hyde & Shriek. Written by Scott Lobdell. Illustrated by Daniel Rendon. Papercutz, 2006. 96pp. ISBN-10: 1-5970702-8-9. ISBN-13: 978-15970702-8-7.

> Joe and Frank are asked to act as bodyguards for a visiting dignitary's daughter. Trouble arises when she is invited to a horror-themed restaurant in New York City and the boys overhear a plot to assassinate their client. Can they stop the assassination, or will they fail for the first time?

Hardy Boys Undercover Brothers Vol. 7: The Opposite Number . . . . Written by Scott Lobdell. Illustrated by Daniel Rendon. Papercutz, 2006. 96pp. ISBN-10: 1-5970703-4-3. ISBN-13: 978-15970703-4-8.

> Traveling cross-country on a modern train, Frank and Joe are framed for murder! Normally they fall back on their secret organization, A.T.A.C., for assistance, but it looks like that was the organization that framed them.

Boxed Sets

The Hardy Boys Undercover Brothers Boxed Set 1: The Ocean of Osyria/ Identity Theft/Madhouse/Malled. **Written by Scott Lobdell. Illustrated by Daniel Rendon. Papercutz, 2006. 384pp. ISBN-10: 1-5970704-0-8. ISBN-13: 978-15970704-0-9.** GR. 4-8

> Collects the first four books in the new graphic novel series.

The Hardy Boys Boxed Set Vol. 2: Sea You, Sea me!/Hyde and Shriek/The Opposite Numbers/Board to Death. **Written by Scott Lobdell. Illustrated by Daniel Rendon. Papercutz, 2007. 432pp. ISBN-10: 1-5970707-5-0. ISBN-13: 978-15970707-5-1.** GR. 4-8

> Collects books five through eight in the new graphic novel set.

Jeremy Creep, Fang Fairy. **Written and illustrated by Andy Smith. Stone Arch Books, 2007. 40pp. ISBN-10: 1-5988989-1-4. ISBN-13: 978-15988989-1-0.** `GR. 2-5`

> Jeremy and his friend Nessy are off to find out who or what snagged Jeremy's little brother's tooth from under his pillow. This book includes a study guide for teachers.

Mercer Mayer's Critter Kids Adventures. `GR. 2-5`

> Though not generally considered to be a graphic novelist, Mercer Mayer has taken his seminal Lil Critter and moved him from picture books to beginner graphic novels. Lil Critter is an unknown type of creature that looks like a woodchuck (Mayer is intentionally vague about Lil Critter's species). He is joined by his friends, Tiger and Gator. The series follows a nontraditional format (akin to a picture book, but using enough elements from graphic novels to move it into that category), but is still a good starting point for reluctant readers.

The Alien from Outer Space: A Graphic Novel. Written and illustrated by Mercer Mayer. School Specialty Publishing, 2006. 32pp. ISBN-10: 0-7696476-3-4. ISBN-13: 978-07697576-3-0.

> On a campout, the Kids see a comet pass over Critterville. They then talk about the town's blackout and eventually take a trip to outer space.

Golden Eagle: A Graphic Novel Adventure. Written and illustrated by Mercer Mayer. Brighter Child, 2006. 32pp. ISBN-10: 0-7696476-4-2. ISBN-13: 978-07696476-4-7.

> Golden Eagle eggs have gone missing! Is it due to depredations of animals, or is someone stealing eggs?

The Jaguar Paw: A Graphic Novel Adventure. Written and illustrated by Mercer Mayer. School Specialty Publishing, 2006. 32pp. ISBN-10: 0-7696476-5-0. ISBN-13: 9780 07696476-5-4.

> The Critter Kids explore the South American rainforest and find an archaeological dig. In the process a priceless Jaguar Paw jade statue is stolen. Can the kids get it back?

Octopus Island: A Graphic Novel Adventure. Written and illustrated by Mercer Mayer. School Specialty Publishing, 2006. 32pp. ISBN-10: 0-7696476-6-9. ISBN-13: 978-07696476-6-1.

> Traveling to the tropics, the Critter kids explore a coral reef and end up shipwrecked. Can they escape the island and its nefarious inhabitant?

The Prince: A Graphic Novel Adventure. Written and illustrated by Mercer Mayer. School Specialty Publishing, 2006. 32pp. ISBN-10: 0-7696476-7-7. ISBN-13: 978-07696476-7-8.

> On a trip to England, the Critter Kids hear a retelling of *The Prince and the Pauper*. In their explorations, will they find out if the Prince was actually thrown in the dungeon?

Salt Water Taffy. **Written and illustrated by Matthew Loux. Oni Press, 2008. 96pp. ISBN-10: 1-9326649-4-7. ISBN-13: 978-19326649-4-2.**

Summer vacation threatens to bore Jack and Benny to death in the coastal town of Chowder Bay, Maine. Once the boys meet Angus O'Neil, a local fisherman who claims to have seen Old Salty, the local sea monster, the summer promises to become much more interesting. With the theft of all the candy from the local taffy shop, Jack and Benny are going to have their hands full.

Scooby-Doo. GR. 3-6

In response to parental groups claiming that cartoons were too violent, this cult hit about four teens and their talking dog who spent their spare time solving mysteries was created as a television cartoon series by Hannah-Barbera studios in the 1960s. Forty years later, Scooby and the gang are still going strong—and as kid-friendly as possible.

Spanning eleven different incarnations, six television specials, thirteen direct-to video films, three live-action films, twelve video games, and two stage plays, Scooby-Doo shows no signs of slowing down, nor do his graphic novels.

Scooby-Doo Vol. 1: You Meddling Kids! Written and illustrated by Various. DC Kids, 2003. 112pp. ISBN-10: 1-4012017-7-6. ISBN-13: 978-14012017-7-7.

> Includes the stories "Scooby in the Booby Hatch," "Scooby Snooze," "The Roswell Riddle," "Stubble Trouble," "The Truth," "Wax Attacks!," "The Old Ways," "How I Spent My Winter Break," "Legend of the Silver Scream," and "The Best Laid Plans."

Scooby-Doo Vol. 2: Ruh-Roh! Written and illustrated by Various. DC Kids, 2003. 112pp. ISBN-10: 1-4012017-8-4. ISBN-13: 978-14012017-8-4.

> The Mystery Inc. crew is back for more crazy disguises, creepy haunting, and calculating criminals. Put on your fake nose and wig, settle into your lair, and enjoy the hair-raising heroics of "Ghost Riders in Disguise," "Repeat Offender," "The Ogre of O'Hare," "Reincarnation Ruckus," "Like a Cracked Mirror," "Kung-Food Fightin'," "Scooby-Voodoo-Krewe," "Costume Caper," "Six Is a Crowd," and "Shaggy's Sasquatch Search."

Scooby-Doo Vol. 3: All Wrapped Up! Written and illustrated by Various. DC Kids, 2005. 112pp. ISBN-10: 1-4012051-3-5. ISBN-13: 978-14012051-3-3.

> The gang is back with more hair-raising adventures of the pseudo-supernatural in such tales as "Hajj Dodger," "Behavior Modification," "The Comic Book Convention Caper," "Gnome Alone," "Welcome to

Monsterville," "No Bones about It!" "I'll Take Manhattan," "Scooby's A-maze-ing Adventure," "Broncos and Boogiemen," and "South Pacific Scooby."

Scooby-Doo Vol. 4: The Big Squeeze! Written and illustrated by Various. DC Kids, 2005. 112pp. ISBN-10: 1-4012051-4-3. ISBN-13: 978-14012051-4-3.

You can't keep a good dog down! Scooby and the whole Mystery Machine crew keep the pressure on the spooks with their fourth volume of terrorific tales, featuring the stories "Almost Live from Big Puce," "Guest Stars!" "Monster Museum," "The Ghost of Christmas Presents," "Are We Scared Yet?" "Sound Stage Spook," "The Curse of the Scary Scarab," "Psychic PsycheOut!" "Wraithecar Driver," and "Ghost in the Machina."

Scooby-Doo Vol. 5: Surf's Up! Written and illustrated by Various. DC Kids, 2006. 112pp. ISBN-10: 1-4012093-6-X. ISBN-13: 978-14012093-6-0.

The gang's back with new adventures. Join Scooby in such tales as "Revenge of the Mudman," "Revenge, Inc.," "Goop on the Loose," "The Curse of Wrangler Field," "The Big Lake Fake," "The Haunted Halibut," "Don't Believe What You See!" "Surf's Up, Monster's Down," "The Phantom of the Mosh Pit," and "Caves of Castle Finn."

Totally Spies: The O.P. **Written and illustrated by Marathon Team. Papercutz, 2006. 96pp. ISBN-10: 1-5970704-4-0. ISBN-13: 978-15970704-4-7.** `GR. 2-7`

In this spin-off of the television series of the same title, three teenage girls are recruited by a mysterious benefactor to work for a secret agency by the name of WOOHP (World Organization of Human Protection). It's like a light, fluffy version of the 1980s TV show *Charlie's Angels*, without the blatant sexual undertones.

Scary Stories

Fear is an emotion that is universal to everyone. There is something primal and thrilling about the sensation of your hair standing on end or being bathed in cold sweat that grabs you and won't let go until an issue is resolved. The books in this section are the kid versions of adult horror and paranormal books. They range from (slightly) scary stories with silly monsters to the grandmaster of horror himself, that desiccated don of the dead: The Crypt-Keeper.

Of course, some young readers enjoy the thrill of being scared more than others, and some things scare some kids more than they scare others. It all depends on the child. Therefore, it is strongly advised that you review these books before suggesting them to patrons or students.

Abracadabra. **Written by Alex Gutteridge. Illustrated by Lucy Su. Stone Arch Books, 2006. 88pp. ISBN-10: 1-5988902-8-X. ISBN-13: 978-15988902-8-0.** `GR. 3-8`

> Tom goes to his cousin's birthday party hoping to see Becca, a girl he likes. Instead, he meets Charlotte, who looks exactly like Becca. The only problem is that Charlotte died 350 years ago!

Curse of the Red Scorpion. **Written by Scott Nickel. Illustrated by Steve Harpster. Stone Arch Books, 2006. 40pp. ISBN-10: 1-5988903-4-4. ISBN-13: 978-15988903-4-1.** `GR. 1-5`

> While looking at a scorpion statue at the museum, someone tells Mitchell about the curse associated with the statue. Now Mitchell is seeing scorpions everywhere.

Dracula.

In the post-<u>Twilight</u> vampire era, it's nice to be able to go back to the roots of a movement and see where it all started. Created at the end of the nineteenth century, the original "demon lover" is still considered to be the best (although female patrons may dispute this!). Dracula has been responsible for more vampire movies, stories, plays, and role-playing books than any other horror icon.

Dracula. Written by Bram Stoker. Adapted and illustrated by Tod Smith. Stone Arch Books, 2008. 72pp. ISBN-10: 1-4342044-8-0. ISBN-13: 978-14342044-8-6. `GR. 2-8`

> Stoker's classic horror tale of undying evil, reinterpreted for a younger audience. Jonathan Harker travels to Transylvania to help a mysterious Count by the name of Dracula. When the Count escapes to London, Jonathan must escape the castle and return home to face this eternal monster.

Dracula. Written by Bram Stoker. Adapted by Michael Mucci. Illustrated by Ben Caldwell. Sterling, 2007. 128pp. ISBN-10: 1-4027315-2-3. ISBN-13: 978-14027315-2-5. `GR. 4-8`

> A fairly faithful adaptation of Bram Stoker's classic vampire tale, aimed at a younger audience.

Frankenstein.

Another horror movie staple, the Monster (often mistakenly called Frankenstein), an amalgam of dead body parts sewn together and then reanimated, draws on ancient Greek mythology about Prometheus, who not only stole fire from the gods to give to man, but was credited with creating man. Although this story is considered science fiction, the creepiness factor places it in scary stories for the purposes of this book. Many stories, movies, plays, and video games have been influenced by Shelley's tale of man playing God, but these two stories are kid friendly.

Frankenstein. Written by Mary Shelley. Illustrated by Frazer Irving. Puffin, 2005. 176pp. ISBN-10:0-1424040-7-1. ISBN-13: 978-01424040-7-2. **GR. 4-8**

The classic "Man playing God" story falls easily into the graphic novel formula in this excellent adaptation. Consciously staying away from the easy violence inherent in the creature, Reed brings forth the sense of foreboding inherent in the book.

Parental Advisory: grave robbery; scary images; surgical procedures.

Frankenstein. Written by Mary Shelley. Adapted and illustrated by Dennis Calero. Stone Arch Books, 2008. 72pp. ISBN-10: 1-5988983-0-2. ISBN-13: 978-15900903-0-9. **GR. 2-8**

Another version of Mary Shelley's classic horror story. Young Victor Frankenstein has created a living being out of dead flesh, but it escapes. Can the scientist stop his creation before the creature's loneliness turns to violence?

Ghostbusters. **GR. 5-8**

Originally created as a comedic movie in the 1980s, *Ghostbusters* has enjoyed an almost cult following over the years. Following a theatrical sequel, two animated cartoon shows, and many video games, *Ghostbusters* is still going strong. Listed below are the latest offerings in print using the Ghostbusters universe.

Ghostbusters: The Other Side. Written by Keith Champagne. Illustrated by Tom Nguyen. IDW Publishing, 2009. 104pp. ISBN-10: 1-6001042-6-6. ISBN-13: 978-16001042-6-8.

Yet another ongoing series featuring the boys in gray, this one finds the Ghostbusters facing off with the spirits of some of the most notorious figures in organized crime. Then they have to escape Purgatory, or spend eternity in hell!

Parental Advisory: depictions of Hell; ghosts; occultism; spirits

Ghostbusters Vol. 1. Written and illustrated by Matt Yamashita and Chrissy Delk. TokyoPop, 2008. 192pp. ISBN-10: 1-4278145-9-7. ISBN-13: 978-14278145-9-3.

In this sort of sequel to the movie *Ghostbusters II*, a vengeful ghost makes a deal with the spirits of New York to take down the Ghostbusters, one by one. To beat this latest threat, Egon is going to have to face the ghosts of his past (literally and figuratively)!

Parental Advisory: ghosts, occultism, spirits

The Real Ghostbusters. **GR. 5-8**

Spun off from the popular cartoon series of the same name (which in turn was influenced by the blockbuster movie), The Real Ghostbusters follows the exploits of three unorthodox scientists and their studies of the paranormal. Joining forces with them are the fourth Ghostbuster, Winston, and their self-appointed "pet," a green ghost by the name of Slimer. Together, the five of these characters must protect the world from the supernatural. This series was a big hit in Europe, but saw little action here in the states.

The Real Ghostbusters: A Hard Day's Fright. Written by Dan Abnett. Illustrated by Anthony Williams. Titan Books, 2005. 96pp. ISBN-10: 1-8457614-0-5. ISBN-13: 978-18457614-0-0.

Who ya gonna call? Join Ray, Egon, Peter, Winston, and Slimer on their adventuresprotecting the universe from evil spirits.

Parental Advisory: ghosts; occultism; spirits

The Real Ghostbusters: This Ghost Is Toast! Written by Dan Abnett. Illustrated by Anthony Williams. Titan Books, 2007. 96pp. ISBN-10: 1-8457614-3-X. ISBN-13: 978-18457614-3-1.

More kid-friendly stories laden with bad puns and British pop culture references that most readers won't get now.

The Real Ghostbusters: Which Witch Is Which? Written by Dan Abnett. Illustrated by Anthony Williams. Titan Books, 2006. 96pp. ISBN-10: 1-8457614-2-1. ISBN-13: 978-18457614-2-4.

This final collection of stories influenced by the hit movie also contains prose stories, Spengler's Spirit Guide entries, and guides to the toys that were created.

The Real Ghost Busters: Who You Gonna Call? Written by Dan Abnett. Illustrated by Anthony Williams. Titan Books, 2006. 96pp. ISBN-10: 1-8457614-1-3. ISBN-13: 978-18457614-1-7.

More adventures with the protectors of protoplasm. This was actually a collection of UK-based stories aimed at a younger audience, collected into book format.

Goosebumps. `GR. 4-8`

In the mid-1980s, R. L. Stine cornered the preteen horror market with his Goosebumps series. It spans more than fifty books, along with two or three different incarnations, a television show, and several made for TV movies. The three anthologies that follow are adapted from Stine's original stories, maintaining the fear levels of the stories that made the original series so gripping.

Goosebumps Vol. 1: Creepy Creatures. Written by R. L. Stine. Illustrated by Gabriel Hernandez, Greg Ruth, and Scott Morse. GRAPHIX, 2006. 144pp. ISBN-10: 0-4398412-5-9. ISBN-13: 978-04398412-5-2.

Collects Stine's stories "The Werewolf of Fever Swamp," "The Scarecrow Walks at Midnight," and "The Abominable Snowman of Pasadena."

Goosebumps Vol. 2: Terror Trips. Written by R. L. Stine. Illustrated by Jill Thompson, Jamie Tolagson, and Amy Kim Ganter. GRAPHIX, 2007. 144pp. ISBN-10: 0-4398578-0-5. ISBN-13: 978-04398578-0-2.

> The second book collects the stories "One Day at Horrorland," "A Shocker on Shock Street," and "Deep Trouble."

Goosebumps Vol. 3: Scary Summer. Written by R. L. Stine. Illustrated by Kyle Baker, Ted Naifeh, and Dean Haspiel. GRAPHIX, 2007. 144pp. ISBN-10: 0-4398578-2-1. ISBN-13: 978-04398578-2-6.

> Includes the stories "The Revenge of the Lawn Gnomes," "The Horror at Camp Jellyjam," and "Ghost Beach."

The Haunting of Julia. Written by M. Hooper. Illustrated by Maureen Gray. Stone Arch Books, 2008. 88pp. ISBN-10: 1-5988982-7-2. ISBN-13: 978-15988982-7-9. GR. 3-8

After a strange incident at her birthday party, Julia begins to think that she's being haunted by a ghost.

Johnny Boo. GR. K-8

Johnny Boo is the best little ghost in the world. The reason he is the best is that he has "boo power"—the ability to shout "BOO" really loud. In these kid-friendly stories, readers see how much fun being yourself can really be.

Johnny Boo Vol. 1: The Best Little Ghost in the World. Written and illustrated by James Kochalka. Top Shelf Productions, 2008. 40pp. ISBN-13: 978-16030901-3-1. ISBN-10: 1-6030901-3-4.

> Johnny Boo's pet ghost Squiggle has "squiggle power," which allows him to fly and do fast loop-the-loops. What happens when they meet a giant pink and yellow Ice Cream Monster?

Johnny Boo Vol. 2: Twinkle Power. Written and illustrated by James Kochalka. Top Shelf Productions, 2008. 40pp. ISBN-13: 978-16030901-5-5. ISBN-10: 1-6030901-5-0.

> Is there a power greater than boo or squiggle power? Could it be wiggle power, or perhaps even giggle power? Squiggle undertakes a quest to learn the secret of twinkle power from the stars, and ultimately a strange and hilarious secret is revealed about Johnny Boo's hair.

The Monster of Lake Lobo. **Written by Scott Nickel. Illustrated by Enrique Corts. Stone Arch Books, 2008. 40pp. ISBN-10: 1-5988983-6-1. ISBN-13: 978-15988983-6-1.** GR. 1-5

Kevin's summer vacation gets pretty hairy when the legend of Lake Lobo shows up. Will Kevin's dog Max help, or is he the problem?

The Monster Piano. **Written by C. Pitcher. Illustrated by Bridget MacKeith. Stone Arch Books, 2007. 72pp. ISBN-10: 1-5988908-7-5. ISBN-13: 978-15988908-7-7. GR. 2-6**

> Lenny's family gets a new grand piano for his little sister to practice on. Lenny is sure that it's evil and is going to eat her. How can he convince them that she's in danger?

Spiral-Bound. **Written and illustrated by Aaron Renier. Top Shelf Productions, 2007. 144pp. ISBN-10: 1-8918305-0-3. ISBN-13: 978-1918305-0-1. GR. 4-8**

> What does the deep, dark secret about the monster that lives in the pond have to do with Turnip the elephant finding his artistic voice, Stucky the dog building a submarine, or Ana the rabbit and her work on the underground newspaper? (Eisner Award)

Stinky. **Written and illustrated by Eleanor Davis. Toon Books, 2008. 36pp. ISBN-13: 978-0-9799238-4-5. ISBN-10: 0-9799238-4-0. GR. K-2**

> Stinky, a purple monster that lives in the swamp, loves pickles and opossums, but is terrified of people. When a new kid enters his swamp, Stinky begins to devise silly plans to chase the stranger off. Ultimately he learns that swamp creatures are not the only friends he can have.

Tales from the Crypt. GR. 5-8

> From the annals of history comes this resurrected series of horror. Revamped for a slightly younger audience, The Crypt-Keeper, The Old Witch, and The Vault-Keeper take turns introducing stories designed to scare the wits out of you, complete with the terrible puns this series was famous for.
>
> **Parental Advisory:** macabre humor; pagan rituals; scary images; violence

Tales from the Crypt Vol. 1: Ghouls Gone Wild. Written by Don McGregor and Mark Bligrey. Illustrated by Exes and Sho Murase. Papercutz, 2007. 112pp. ISBN-10: 1-5970708-3-1. ISBN-13: 978-15970708-3-6.

> After a fifty-year hiatus, the comical wisecracker and his cadre of groovy ghoulies are back, spinning scary stories for younger audiences. In "Body of Work," a nosy and somewhat murderous couple discover the inspiration for their neighbor's gruesome artwork. "Runway Roadkill" gives readers a behind-the-scenes look at a fashion designer's last show. "For Serious Collectors Only" explains why it is always important to read the labels on packaging, even if you are a connoisseur. Finally, "The Tenant" shows what happens to a slumlord who allowed a tenant to die in his building.

Tales from the Crypt Vol. 2: Can You Fear Me Now? Written by Neil Kleid and Stefan Petrucha. Illustrated by Exes and Chris Noeth. Papercutz, 2007. 112pp. ISBN-10: 1-5970508-5-8. ISBN-13: 978-15970708-5-0.

> More livid laughs and putrid puns in the second installment of the horror franchise. In "The Garden," Richard has been promised a beautiful woman who will wait on him hand and foot in paradise; all he has to do is one simple task. In "Crystal Clear," a gangster with cell phone technology imbedded in

his head can't seem to get away from one of his victims who is seeking revenge. Finally, see what can happen if you sell a priceless collector's comic book to the wrong dealer in "Slabbed."

Tales from the Crypt Vol. 3: Zombielicious. Written by Mort Todd, Marc Bilgrey, Jared Gniewek, Jim Salicrup, and Allison Acton. Illustrated by Rick Parker, Steve Mannion, and Exes. Papercutz, 2008. 112pp. ISBN-10: 1-5970709-0-4. ISBN-13: 978-15970709-0-4.

Andy Dabbstein loves the game *Ogre Continent*, but his worst nightmare comes to life when his virtual world starts interposing on his real life in "Extra Life." A would-be horror novelist meets her favorite writer and learns the shocking secret of "The Queen of the Vampires," and even breakfast cereal isn't safe: Find out the real reason why kids must eat their Chocolate Stuffed Fruit Grain Cereal in "Kid Tested, Mother Approved."

Tales from the Crypt Vol. 4: Crypt-Keeping It Real. Written by Fred Van Lente, Christian Zanier, Ari Kaplan, Keith R. A. DeCandido, and Jim Salicrup. Illustrated by Christian Zanier, Steve Mannion, Exes, Rick Parker, and Chris Noeth. Papercutz, 2008. 112pp. ISBN-10: 1-5970510-4-8. ISBN-13: 978-15970710-4-8.

The wildest and scariest collection yet includes such gems of tale telling as "She Who Would Rule the World," in which a homeless woman has been turned into a nearly invincible, power-hungry being by a pair of misguided scientists. A cursed gigolo is forced to remain alive as his body slowly becomes zombiefied in "Ignoble Rot." "Jumping the Shark" finds a deceased reality TV series producer continuing to pitch shows from beyond the grave. Finally, "Spam!" is a deliciously deadly tale about the dangers of junk e-mail.

Tales from the Crypt Vol. 5: Yabba Dabba Voodoo. Written by Fred Van Lente, Tony Isabella, Marc Bilgrey, and Jim Salicrup. Illustrated by Steve Mannion, Exes, Chris Noeth, and Rick Parker. Papercutz, 2009. 96pp. ISBN-10: 1-5970711-6-1. ISBN-13: 978-15970711-6-1.

Just when you thought it couldn't get any scarier, the ghoulish gang is back with more FEAR-Y TALES to frighten you! In "Glass Heads," a man receives telepathic signals from a young woman, but it all turns out terribly wrong. A couple of voodoo inspired tales, "Chicken Man" and "Voodoo Redux," will make your head spin . . . right off!

Tales from the Crypt Vol. 6: You-Tomb. Written by Fred Van Lente, Mort Todd, John L. Lansdale, and Jim Salicrup. Illustrated by Steve Mannion, Chris Noeth, and Rick Parker. Papercutz, 2009. 96pp. ISBN-10: 1-5970713-7-4. ISBN-13: 978-15970713-7-6.

The only thing better than the latest collection of fear-filled tales? How about combining the thrills and chills of *Tales from the Crypt* with the short and funny style of online videos? If you call it You-Tomb, it'll pack even more monsters, psychos, vampires, werewolves, and zombies into the book than before.

Tales from the Crypt Vol. 7: Something Wicca This Way Comes. Written by John L. Lansdale, Fred Van Lente, Greg Farshtey, David Gerrold, and Jim Salicrup. Illustrated by James Romberger, Steve Mannion, Exes, Chris Noeth, and Rick Parker. Papercutz, 2009. 96pp. ISBN-10: 1-5970715-1-X. ISBN-13: 978-15970715-1-2.

> This volume debuts the departure of the "original" cover art with The Crypt-Keeper, The Old Witch, and The Vault-Keeper in little circles on the righthand side and begins to spoof other graphic novel covers. This one spoofs *Watchmen*. The main story, "Hex and the City," concerns a rich businessman and his three stuck-up, materialistic, and shallow female employees. When they find out he has a "thing" for witchy women, they pretend to be witches in order to defraud him of his money. When they summon the Great Horned God, they actually get exactly what they want, but not the way they want it.

Tales from the Crypt Vol. 8: Diary of a Stinky Dead Kid. Written by David Gerrold, John L. Lansdale, Rob Vollmar, Stefan Petrucha, and Jim Salicrup. Illustrated by Robert Hack, James Romberger, Tim Smith 3, Exes, and Rick Parker. Papercutz, 2009. 96pp. ISBN-10: 1-5970916-3-3. ISBN-13: 978-15970716-3-5.

> The series spoofs the super-popular *Diary of a Wimpy Kid* by Jeff Kinney this time, as well as *Guitar Hero* and the Twilight series. The Crypt-Keeper and crew tell the tale of Stinky Dead Kid: first, how he became a Stinky Dead Kid, and then his battle with "Guitar Demon," a popular musical toy that has become possessed by an evil entity. "Dielite" tells the tale of a misunderstood misfit who falls in love with a pale boy, and the ever-doomed Thomas Donnelly shows up again for his most bizarre tale yet.

Boxed Sets

Tales from the Crypt: Vols. 1–4. **Edited by Jim Salicrup. Written and illustrated by Various. Papercutz, 2008. 448pp. ISBN-10: 1-5970712-7-7. ISBN-13: 978-15970712-7-7.** `GR. 5-8`

> Collects the first four books in the re-released series, detailing humorous horror tales and groovy ghoulies. Contains the stories "Body of Work," "Runway Roadkill," "For Serious Collectors Only!" "The Tenant," "The Garden," "Crystal Clear," "Slabbed," "Extra Life," "The Queen of the Vampires," and "Kid Tested, Mother Approved."

Tales from the Crypt: Vols. 5–8. **Edited by Jim Salicrup. Written and illustrated by Various. Papercutz, 2009. 384pp. ISBN-10: 1-5970717-5-7. ISBN-13: 978-15970717-5-8.** `GR. 5-8`

Collects the second group of books in the spooky story series. Includes the stories "Hex and the City," "Guitar Demon," and "Dielite," as well as scarily silly spoofs of YouTube videos.

Trevor Walton: Zombie Fighter.

Trevor Walton is just your average elementary school kid, except that his classmates keep getting turned into zombies! Join Trevor as he continually fights against the evil Dr. Brainium, who wants to turn all the kids into mindless zombies who like to eat their vegetables and do math problems!

Day of the Field Trip Zombies. Written by Scott Nickel. Illustrated by Cedric Hohnstadt. Stone Arch Books, 2007. 40pp. ISBN-10: 1-5988989-0-6. ISBN-13: 978-15988989-0-3. `GR. 2-4`

When his class takes a trip to the aquarium, Trevor finds something fishy: zombies! Can Trevor thwart Dr. Brainium and his latest plan to force kids to do homework and other boring stuff?

Invasion of the Gym Class Zombies. Written by Scott Nickel. Illustrated by Matt Luxich. Stone Arch Books, 2008. 40pp. ISBN-10: 1-4342050-3-7. ISBN-13: 978-14342950-3-2. `GR. 2-4`

With Dr. Brainium behind bars, Trevor feels that he can finally retire from fighting zombies. Unfortunately his new gym teacher, Mr. Brainium, has other plans. Can Trevor defeat this new menace, or is he going to be stuck in gym class forever?

Night of the Homework Zombies. Written by Scott Nickel. Illustrated by Steve Harpster. Stone Arch Books, 2006. 40pp. ISBN-10: 1-5988903-5-2. ISBN-13: 978-15988903-5-8. `GR. 1-5`

Trevor's classmates are in trouble. They've been programmed to love homework, and it's up to Trevor to knock them out of their zombie trance.

Secret of the Summer School Zombie. Written by Scott Nickel. Illustrated by Matt Luxich. Stone Arch Books, 2009. 40pp. ISBN-10: 1-4342076-0-9. ISBN-13: 978-14342076-0-9. `GR. 1-5`

Trevor thought nothing could be worse than spending the entire summer in school, but when his teachers are turned into homework-loving zombies by an alien creature, Trevor and his friend Filbert must find out a way to defeat this menace.

Nate's Picks

- <u>Jimmy Sniffles series</u> by Scott Nickel and Steve Harpster. Another silly series from Stone Arch Books.

- <u>Johnny Boo</u> by James Kolchalka. For youngest readers, Johnny Boo is an excellent entry into graphic novels. Silly ghost stories without any of the scariness.

- <u>Tales from the Crypt</u> by Various. An homage to the EC Comics of the 1950s, this is a great series for older readers, especially reluctant ones.

Chapter 6

Contemporary Life

Though usually found in graphic novels for older audiences, especially teens, protagonists with real-life problems are becoming increasingly popular with younger audiences. Just because kids haven't hit puberty yet doesn't mean they don't have problems, and the books in this section strive to address them.

Kids may not have to worry about impressing the cute guy/girl, or face pressure from drugs or gangs, but they still have to face problems, such as the lost of a loved one, divorce, or even having a bad hair (or whisker) day.

These types of books are good for kids who prefer slice-of-life stories—with characters like themselves, as opposed to superheroes, aliens, or fantastical beasts. Some subject matter may be controversial, so familiarize yourself with the titles here; that will help you better pair books with young readers, as well as explain to parents what situations a book handles and how.

Boy's Life/Girl's Life

As the traditional audience for comic books in the United States, boys are an easy audience for graphic novels. However, boys don't necessarily like to read about "real life." Heck, common knowledge holds that boys much of the time don't like to read, period. Much has been made of this, but the simple fact is that unless reading has to do with sports, explosions, or some cool concept, most of the time boys are not going to be interested.

On the other hand, girls don't read graphic novels as much as boys, because the traditional genres (e.g., superheroes, adventure stories) are directed to young male readers and don't usually appeal to them. It can be frustrating to try to get kids of either sex to read graphic novels.

The books listed in this section are especially good choices for those kids who are reluctant to read anything, especially about things that probably have no connection to their lives.

Amelia Rules! `GR. 3-8`

Poor Amelia; not only is she having to adjust to a new life with her mom and her cool Aunt Tanner, she also has to deal with moving from Manhattan to a small town, new friends, a new school, and new adversaries. Told with from a kid's-eye view, with a child's innocence, Amelia Rules! is a must have series for any collection.

Amelia Rules! Funny Stories. Written and illustrated by Jimmy Gownley. Renaissance Press, 2008. 128pp. ISBN-10: 0-97960520-2. ISBN-13: 978-09796052-0-8.

> This compilation of the best stories from the first four books, includes the stories "The Sneeze Barf Incident" and "The Ugly Truth" as well as the never-before-reprinted origin story from *Amelia Rules! #0*.

Amelia Rules! Vol. 1: The Whole World's Crazy. Written and illustrated by Jimmy Gownley. Renaissance Press, 2006. 176pp. ISBN-10: 0-97121692-4. ISBN-13: 978-09712169-2-1.

> Amelia and her friends take on bullies, barely survive gym class, learn the truth about Santa, and break down the dubious merits of the elusive "Sneeze Barf."

Amelia Rules! Vol. 2: What Makes You Happy. Written and illustrated by Jimmy Gownley. Renaissance Press, 2006. 176pp. ISBN-10: 0-97121694-0. ISBN-13: 978-09712169-4-5.

> G.A.S.P. (the Gathering of Awesome Super Pals) learns more about Amelia's mysterious rock star aunt Tanner, how to deal with first love, and what it takes to be a superhero, and they prove that eggs aren't just part of a balanced breakfast.

Amelia Rules! Vol. 3: Superheroes. Written and illustrated by Jimmy Gownley. Renaissance Press, 2006. 176pp. ISBN-10: 0-97121696-7. ISBN-13: 978-09712169-6-9.

> Amelia McBride is facing more challenges: her Aunt Tanner is moving, her new friend Trish is hiding a terrible secret, and superhero wannabe Reggie has vowed to destroy the evil Legion of Steves. (It's a well known fact that everyone named Steve is up to no good, right?)

Amelia Rules! Vol. 4: When the Past Is a Present. Written and illustrated by Jimmy Gownley. Renaissance Press, 2007. 176pp.ISBN-10: 0-9712169-9-1. ISBN-13: 978-09712169-9-0.

> Amelia is going to her first dance (with a boy!), but she's not the only one with a date. Is Amelia's mom seeing someone, too? It's not all fun and games for the ten-year-old spitfire. A good friend reveals that her father is being sent to a dangerous country with his job in the military, which causes Amelia to think about her own family, her past, and what it all means for the present.

The Baby-Sitters Club. `GR. 4-7`

Originally written in the mid-1980s, <u>The Baby-Sitters Club</u> grew from a small series into a raging juggernaut consisting of 100+ books, a television series, and a movie. Adaptor and illustrator Telgemeier updates the series into a more "modern" setting while still keeping the feeling of the original. Though aimed at girls, this series has been well received by boys of various ages.

The Baby-Sitters Club: Claudia and Mean Janine. Written by Ann M. Martin. Adapted and illustrated by Raina Telgemeire. GRAPHIX, 2006. 176pp. ISBN-10: 0-4398851-7-5. ISBN-13: 978-04398851-7-1.

> Claudia and her sister, Janine, may as well be from two different planets. Claudia pays more attention to her art than her grades, while Janine studies nonstop to get straight As. The girls are nothing alike, and they can't agree on anything. When something bad happens to their grandmother, the two sisters discover they're more alike than they thought.

The Baby-Sitters Club: Kristy's Great Idea. Written by Ann M. Martin. Adapted and illustrated by Raina Telgemeier. GRAPHIX, 2006. 192pp.

> After Kristy gets her idea for a baby-sitters club and gets her friends to help out, things really start getting interesting. Not only does she have to accept her new stepdad-to-be, but the newest member of the gang, Stacey, seems to be hiding something. (ALA Great Graphic Novel)

The Baby-Sitters Club: Mary Anne Saves the Day. Written by Ann M. Martin. Adapted and illustrated by Raina Telgemeier. GRAPHIX, 2007. 160pp. ISBN-10: 0-4398851-6-7. ISBN-13: 978-04398851-6-4.

> A huge fight breaks out among the four friends, and Mary Anne is left to her own devices. Now she has to sit by herself at lunch, make new friends, and deal with her overprotective father without advice from the gang. The worst part is when she faces a terrible predicament with baby-sitting, and she can't find any help. Will she be able to pull through?

The Baby-Sitters Club: The Truth about Stacey. Written by Ann M. Martin. Adapted and illustrated by Raina Telgemeier. GRAPHIX, 2006. 144pp. ISBN-10: 0-4398393-6-5. ISBN- 13: 978-04397393-6-8.

> Poor Stacey; even though she has moved to a new town, she's still having troubles. Not only does she have to deal with diabetes and her best friend from her old town completely alienating her, a rival baby-sitting club has set up shop. Fortunately, she and her four new friends can beat anything!
>
> **Parental Advisory:** allusions to eating disorders and medical issues

Benny and Penny in Just Pretend. **Written and illustrated by Geoffrey Hayes. Toon Books 2008. 32pp. ISBN-13: 978-0-9799238-0-7. ISBN-10: 0-9799238-0-8. GR. K-2**

Benny wants to play pirates, but he is constantly being annoyed by his little sister Penny. Penny wants to play with Benny, but she's a princess, and all she wants to do is give her big brother a hug. Can they work out their differences?

The Boy Who Burped Too Much. **Written by Scott Nickel. Stone Arch Books, 2006. 40pp. ISBN-10: 1-5988903-7-9. ISBN-13: 978-15988903-7-2. GR. 1-5**

Bobby constantly burps. He burps at school, he burps at home, and he even burps at the movies, recitals, and plays! When he enters the school spelling bee, will his Grandpa's strange treatment solve Bobby's problem, or will he burp his way through the competition?

Castaway. **Written by C. Pitcher. Illustrated by Peter Dennis. Stone Arch Books, 2006. 88pp. ISBN-10: 1-5988902-9-8. ISBN-13: 978-15988902-9-7. GR. 3-8**

Six kids are dared to travel out on a boat at night. After an accident, they end up stranded on a desert island. In their attempts to get home one of them is injured, and the rest have to work together to get off the island and back home.

The Day Mom Finally Snapped. **Written by Bob Temple. Illustrated by Steve Harpster. Stone Arch Books, 2006. 40pp. ISBN-10: 1-5988903-8-7. ISBN-13: 978-15988903-8-9. GR. 1-5**

All Willy, Tom, and Grace want to do is help their mom out, but why is there smoke coming out of her ears? Could it have something to do with the kids painting their bedrooms, washing the dog with their mother's shampoo, making chocolate chip cookies, or redecorating the house with glitter?

Grampa & Julie: Shark Hunters. **Written and illustrated by Jef Czekaj. Top Shelf Productions, 2004. 128pp. ISBN-10: 1-8918305-2-X. ISBN-13: 978-18918305-2-5. GR. 3-7**

When Julie and her crazy, world-famous Grampa search the high seas for the largest shark in the world, they meet up with many odd characters, including musical squirrels, business-minded penguins, and undersea simians. But will they ever find Stephen the shark? Or will they end up in perpetual peril?

Hot Air. **Written by Anthony Masters. Illustrated by Mike Perkins. Stone Arch Books, 2007. 72pp. ISBN-10: 1-5988908-6-7. ISBN-13: 978-15988908-6-0. GR. 2-6**

Steve is super excited to go on a hot air balloon ride with his uncle and two younger cousins, but when his uncle collapses, the boys begin to drift toward the ocean. Forced to take the initiative, Steve has to figure out how to save all of them. Will he succeed, or will they be lost at sea?

Into the Volcano. **Written and illustrated by Don Wood. Blue Sky Press, 2008. 176pp. ISBN-10: 0-4397267-1-9. ISBN-13: 978-04397267-1-9. GR. 5-8**

Two brothers, Duffy and Sumo, have to spend the summer in Hawaii with their strange aunt. Once they arrive, she takes them into the bowels of an erupting volcano to find something important. The crew is capable, but untrustworthy, and what the boys find will change them forever. Although this can be considered an adventure tale, the interaction between the two brothers is the main focus of the story.

Parental Advisory: dark themes; scenes of intense peril

Joker. **Written by Anthony Masters. Illustrated by Michael Reid. Stone Arch Books, 2006. 72pp. ISBN-10: 1-5988902-4-7. ISBN-13: 978-15988902-4-2.** `GR. 2-6`

Mel is a joker, so when his father is kidnapped, everyone thinks it's another prank. Can Mel get anyone to believe him and save his dad? (Not to be confused with the DC Villain by the same name.)

Lost: A Tale of Survival. **Written by Chris Kreie. Illustrated by Marcus Smith. Stone Arch Books, 2008. 88pp. ISBN-10: 1-5988982-8-0. ISBN-13: 978-15988982-8-6.** `GR. 3-8`

Eric and his dad go camping in Minnesota every summer. This year Eric brings his friend. When they go out exploring and Cris gets injured, Eric heads back to camp to get help, but soon discovers he's lost.

Mink. `GR. 3-7`

In the vein of Miley Cyrus's character "Hannah Montana," Mink tells the story of a fourteen-year-old girl who receives a strange CD. After using the CD, a cybernetic version of Mink pops out of the computer and merges with Mink to become a pop music star. Only her two friends who were with her at the time of the event are allowed to know her identity; if anyone else finds out, she risks being deleted for using technology from the future.

Mink Vol. 1. Written and illustrated by Megumi Tachikawa. TokyoPop, 2004. 184pp. ISBN-10: 1-5918271-5-9. ISBN-13: 978-15918271-5-3.

Mink and her friends are out shopping for CDs when Mink finds one that allows her to become whatever she wants. After Mink and her friends program a "Cyber Idol" (pop star), it fuses with Mink and she becomes an instant rock star.

Mink Vol. 2. Written and illustrated by Megumi Tachikawa. TokyoPop, 2004. 192pp. ISBN-10: 1-5918271-6-7. ISBN-13: 978-15918271-6-0.

Mink has begun to follow her dream of becoming a teen idol, but things are not always what they seem. Mink's role model, Azumi Mizuhara, is picking on her, and a gossip columnist starts following her around trying to get a scoop.

My First Graphic Novel. `GR. K-2`

A series specifically aimed at beginning readers, these books all use familiar topics, repeating patterns, and core vocabulary words appropriate for a reader who is just starting out. They combine an entertaining story with comic book panels, exciting action elements, and bright colors; young readers will be enthralled and want to read more.

Airplane Adventure. Written by Cari Meister. Illustrated by Marilyn Janovitz. Stone Arch Books, 2010. 32pp. ISBN-10: 1-4342161-8-7. ISBN-13: 978-14342161-8-2.

> Aimed at much younger children, this gentle tale about Juan and Anna flying to Mexico to see their grandmother is good for very young audiences. Follow them on their trip from the airport to the sky. A good book for children who may be flying for the first time.

Bella's Boat Surprise. Written by Christianne C. Jones. Illustrated by Mary Sullivan. Stone Arch Books. 2010. 32pp. ISBN-10: 1-4342161-7-9. ISBN-13: 978-14342161-7-5.

> Bella is all ready to go on a boating trip with her family, but will she change her mind when she sees the boat they picked out?

Dump Truck Day. Written by Cari Meister. Illustrated by Michael Emmerson. Stone Arch Books, 2010. 32pp. ISBN-10: 1-4342162-1-7. ISBN-13: 978-14342162-1-2.

> For as long as he can remember, Jacob has wanted to ride in a dump truck with his uncle. Finally he gets his wish when his uncle invites him to the pit mine.

Secret Scooter. Written by Christianne C. Jones. Illustrated by Mary Sullivan. Stone Arch Books, 2010. ISBN-10: 1-4342161-9-5. ISBN-13: 978-14342161-9-9.

> Jackson sees someone on a scooter go shooting by every day. Will he ever discover the identity of the red blur?

The Rescue. Written by Anthony Masters. Illustrated by Mike Perkins. Stone Arch Books, 2008. 72pp. ISBN-10: 1-4342045-6-1. ISBN-13: 978-14342045-6-1. `GR. 2-6`

After discovering an injured fox, Justin needs to find someplace to hide it so it can recover without being injured by the Baxter brothers, who want to hurt it more. The only place Justin knows of is an old, haunted barn.

Swan. `GR. 6-8`

Masumi, a young lady from rural Japan, dreams of becoming a prima ballerina. After being chosen to be part of a national ballet competition, Masumi discovers that although she has the passion and talent to be great, her training isn't what it should be.

Originally written in the 1970s, Swan is a story that transcends time and is aimed specifically at a female audience. The series ran for twenty-one books and is currently being translated for English audiences. These entries are for the

English-language translations. Although this is manga, the character development is more in focus than in traditional manga.

Swan Vol. 1. Written and illustrated by Kyoko Ariyoshi. CMX, 2005. 200pp. ISBN-10: 1-4012053-5-6. ISBN-13: 978-14012053-5-5.

> After the lead ballet dancer injures her ankle, it is up to Masumi to represent Japan against two Russian dance prodigies. When the stress gets to be too much, Masumi loses her hearing; can she dance without music to inspire her?

Swan Vol. 2. Written and illustrated by Kyoko Ariyoshi. CMX, 2005. 208pp. ISBN-10: 1-4012053-6-4. ISBN-13: 978-14012053-6-2.

> Masumi has won a spot in the ballet company, but can she keep it? So far, she has survived the competition and has resolved to work hard and stay focused. All of that gets thrown into jeopardy when a handsome new foreign student arrives. Will he support her quest, or will romantic entanglements become a distraction?

Swan Vol. 3. Written and illustrated by Kyoko Ariyoshi. CMX, 2005. 208pp. ISBN-10: 1-4012053-7-2. ISBN-13: 978-14012053-7-9.

> Masumi makes her way to London, stopping over in Moscow to see her friends, Sayoko and Kusakabe, perform in a Bolshoi Ballet production. Unfortunately Sayoko is severely injured, ending her career as a ballerina. Though everyone is devastated, Japan still has to save face, so Masumi must take her place. Will she have what it takes to win the audition and beat Russia's best?

Swan Vol. 4. Written and illustrated by Kyoko Ariyoshi. CMX, 2005. 200pp. ISBN-10: 1-4012053-8-0. ISBN-13: 978-14012053-8-6.

> Masumi faces tough personal challenges this time, from learning how to be independently creative to understanding personal sacrifice. Masumi begins to realize her feelings for Kusakabe and returns to Moscow for the Bolshoi auditions.

The Walking Man. **Written and illustrated by Jiro Taniguchi. Toptron Ltd. T/A Fanfare, 2006. 160pp. ISBN-10: 8-4933409-9-5. ISBN-13: 978-84922409-9-5.** **GR. 3-8**

Instead of leading a fast-paced, frenetic life like others do, Walking Man actually takes the time to climb a tree in his bare feet, or play in puddles after a storm, or even go to the sea to return a shell. Sparse dialogue allows the pictures, and Walking Man's daydreams, to tell the stories.

WJHC: On the Air. **Written by Jane Smith Fisher. Illustrated by Kristen Petersen. Wilson Place Comics Inc, 2003. 96pp. ISBN-10: 0-97442350-5. ISBN-13: 978-09744235-0-0.** **GR. 4-8**

Some high school kids from decidedly different backgrounds start a radio station. This character study directed to a younger audience explores issues of student power, cliques, puppy love, and others that kids transitioning from elementary school to middle or high school are interested in. Though dealing with "sensitive" issues, this book is highly unlikely to offend.

Yikes, It's a Yeti! **Written by Karen Wallace. Illustrated by Mick Reid. Stone Arch Books, 2008. 72pp. ISBN-10: 1-4342045-9-6. ISBN-13: 978-14342045-9-2. `GR. 2-6`**

A vacation with his grandma? Norman would rather die! But she's taking him on an amazing adventure in search of a mysterious monster.

Yotsuba&! **Written and illustrated by Azuma Kiyohiko. ADV Manga, 2005. 232pp. ISBN-10: 1-4139031-7-7. ISBN-13: 978-14139031-7-1. `GR. 4-8`**

Taking elements of *Dennis the Menace, Yotsuba&!* Is an episodic tale of a young girl, Yotsuba, the adventures she has, and her irrepressible spirit. Deemed "weird" by the neighbors in her new apartment building, Yotsuba has a decidedly distinct worldview and finds wonder in the simplest things. (ALA Great Graphic Novel)

Anthropomorphic Animals

Just because a protagonist is not human does not mean it cannot (and does not) face real human issues. By putting a nonhuman face on the characters, the story may shed light on a familiar theme in an entirely new way.

Babymouse. `GR. 2-6`

Babymouse is a sassy young rodent who, like most kids, has a very active imagination. From her empty school locker, which becomes a black hole that sucks her into space, to a Wild West adventure spawned from a boring party, Babymouse and her imagination pursue an exciting adventure that kids absolutely adore. The series is very popular and highly suggested for girls.

Babymouse Vol. 1: Queen of the World! Written by Jennifer Holm. Illustrated by Matthew Holm. Random House Books for Young Readers, 2005. 96pp. ISBN-10: 0-3758322-9-7. ISBN-13: 978-03758322-9-1.

Babymouse wants nothing more than to be invited to Felicia Furrypaw's sleepover, but when she gets invited to the party at the expense of her friendship with Wilson Weasel, will Babymouse decide if it was worth it or not?

Babymouse Vol. 2: Our Hero. Written by Jennifer Holm. Illustrated by Matthew Holm. Random House Books for Young Readers.2005. 96pp. ISBN-10: 0-358323-0-0. ISBN-13: 78-035832-0-7.

That pink-loving little mouse is back in her next adventure. This time she has to face her greatest fear: dodgeball! What's worse is that Felicia Furrypaws has the fastest throw in school and has targeted a certain mouse.

Babymouse Vol. 3: Beach Babe. Written by Jennifer Holm. Illustrated by Matt Holm. Random House Books for Young Readers, 2006. 96pp. ISBN-10: 0-3758323-1-9. ISBN-13: 978-03758323-1-4.

> Babymouse and family travel to the beach, and in her own inimitable fashion, she sets out on a disastrous surfing career. At the same time, Babymouse's little brother keeps getting underfoot. When he disappears, will Babymouse realize how important he is to her?

Babymouse Vol. 4: Rock Star. Written by Jennifer Holm. Illustrated by Matt Holm. Random House Books for Young Readers, 2006. 96pp. ISBN-10: 0-3758323-2-7. ISBN-13: 978-03758323-2-1.

> In her imagination, Babymouse is a total rock star whose concerts sell out all over the world. In real life, she's having trouble getting her flute to work properly. Will she ever realize her dreams of becoming a music star (or at least get out of the last chair?)

Jellaby. **Written and illustrated by Kean Soo. Hyperion Book CH, 2008. 100pp. ISBN-10: 1-4231030-3-3. ISBN-13: 978-14231030-3-5.** `GR. 4-7`

> Jellaby, a huge purple monster, tries to eat Portia Bennett's flashlight one night while she's out in the woods. Portia decides to take Jellaby home with her, and her life gets more interesting as Portia tries to keep Jellaby a secret.

Monster and Me.

> Most kids have monsters in their closet or under their bed, but Gabby refuses to keep her monster, Dwight, hidden away. How will the town react to Dwight the friendly monster?

Monster and Me. Written by Robert Marsh. Illustrated by Tom Percival. Stone Arch Books, 2010. 40pp. ISBN-10: 1-4342158-9-X. ISBN-13: 978-14342158-9-5. `GR. 2-5`

> Twelve-year-old Gabby is like most kids in town. She goes to school, hangs out with her friends, and has a pet monster. However, unlike most kids, she refuses to keep Dwight in the closet. Instead, she takes him to school. Now Gabby's drama teacher wants Dwight to play Ebenezer Scrooge in the school play.

Monster in the Outfield. Written by Robert Marsh. Illustrated by Tom Percival. Stone Arch Books, 2010. 40pp. ISBN-10: 1-4342159-0-3. ISBN-13: 978-14342159-0-1. `GR. 1-5`

> What starts out as a friendly game of faculty vs. students gets nasty when the teachers start cheating. Can Gabby and Dwight win the game, especially when Dwight is not very good?

Peanutbutter & Jeremy's Best Book Ever. **Written and illustrated by James Kochalka. Alternative Comics, 2003. 280pp. ISBN-10: 1-8918674-6-6. ISBN-13: 978-18918674-6-0.** `GR. 3-8`

> The hardworking Peanutbutter is an office cat; Jeremy is a troublemaking crow. The adventures they get into not only serve to entertain children, but also cleverly critique modern society.

Robot Dreams. **Written and illustrated by Sara Varon. : First Second, 2007. 208pp. ISBN-10: 1-5964310-8-3. ISBN-13: 978-15964310-8-9.** `GR. 3-6`

> In this virtually wordless book, a story is told about a dog that makes a robot friend and has several adventures. After a bad decision on both of their parts, they part ways. What follows is a series of stories that poignantly explore relationships and loss. (ALA Great Graphic Novels)

Sea Princess Azuri. `GR. 4-7`

> Queen Onyxis of the Kingdom of Orca's only daughter, the princess Azuri, is next in line for the matriarchal throne. She's also subject to something that hasn't been heard of since the olden days, an arranged marriage. She is betrothed from a young age to the prince Unagi from the Eel kingdom of Gillenok. As her wedding day approaches, Azuri begins to freak out and confides in her best friend, a young Orcan boy by the name of Thalo, who is now a member of the Royal Guard. Everyone around the two young Orcans can tell they are falling in love, but Azuri and Thalo are completely oblivious. Will Azuri or Thalo realize before Unagi arrives and is made aware of what is going on? Will Azuri be able to save the two kingdoms and prevent an all-out war?

Sea Princess Azuri Vol. 1. Written and illustrated by Erica Reis. TokyoPop, 2006. 96pp. ISBN-10: 1-5981640-1-5. ISBN-13: 978-15981640-1-5.

> Azuri, the princess of the Orcans (a type of whale-merpeople) is betrothed to Prince Unagi, who is the leader of the Eel people. The marriage is to bring peace to the two groups, but Azuri falls in love with an Orcan Guard. Will she choose love, or will she save the world? Though easily considered a contemporary fantasy, in this series the relationships between the characters are heavily emphasized.

Sea Princess Azuri Vol. 2. Written and illustrated by Erica Reis. TokyoPop, 2007. 96pp. ISBN-10: 1-5981640-2-3. ISBN-13: 978-15981640-2-2.

> The decorations are being strung. The cake is being baked. The date has been set. It seems that nothing will stand in the way of the Prince Unagi and Princess Azuri's wedding—except Azuri herself! Realizing that life without love isn't much of a life at all, Azuri is having second thoughts. Will Thalo be the wedding crasher of Azuri's dreams?

Yam. **Written and illustrated by Corey Barba. Top Shelf Productions, 2008. 88pp. ISBN-13: 978-1-6030901-4-8. ISBN-10: 1-6030901-4-2.** **GR. K-8**

> In this story told strictly through pictures (no text), Yam and his friends live on a remote tropical island called Leche de la Luna (Milk of the Moon) and always manage to get mixed up in surreal adventures. This edition also contains several short stories originally printed in *Nickelodeon Magazine*.
>
> **Parental Advisory:** bullying

Sports

A relatively new subgenre in the past few years (at least to Western audiences), sports graphic novels focus on various aspects of sports, from the mechanics of the game itself to the ideologies of the players. Sports-based graphic novels are a great way to get kids who are deeply into sports, but turn their noses up at books, to read.

Archie's Amazing Game. **Written by Michael Hardcastle. Illustrated by Michael Reid. Stone Arch Books, 2006. 72pp. ISBN-10: 1-5988902-5-5. ISBN-13: 978-15988902-5-9.** **GR. 2-6**

> Archie's been banned from playing soccer by his mom. He comes up with a plan to get back in the game, but he needs support from his sister and best friend. Archie makes lots of promises, but can he keep them all? Not to be confused with the other Archie of *Archie Comics* fame.

Harlem Beat/Rebound. **GR. 4-8**

> This basketball based manga follows the story of Nate Torres, an unlikely basketball player. A perennial benchwarmer, Nate lacks two very important things: coolness and talent. Another series that focuses on an underdog with a raw ability for the sport, <u>Harlem Beat</u> spanned twenty-nine volumes in Japanese, but only nine have been translated into English.
>
> The series was renamed <u>Rebound</u> starting with volume 12. Volumes 10 and 11 have not been translated, and because of poor sales, probably will not be translated.

Harlem Beat Vol. 1. **Written and illustrated by Yurkio Nishiyama. TokyoPop, 1999. 162pp. ISBN-10: 1-8922130-4-4. ISBN-13: 978-18922130-4-4.**

> Nate Torres is your typical kid growing up in the big city. In between his clumsiness, dealing with gangs, school work, and girls, he still devotes himself to improving his jump shot in the world of street hoops.

Harlem Beat Vol. 2. Written and illustrated by Yurkio Nishiyama. TokyoPop, 1999. 184pp. ISBN-10: 1-8922131-7-6. ISBN-13: 978-18922131-7-4.

> After scoring on one of the best street players around, Nate decided that he's going to pursue street basketball. Now his adventures continue as he trains long and hard in street hoops to join the ultimate 3-on-3 tournament.

Harlem Beat Vol. 3. Written and illustrated by Yurkio Nishiyama. TokyoPop, 2000. 181pp. ISBN-10: 1-8922132-3-0. ISBN-13: 978-18922132-3-5.

> Nate and team Scratch make it to the semifinals of a local tournament, but the team they're facing is brand new. Will they be able to beat this new team and continue their streak, or will the mysterious team Icepick shut them down?

Harlem Beat Vol. 4. Written and illustrated by Yurkio Nishiyama. TokyoPop, 2000. 192pp. ISBN-10: 1-8922133-4-6. ISBN-13: 978-18922133-4-1.

> Nate's friend Sawamura has been running with the Icepicks, and Nate decides to try to stop him. In response, the Icepicks attack Nate, beating him up. Only when Kyle and Team Scratch, along with former rivals Mermaid Force, show up do the Icepicks leave Nate alone.

Rebound Vol. 1. Written and illustrated by Yurkio Nishiyama. TokyoPop, 2003. 192pp. ISBN-10: 1-9315140-2-X. ISBN-13: 978-19315140-2-6.

> The "sequel" to Harlem Beat finds the team traveling around the world to face international opponents. Their first stop is to face off against the high school team from Kyan High in Japan. If they're going to beat this team, they'll have to break with structure and fall back on their street moves.

Rebound Vol. 2. Written and illustrated by Yurkio Nishiyama. TokyoPop, 2003. 192pp. ISBN-10: 1-5918207-4-X. ISBN-13: 978-15918207-4-1.

> Jonan and the team are getting run ragged by the team from Okinawa, but even though they may be down twenty-five points, they're not going down with a fight!

Rebound Vol. 3. Written and illustrated by Yurkio Nishiyama. TokyoPop, 2003. 192pp. ISBN-10: 1-5918222-1-1. ISBN-13: 978-15918222-1-9.

> Making it through the first round, Nate and his team now face off against their archrivals, Tsukuba High. Will personal issues with the team and unresolved problems ruin their chances against their opponents?

The Haunted Surfboard. **Written by Anthony Masters. Illustrated by Peter Dennis. Stone Arch Books, 2007. 88pp. ISBN-10: 1-5988908-0-8. ISBN-13: 978-15988908-0-8.** `GR. 3-8`

Jack hates his new school, except for the fact that it's close to the ocean, which gives him a chance to surf every day. One day Jack meets a daredevil who insists on risking his life every time he enters the water. Has Jack gotten in over his head?

Hit It! **Written by Michael Hardcastle. Illustrated by Bob Moulder. Stone Arch Books, 2006. 88pp. ISBN-10: 1-5988902-7-1. ISBN-13: 978-15988902-7-3. `GR. 3-8`**

Scott and Kel are rivals on the same soccer team, but when they decide to find out who the top scorer is, they realize they have to make a big decision: What's more important; their personal goals or teamwork?

Horror of the Heights. **Written by Anthony Masters. Illustrated by Peter Dennis. Stone Arch Books, 2006. 88pp. ISBN-10: 1-5988903-0-1. ISBN-13: 978-15988903-0-3. `GR. 3-8`**

Dean Lambert is terrified of diving. Complicating things is the fact that his fear is getting worse, especially now that he thinks someone is sabotaging the diving board at the fitness center.

My Brother's a Keeper. **Written by Michael Hardcastle. Illustrated by Bob Moulder. Stone Arch Books, 2007. 88pp. ISBN-10: 1-5988908-1-6. ISBN-13: 978-15988908-1-5. `GR. 3-8`**

Carlo's soccer team, the Raiders, is in trouble. Their goalie has been injured, and they don't have anyone to replace him, until Carlo's new stepbrother reveals that he plays goalie.

My First Graphic Novel: Sports. `GR. K-2`

An introductory series from Stone Arch books presents easy-to-read stories that not only keep the storytelling simple, but also introduce the "proper" way to read graphic novels.

Bree's Bike Jump. Written by Lori Mortensen. Illustrated by Mary Sullivan. Stone Arch Books, 2010. 32pp. ISBN-10: 1-4342162-0-9. ISBN-13: 978-14342162-0-5.

Yikes! Bree just can't do it. The big bike jump is too big, too steep, and too scary. Is there any way for Bree to pedal through her fears?

The End Zone. Written by Lori Mortensen. Illustrated by Mary Sullivan. Stone Arch Books, 2009. 32pp. ISBN-10: 1-4342128-9-0. ISBN-13: 978-14342128-9-4.

Olivia wants to play flag football with the boys, but the other boys always tell her to go jump rope. When the boys are short a player, will they give Olivia a shot?

Goalkeeper Goof. Written by Cari Meister. Illustrated by Cori Doerrfeld. Stone Arch Books, 2009. 32pp. ISBN-10: 1-4342129-2-0. ISBN-13: 978-14342129-2-4.

Although David likes to play soccer, he hates being goalie. When he has to take a turn as goalie, he has a new trick he wants to try. Will it work?

The Kickball Kids. Written by Cari Meister. Illustrated by Julie Olson. Stone Arch Books, 2009. 32pp. ISBN-10: 1-4342141-0-9. ISBN-13: 978-14342141-0-2.

A group of first-grade kids play kickball in a tournament. Eventually they face off against the fifth-grade champions.

Lily's Lucky Leotard. Written by Cari Meister. Illustrated by Jannie Ho. Stone Arch Books, 2009. 32pp. ISBN-10: 1-4342129-6-3. ISBN-13: 978-14342129-6-2.

Lily loves gymnastics, but she's afraid of jumping off the balance beam. After she gets a new leotard, she knows she can do it.

Rah-Rah Ruby! Written by Christianne C. Jones. Illustrated by Cori Doerrfeld. Stone Arch Books, 2009. 32pp. ISBN-10: 1-2423129-8-X. ISBN-13: 978-14342129-8-6.

Ruby wants to be a cheerleader. She's great at tumbling, shouting, and working with the team, but she has trouble spelling. Will she be able to learn how to spell in time for tryouts?

T-Ball Trouble. Written by Cari Meister. Illustrated by Jannie Ho. Stone Arch Books, 2009. 32pp. ISBN-10: 1-4342130-0-5. ISBN-13: 978-14342140-0-6.

Marco loves baseball, on the television, at the park; he can't get enough. Finally he joins a T-ball team; will he be good enough?

The Prince of Tennis. GR. 4-8

Another sports manga that has swept through Japan and America, The Prince of Tennis series follows the story of Ryoma Echizen, a tennis prodigy who has won four straight America junior tournament titles. Enrolling in Seishum Gakuen Middle School, Ryoma joins the tennis team and becomes a rising star. Ryoma inspires younger players and angers older players by challenging the rule that freshmen cannot represent the team in tournaments until summer.

The series has spawned a sequel series, an anime series that ran for 178 episodes, an animated theatrical release, a live-action movie, a radio show, and video games, as well as more than fifteen stage musicals.

The Prince of Tennis Vol. 1. Written and illustrated by Takeshi Konomi. VIZ Media LLC, 2004. 192pp. ISBN-10: 1-5911643-5-4. ISBN-13: 978-15911643-5-7.

Ryoma Echizen is a prodigy tennis star with the potential to surpass even the career of his father, if only the rest of his new tennis team knew it. Because Ryoma is at a new school, to get on the team, he has to beat players much older than he is, and if he beats them, they're liable to beat him, with their rackets if they have to!

The Prince of Tennis Vol. 2. Written and illustrated by Takeshi Konomi. VIZ Media LLC, 2004. 200pp. ISBN-10: 1-5911643-6-2. ISBN-13: 978-15911643-6-4.

> Ryoma has managed to prove himself to the captain of the tennis team, but the rules state that seventh graders are not allowed to play in tournaments. After some wheeling and dealing by the captain, Ryoma is set to join ranking matches; will he have what it takes to truly be called the "Prince of Tennis?"

The Prince of Tennis Vol. 3. Written and illustrated by Takeshi Konomi. VIZ Media LLC, 2004. 200pp. ISBN-10: 1-5911643-7-0. ISBN-13: 978-15911643-7-0.

> Ryoma is in the district preliminaries, but he also has to play doubles matches. Although Ryoma is a master of singles events, can he and his teammate Momo work out their differences and dominate?

The Prince of Tennis Vol. 4. Written and illustrated by Takeshi Konomi. VIZ Media LLC, 2004. 200pp. ISBN-10: 1-5911643-8-9. ISBN-13: 978-15911643-8-8.

> Ryoma runs across a tennis player just as good as he is, but doesn't play him. Instead, Ryoma and Momo get caught up in a street-style tennis match. If these two can't get their problems worked out, they'll be out of the tournament before it even begins in earnest.

The Prince of Tennis Vol. 5. Written and illustrated by Takeshi Konomi. VIZ Media LLC, 2004. 200pp. ISBN-10: 1-5911643-9-7. ISBN-13: 978-15911643-9-5.

> Seishun Academy is only one win away from advancing to the city tournaments, so Ryoma is chosen to face off against the mysterious and difficult-to-understand Shinji of the Fudomine Team. When Ryoma develops a muscle paralysis called "Spot," will he be able to beat this competitor when he's almost too weak to even hold his racket?

Raven's Revenge. **Written by Anthony Masters. Illustrated by Peter Dennis. Stone Arch Books, 2007. 88pp. ISBN-10: 1-5988908-2-4. ISBN-13: 978-15988908-2-2.** GR. 3-8

In an effort to forget about the nightmares he's been having, Andy goes kayaking. Unfortunately, real life can be a lot scarier than bad dreams.

Ridge Riders. GR. 2-5

This series aimed at reluctant readers fuses extreme sports and kid-friendly dialogue. As do all Stone Arch Books, these books have writing prompts, discussion prompts, and a teacher's guide at the end of each book. The stories detail the trials and tribulations of a group of downhill mountain bikers called the "Ridge Riders." From dealing with cheaters to bad accidents, the Ridge Riders face it all with adrenaline, racing, and friendship.

Ridge Riders: Block Buster. Written by Chris Lawrie and Robin Lawrie. Illustrated by Robin Lawrie. Stone Arch Books, 2008. 40pp. ISBN-10: 1-4342048-4-7. ISBN-13: 978-14342048-4-4.

> The Ridge Riders each face a new challenge, so Dozy comes up with blockbuster ideas for each of them while engaging in downhill mountain bike racing. Will his psychology work, or are the Ridge Riders doomed?

Ridge Riders: Chain Reaction. Written by Chris Lawrie and Robin Lawrie. Illustrated by Robin Lawrie. Stone Arch Books, 2008. 40pp. ISBN-10: 1-4342048-3-9. ISBN-13: 978-14342948-3-7.

> Slam thinks the mountain biking team is jinxed, as one bad event after another occurs. Is the team really doomed, or can they work as a team to fix the problems?

Ridge Riders: Cheat Challenge. Written by Chris Lawrie and Robin Lawrie. Illustrated by Robin Lawrie. Stone Arch Books, 2007. 40pp. ISBN-10: 1-5988934-7-5. ISBN-13: 978-15988934-7-2.

> Slam and the gang enter a mountain biking race, but Slam faces a dilemma: He has seen the map of the race and realizes that some things on the course could endanger his teammates. Does he keep his mouth shut and play fair, or does he cheat and protect his friends from danger?

Ridge Riders: Fear 3.1. Written by Chris Lawrie and Robin Lawrie. Illustrated by Robin Lawrie. Stone Arch Books, 2007. 40pp. ISBN-10: 1–5988934-8-3. ISBN-13: 978-15988934-8-9.

> Slam Duncan used to love rock climbing, until his fall. Now, not only can he not climb, he can't ride the path he has ridden for years, because he is freaked out. Can his friend Dozy discover a way to help Slam conquer his fear of heights?

Ridge Riders: First Among Losers. Written by Chris Lawrie and Robin Lawrie. Illustrated by Robin Lawrie. Stone Arch Books, 2007. 40pp. ISBN-10: 1-5988912-5-1. ISBN-13: 978-15988912-5-6.

> Slam and the gang are bound and determined to defeat their rival, Punk Tier. However, Punk thinks he can buy the race off, until he gets into an impossible situation. Now it's up to the Ridge Riders to teach Punk what it means to race like a team.

Ridge Riders: Paintball Panic. Written by Chris Lawrie and Robin Lawrie. Illustrated by Robin Lawrie. Stone Arch Books, 2007. 40pp. ISBN-10: 1-5988912-6-X. ISBN-13: 978-15988912-6-3.

> Property developers are trying to take over the hill where the Ridge Riders practice their downhill racing. Will Slam and the gang be able to keep their practice area?

Ridge Riders: Radar Riders. Written by Chris Lawrie and Robin Lawrie. Illustrated by Robin Lawrie. Stone Arch Books, 2007. 40pp. ISBN-10: 1-5988912-7-8. ISBN-13: 978-15988912-7-0.

> The Ridge Riders build a new mountain biking course in an abandoned quarry. What could possibly go wrong?

Ridge Riders: Slamming Success. Written by Chris Lawrie and Robin Lawrie. Illustrated by Robin Lawrie. Stone Arch Books, 2008. 40pp. ISBN-10: 1-4342048-2-0. ISBN-13: 978-14342048-2-0.

> Slam needs to win the downhill race to get points to help out the team, but everyone he runs into on the course needs his help. Will he be able to help out and still win?

Ridge Riders: Snow Bored. Written by Chris Lawrie and Robin Lawrie. Illustrated by Robin Lawrie. Stone Arch Books, 2007. 40pp. ISBN-10: 1-5988934-9-1. ISBN-13: 978-15988934-9-6.

> Snow has fallen, and the Ridge Riders can't ride. Nobody can do anything until Dozy comes up with a homemade snowboard, then it's back to the slopes. However, Fiona's horse hurts itself in the snow, and it's up to Slam to get to the vet. Will he make it, or is the horse doomed?

Ridge Riders: Sweet Revenge. Written by Chris Lawrie and Robin Lawrie. Illustrated by Robin Lawrie. Stone Arch Books, 2008. 40pp. ISBN-10: 1-4342048-5-5. ISBN-13: 978-14342048-5-1.

> After Stick and Spanner steal Slam's shocks before a big downhill race, the Ridge Riders concoct a spooky scheme to get the shocks back and teach the thieves a lesson.

Ridge Riders: Treetop Trauma. Written by Chris Lawrie and Robin Lawrie. Illustrated by Robin Lawrie. Stone Arch Books, 2007. 40pp. ISBN-10: 1-5988912-8-6. ISBN-13: 978-15988912-8-7.

> Time is running out for the Ridge Riders to save their local hill from property developers. In a bold move, the team decides to sacrifice their chances at winning one of the last races in the series to hold a treetop protest. When their plan goes horribly wrong, who's going to save the hill?

Ridge Riders: White Lightning. Written by Chris Lawrie and Robin Lawrie. Illustrated by Robin Lawrie. Stone Arch Books, 2007. 40pp. ISBN-10: 1-5988935-0-5. ISBN-13: 978-15988935-0-2.

> The Ridge Rider's practice jumps have all been smashed, and they think Fiona and her horse-riding friends are to blame. After the boys are extremely mean to Fiona, can Slam find some way to make it up to her?

Sam's Goal. **Written by Michael Hardcastle. Illustrated by Tony O'Donnell. Stone Arch Books, 2007. 72pp. ISBN-10: 1-5988908-8-3. ISBN-13: 978-15988908-8-4.** `GR. 2-6`

Sam has always dreamed of playing professional soccer. When the best soccer player in the country invites Sam to his next game, Sam can't believe it. The problem is, neither can Sam's friends. Can Sam convince them that he's telling the truth?

Whistle! `GR. 3-7`

A popular soccer-based manga from Japan, translated for English audiences, tells the story of Shō Kazamatsuri, a young man who wants to play soccer, so he transfers to Sakura Josui Junior High in an attempt to join the team. Shō's problem is that he is a small kid and didn't get much field time at his old school; Musashinomori, home of the famed soccer team. Can Shō improve his game and prove that even though he's small, he can dominate?

A good series that emphasizes that talent and perseverance always beat physical shortcomings. It has spawned video game versions on the Game Boy Advance and Playstation console systems.

The following list includes only the library binding editions.

Whistle! 1: Break Through. Written and illustrated by Daisuke Higuchi. VIZ Media LLC, 2008. 208pp. ISBN-10: 1-4352420-2-X. ISBN-13: 978-14352320-2-0.

Shō has always loved soccer, but due to his short stature, he was always a third string bench warmer. After transferring to a new school, his is mistaken for a striker (lead attacker) and made a fool of. Joining forces with Mizuno Tatsuya, they set out to prove that the alternates (replacement players) can beat the seniors at their own game.

Whistle! 2: On Your Marks. Written and illustrated by Daisuke Higuchi. VIZ Media LLC, 2008. 208pp. ISBN-10: 1-4352520-3-8. ISBN-13: 978-14352320-3-7.

Shō and the team managed to beat the seniors, and now Mizuno leads the team. However, in response, the majority of the team has quit! With only seven players on the new team, they're going to have to work twice as hard with the state finals coming up.

Nate's Picks

- The Babysitter's Club by Ann M. Martin and Raina Telgemeyer. Originally written for girls, this new series has played well with boys, too.

- Babymouse by Jennifer Holm and Matthew Holm. Another title that is aimed at girls, but boys will like it too, even if they won't admit it.

- *Stuck in the Middle*: *17 Tales from an Awkward Age* by Ariel Schrag. Helps middle school age readers understand that what they're beginning to go through is not unique to them.

Chapter 7

Literary Classics

We all remember those classics we had to read in school, slogging through archaic language, often with stilted writing or outdated ideas. But what made these books "classics" is that underneath it all, there is something about the stories that speaks to us and holds our attention, even when they are difficult to get through.

The books listed in this chapter attempt to make it more enjoyable to read these stories, adding a visual element that was missing from the original ones.

Literary Classics

You may remember slogging through the American Literary Classics brand of comics when you were younger (none of which are still in print). Though interesting in conception, their execution often left something to be desired. However, with graphic novel adaptations, readers can now see what life was like in these classic novels instead of having to try to imagine what something would look like.

Most of these books have been adapted for younger readers; nevertheless, exercise caution when recommending certain titles, and review them before suggesting them to young readers.

20,000 Leagues under the Sea.

Jules Verne's classic story about a noted French marine biologist, a Canadian master harpoonist, and the mysterious captain of the magnificent submarine the *Nautilus*. Cutting edge for its time (the book was written decades before submarines the size of the *Nautilus* were created), Verne can be categorized as either literary classic or science fiction.

20,000 Leagues under the Sea. Written by Jules Verne. Adapted and illustrated by Tod Smith. Stone Arch Books, 2008. 72pp. ISBN-10: 1-4342044-7-2. ISBN-13: 978-14342044-7-9. `GR. 2-8`

> Jules Verne's classic story of a high-tech submarine and its mysterious creator, Captain Nemo, rewritten for younger readers. Scientist Pierre Aronnax and his trusty servant set sail to hunt a sea monster. With help from the world's greatest harpooner, the men discover that the creature is really a high-tech submarine with a mysterious leader, Captain Nemo.

20,000 Leagues under the Sea. Written and illustrated by YKids. YoungJin Singapore Pte. Ltd, 2008. 144pp. ISBN-10: 9-8105755-6-4. ISBN-13: 978-98105755-6-4. `GR. 4-8`

> An interpretation of Jules Verne's classic about the obsessive Captain Nemo and the team who must stop him. After reports start coming in about warships being destroyed by a giant sea monster, Pierre Aronnax heads out to sea to destroy the menace. Only after his own ship is destroyed does he discover the truth: The monster is actually a huge submarine, and the captain plans on destroying the world's navies!

Alice in Wonderland. **Written by Lewis Carroll. Illustrated by Daniel Perez. Stone Arch Books, 2010. 72pp. ISBN-10: 1-4342158-5-7. ISBN-13: 978-14342158-5-7.** `GR. 2-8`

After spying on and chasing after a rabbit in human clothes, young Alice tumbles down a rabbit hold into a magical wonderland. There she meets many strange characters, including a mad hatter, an imperious caterpillar, a cat that is not always there (or not all at once), and the haughty Queen of Hearts. When the Queen turns on Alice, the adventures begin. This classic literary tale can also be considered a fantasy.

Black Beauty. **Written by Anna Sewell. Adapted and illustrated by June Brigman and Roy Richardson. Puffin, 2005. 176pp. ISBN-10: 0-1424040-8-X. ISBN-13: 978-01424040-8-9.** `GR. 3-7`

An autobiographical memoir told from a horse's point of view, from carefree days on an English farm, to a difficult life pulling cabs in London, to a happy retirement in the country. The nineteenth-century story translates well to the graphic novel format, but moral lessons and antiquated language may turn off reluctant readers.

Parental Advisory: animal cruelty

Call of the Wild. **Written by Jack London. Adapted by Neil Kleid. Illustrated by Alex Niño. Puffin, 2006. 176pp. ISBN-10: 0-1424057-1-X. ISBN-13: 978-01424057-1-0.** `GR. 6-8`

A heavily digested version of the Jack London classic, still a worthwhile, if slightly confusing, read. Easier to locate than the original Classic Comics series from the early to mid-1980s. Buck is a somewhat pampered domesticated dog who goes feral after he becomes a sled dog in the frozen Yukon during the Klondike Gold Rush.

Parental Advisory: animal cruelty

Charles Dickens and Friends. **Written by Charles Dickens. Adapted and illustrated by Marcia Williams. Candlewick, 2006. 48pp. ISBN-10: 0-7636319-8-1. ISBN-13: 978-07636319-8-7.** `GR. 4-7`

Heavily truncated adaptations of Dickens's most popular tales (*Oliver Twist, Great Expectations, A Tale of Two Cities, David Copperfield,* and *A Christmas Carol*) are compacted into easy-to-digest stories that still maintain the spirit of the originals.

Gulliver's Travels. **Written by Jonathan Swift. Adapted and illustrated by Cynthia Martin. Stone Arch Books, 2008. 72pp. ISBN-10: 1-4342044-9-9. ISBN-13: 978-14342044-9-3.** `GR. 2-8`

Lemuel Gulliver always dreamed of traveling, but once he gets out on the open sea, his adventures take him to places he never knew existed. If he survives, his travels could be the greatest ever told!

The Hunchback of Notre Dame. **Written by Victor Hugo. Adapted by L. L. Owens. Illustrated by Greg Rebis. Stone Arch Books, 2007. 72pp. ISBN-10: 1-5988904-7-6. ISBN-13: 978-15988904-7-1.** `GR. 2-8`

Quasimodo, a deformed hunchback, lives in the bell tower of Notre Dame and is treated like a monster. When a gypsy girl by the name of Esmeralda shows him kindness, Quasimodo discovers what it takes to become a hero.

The Invisible Man. **Written by H. G. Wells. Adapted by Terry Davis. Illustrated by Dennis Calero. Stone Arch Books, 2008. 72pp. ISBN-10: 1-5988983-1-0. ISBN-13: 978-15988983-1-6.** `GR. 2-8`

One night a stranger covered in bandages appears in a town. Growing suspicious of the man, the villagers decide to arrest him; only then do they discover his awful secret: He's invisible! A classic scary story.

Journey to the Center of the Earth. **Written by Jules Verne. Adapted by Davis Worth Miller and Katherine Mclean Brevard. Illustrated by Greg Rebis. Stone Arch Books, 2008. 72pp. ISBN-10: 1-5988983-2-9. ISBN-13: 978-15988983-2-3.** `GR. 2-8`

Finding a note that describes a path to the earth's center, Axel and his uncle follow it. Deep inside a volcano, they discover amazing wonders as well as dangers that could trap them below the surface forever.

The Last Knight: An Introduction to Don Quixote. **Written by Miguel de Cervantes Saavedra. Adapted and illustrated by Will Eisner. Nantier Beall Minoustchine Publishing, 2000. 32pp. ISBN-10: 1-5616325-1-1. ISBN-13: 978-15616325-1-0.** `GR. 5-8`

> Eisner condenses the classic and comical story of a deluded knight into an easy-to-approach introduction to Cervantes's classic. Don Quixote sees himself as a latter day knight, saving the honor of barmaids and tilting at windmills, which he sees as ogres. Told from the point of view of his faithful friend and servant, Sancho Panza.

The Legend of Sleepy Hollow. **Written by Washington Irving. Adapted and illustrated by Tod Smith. Stone Arch Books, 2008. 72pp. ISBN-10: 1-4342-044-6-4. ISBN-13: 978-14342044-6-2.** `GR. 2-8`

> Irving's classic Halloween story about a beautiful woman, a nervous schoolteacher, and a jealous rival. (**Note:** This is from Stone Arch, so the terror factor of this is very mild.)

Macbeth. **Written by William Shakespeare. Adapted by Arthur Byron Cover. Illustrated by Tony Leonard Tamai. Puffin, 2005. 176pp. ISBN-10: 0-1424040-9-8. ISBN-13: 978-01424040-9-6.** `GR. 6-8`

> A futuristic take on Shakespeare's classic tragedy. Macbeth is told that he will become king and cannot be defeated by "any man born of woman." But for Macbeth to become king, King Duncan must first die. Will Lady Macbeth drive her husband to the ultimate betrayal?

Pinocchio. **Written by Carlo Collodi. Adapted and illustrated by Alfonso Ruiz. Stone Arch Books, 2010. 72pp. ISBN-10: 1-4342158-3-0. ISBN-13: 978-14342158-3-3.** `GR. 2-8`

> This perennial children's favorite is the story of a wooden boy who wants nothing more than to be real. The only problem is that he keeps doing naughty things.

Red Badge of Courage. **Written by Stephen Crane. Adapted and illustrated by Wayne Vansant. Puffin, 2005. 176pp. ISBN-10: 0-1424041-0-1. ISBN-13: 978-01424041-0-2.** `GR. 4-8`

> Henry Fleming is a private in the Union Army during an unnamed battle during the American Civil War. Fearing the battle lost, Henry flees into the forest, meeting up with injured soldiers, only to run from them because he has no injuries. Joining back up with his battalion (which won the battle), Henry overhears his commanding officer planning on sacrificing the battalion. Fueled by an intense drive to prove the man wrong, Henry charges into the next battle, becoming not only one of the best fighters, but also the flag bearer. Faithfully introducing the plot, characters, and primary themes, this adaptation is a good introduction to the book without delving into its multilayered character studies.
>
> **Parental Advisory:** war-related violence

The Strange Case of Dr. Jekyll and Mr. Hyde. **Written by Robert Louis Stevenson. Retold by Carl Bowen. Illustrated by Daniel Perez. Stone Arch Books, 2009. 72pp. ISBN-10: 1-4342-0745-4-4. ISBN-13: 978-14342075-4-8.** `GR. 2-8`

> In an effort to isolate the evil side of man's mind, Dr. Henry Jekyll attempts a strange experiment. It backfires, unleashing the monstrous Mr. Hyde. A scary story that became a classic.

The Swiss Family Robinson. **Written by Johann D. Wyss. Retold by Martin Powell. Illustrated by Gerardo Sandoval. Stone Arch Books, 2009. 72pp. ISBN-10: 1-4342075-6-0. ISBN-13: 978-14342075-6-2.** `GR. 2-8`

> The grand tale of shipwreck and survival on a distant island. After their ship is swept off course, a Swiss pastor, his wife, and their four young sons end up shipwrecked on an uncharted tropical island. As they adapt to their environs, they learn not only to survive, but to thrive.

Tom Sawyer.

> Mark Twain's tale of mischief and hijinks of the irrepressible Tom Sawyer and his best friend (and shiftless layabout) Huckleberry Finn. Often required reading in schools, the original story is great fun, but with graphic images to go along with it, these books are impossible to put down.

The Adventures of Tom Sawyer. Written by Mark Twain. Adapted by Matt Josdal. Illustrated by Brian Shearer. Campfire Books, 2010. 72pp. ISBN-10: 8-190693-7-8. ISBN-13: 978-81906963-7-1. `GR. 3-8`

> Follow Tom and Huck's adventures as Tom cons his fellow boys into whitewashing his fence and falls in love with the new girl in town, and he and Huck become pirates and witness a murder. Will Tom and Huck be able to stay alive long enough to point out the real killer?

The Adventures of Tom Sawyer. Written by Mark Twain. Adapted and illustrated by Daniel Strickland. Stone Arch Books, 2006. 72pp. ISBN-10: 1-5988922-0-7. ISBN-13: 978-15988922-0-8. `GR. 4-8`

> After witnessing a murder, Tom Sawyer and Huckleberry Finn find themselves in a series of adventures that lead them into some frightening situations. Will Tom and Huck do the right thing and absolve Muff Potter of the killing of a doctor?

Tom Sawyer. Written by Mark Twain. Adapted by Tim Mucci. Illustrated by Rad Sechrist. Sterling, 2008. 128pp. ISBN-10: 1-4027339-9-2. ISBN-13: 978-14027339-9-4. `GR. 4-8`

> A close adaptation of Mark Twain's classic. Tom manages to talk the local boys into painting his fence for him; he also falls in love with the new girl in town, becomes a pirate with Huck Finn, witnesses the murder of a doctor by Injun Joe, and comes across hidden treasure.

Treasure Island.

Robert Louis Stevenson's coming-of-age tale about pirate treasure, action, and the ambiguity of morality (which is unusual in children's literature from any era) is one of the most frequently dramatized stories ever created. A classic adventure.

Treasure Island. Written by Robert Louis Stevenson. Illustrated by Tim Hamilton. Puffin Books, 2005. 176pp. ISBN-10: 0-1424047-0-5. ISBN-13: 978-01424047-0-6. **GR. 4-8**

Young Jim Hawkins gets caught up in the adventure of a lifetime when a treasure map comes into his possession that allegedly leads to a major treasure trove. Along the way he befriends the pirate of pirates, Long John Silver, and discovers a mutiny brewing, led by none other than Silver himself.

Treasure Island. Written by Robert Louis Stevenson. Retold by Wim Coleman and Pat Perrin. Illustrated by Greg Rebis. Stone Arch Books, 2007. 72pp. ISBN-10: 1-5988905-0-6. ISBN-13: 978-15988905-0-1. **GR. 2-8**

Follow young Jim Hawkins as he discovers an old treasure map and runs afoul of the sly pirate, Long John Silver.

The Wind in the Willows. **Written by Kenneth Grahame. Illustrated by Michel Plessix. Papercutz, 2008. 144pp. ISBN-10: 1-5970709-6-3. ISBN-13: 978-15970709-6-6. GR. 3-7**

Join Mole, Ratty, and the driving-impaired Mr. Toad in all of their adventures. Mole has never been above ground, but one day he decides to check it out, discovering a big river near his house. Near the river he meets Water Rat, who invites Mole on a boat ride and picnic. Later Mole and Ratty pay a visit to Mr. Toad, who is completely taken with racing automobiles and almost gets them killed. What other adventures will the three friends engage in?

Nate's Picks

- *The Strange Case of Dr. Jekyll and Mr. Hyde* by Robert Louis Stevenson. The classic tale of the battle between good and evil has never been so entertaining.

- Tom Sawyer by Mark Twain. This early look at youth in America still stands the test of time.

- Treasure Island by Robert Louis Stevenson. Proof that a bad guy can still have a soft spot for a kid.

Chapter 8

Educational

One of the most exciting developments in graphic novels is the publication of educational books that not only help engage young readers, but also allow them to learn at the same time. These books cover scientific theories, historical fact and fiction, nonfiction and educational books. Especially useful in educational settings, these stories also appeal to children with avid interests in these subjects or who enjoy "true stories." Though some of the titles here are fictionalized, they are based on true events.

Science

When it comes to graphic novels, even the natural sciences are not impervious to treatment. From the works of Dr. Jay Hostler to the mechanics of science with <u>Max Axiom</u>, these books prove that even science can be fun to learn. Most of the books in this section have a teacher's guide or section for class discussion and/or experiments that can be performed.

***Clan Apis*. Written and illustrated by Jay Hosler, Ph.D. Active Synapse, 2000. 158pp. ISBN-10: 0-9677255-0-X. ISBN-13: 978-09677255-0-5.** `GR. 4-8`

Hosler, a PhD, presents the singular story of the honeybee's life cycle in such a way that children will not realize they are learning more than they ever wanted to about bees. Exhaustively researched and documented, this is recommended for elementary school science classes.

Max Axiom. `GR. 3-7`

Max Axiom was a regular guy until a freak accident gave him all sorts of really cool powers. Now Max demonstrates and explains scientific phenomena in ways not possible in the classroom!

Adventures in Sound with Max Axiom, Super Scientist. Written by Emily Sohn. Illustrated by Cynthia Martin. Capstone Press, 2007. 32pp. ISBN-10: 0-7368683-6-4. ISBN-13: 978-07368683-6-5.

> From viewing sound as a wave to exploring the inner workings of the human ear, Max explains the science behind sound.

A Crash Course in Forces and Motion with Max Axiom, Super Scientist. Written by Emily Sohn. Illustrated by Steve Erwin. Capstone Press, 2007. 32pp. ISBN-10: 0-7368683-7-2. ISBN-13: 978-07368683-7-2.

> Ride along as Max bungee jumps and roller coasters his way through a crash course in speed, acceleration, inertia, friction, gravitational pull, and much more.

Exploring Ecosystems with Max Axiom, Super Scientist. Written by Agnieszka Biskup. Illustrated by Tod Smith. Capstone Press, 2007. ISBN-10: 0-7368684-2-9. ISBN-13: 978-07368684-2-6.

> Max travels through various ecosystems, explaining how everything works within a system and what would happen if we didn't have scavengers and decomposers.

A Journey into Adaptation with Max Axiom, Super Scientist. Written by Agnieszka Biskup. Illustrated by Cynthia Martin. Capstone Press, 2007. 32pp. ISBN-10: 0-7368-684-0-2. ISBN-13: 978-07368684-0-2.

> How does changing skin color help a chameleon survive? Why do certain plants survive with little water, while others need lots of water? Hang out with Max as he explores the science behind adaptation in the living world.

Lessons in Science Safety with Max Axiom, Super Scientist. Written by Donald Lemke and Thomas Adamson. Illustrated by Tod Smith. Capstone Press, 2007. ISBN-10: 0-7368683-4-8. ISBN-13: 978-07368683-4-1.

> Max explains the importance of science safety and safety equipment and shows how to deal with accidents that may occur.

The Shocking World of Electricity with Max Axiom, Super Scientist. Written by Liam O'Donnell. Illustrated by Richard Dominguez. Capstone Press, 2007. 32pp. ISBN-10: 0-7368683-5-6. ISBN-13: 978-07368683-5-8.

> Max explains how dangerous electricity can be, how energy is converted into electricity, and what electricity can be used for, among other topics.

Understanding Photosynthesis with Max Axiom, Super Scientist. Written by Liam O'Donnell. Illustrated by Richard Dominguez. Capstone Press, 2007. 32pp. ISBN-10: 0-7368684-1-0. ISBN-13: 978-07368684-1-9.

> Photosynthesis is the process by which plants convert sun into food, and Max shows how this process is beneficial not only to the plant itself, but also humans and the earth.

The World of Food Chains with Max Axiom, Super Scientist. Written by Liam O'Donnell. Illustrated by Cynthia Martin. Capstone Press, 2007. 32pp. ISBN-10: 0-7368683-9-9. ISBN-13: 978-07368683-9-6.

> What gives you the energy you need to study for a test or play basketball? Sure, you need food, but how does that food convert into the energy you need to keep going? Find out with Max!

Optical Allusions. **Written and illustrated by Jay Hosler, Ph.D. Active Synapse, 2008. 127pp. ISBN-10: 0-9677255-2-6. ISBN-13: 978-09677255-2-9.** `GR. 4-8`

> Wrinkles the Wonder Brain has done it this time: He's managed to lose his boss's eye! To find it, he's going to need to trek across the length of human imagination. Along the way, he faces off against biology and ends up (along with the reader) learning more about the eyes and the evolution of vision than is probably healthy. An essential resource for health class when discussing optics.

The Sandwalk Adventures: An Adventure in Evolution Told in Five Chapters. **Written and illustrated by Jay Hosler, Ph.D. Active Synapse, 2003. 159pp. ISBN-10: 0-9677255-1-8. ISBN-13: 978-09677255-1-2.** `GR. 5-8`

> The theory of evolution has never been as entertaining or informative as this! Follow the fictional story, with Charles Darwin explaining the theory of evolution to two hair mites in his eyebrow, and see how he disabuses them of their notions about who he really is.
>
> **Parental Advisory:** discussion of evolution

Historical Fiction

History often works best when a visual interpretation is available to go along with the text. Graphic novels serve to help the reader interpret not only the story, but also the setting that it is taking placing in, which is useful because usually things have changed a great deal between the time the event occurred and when the audience is reading the book. The books in this section cover actual historical events, but incorporate fictional elements for storytelling purposes.

Some stories cover major tragedies in American (if not world) history, so parental advisory is suggested for most titles in this section.

After the **Challenger:** *A Story of the Space Shuttle Disaster.* **Written by Robert Marsh. Illustrated by Marcelo Baez. Stone Arch Books, 2009. 56pp. ISBN-10: 1-4342116-1-4. ISBN-13: 978-14342116-1-3.** `GR. 2-8`

> A fictional story about the tragic NASA *Challenger* disaster. Fifteen-year-old Dustin Martinez has always been a big fan of the space program, and today is especially exciting: This launch includes the very first schoolteacher to go into space. But something goes terribly wrong.

Blackbeard's Sword: the Pirate King of the Carolinas. **Written by Liam O'Donnel. Illustrated by Mike Spoor. Stone Arch Books. 2007. 56pp.** `GR. 2-8`

Lieutenant Maynard and his men of the Royal Navy plan to capture the notorious pirate Blackbeard. Have they made a mistake by enlisting the help of a young local fisherman by the name of Jacob Webster?

Captured off Guard: the Attack on Pearl Harbor. **Written by Donald B. Lemke. Illustrated by Claude St. Aubin. Stone Arch Books, 2008. 56pp. ISBN-10: 1-4342044-3-X. ISBN-13: 978-14342044-3-1.**

Hank and James hear loud explosions while camping outside Pearl Harbor. James wants to hide, but Hank wants to photograph the battle. Will they risk their lives for photos of the Japanese attack?

Fire and Snow: A Tale of the Alaskan Gold Rush. **Written by Jessica Gunderson. Illustrated by Shannon Townsend. Stone Arch Books, 2007. 56pp. ISBN-10: 1-5988931-0-6. ISBN-13: 978-15988931-0-6.** `GR. 2-8`

Follow Ethan and his family as they leave everything they know in search of gold on the Alaskan frontier during the 1897 Gold Rush.

Fire in the Sky: A Tale of the **Hindenburg** *Explosion.* **Written by J. Gunderson. Illustrated by Claude St. Aubin. Stone Arch Books, 2009. 56pp. ISBN-10: 1-4342116-3-0. ISBN-13: 978-14342116-3-7.** `GR. 2-8`

Fifteen-year-old Michael Roth and his family are headed toward America in 1936. They're fleeing Frankfurt, Germany, to escape the Nazi government and start a better life. Michael is even more excited about the trip because they'll be traveling in the airship *Hindenburg*.

The First and Final Voyage: The Sinking of the **Titanic.** **Written by Stephanie Peters. Illustrated by Jon Proctor. Stone Arch Books, 2008. 56pp. ISBN-10: 1-4342044-4-8. ISBN-13: 978-14342044-4-8.** `GR. 2-8`

Christopher Watkins and his family board the *Titanic* on April 10, 1912. While crossing the Atlantic, disaster strikes! Can Christopher find a way to save his family?

Freedom Songs: A Tale of the Underground Railroad. **Written by Trina Robbins. Illustrated by Jason Millet. Stone Arch Books, 2008. 56pp. ISBN-10: 1-4342044-5-6. ISBN-13: 978-14342044-5-5.** `GR. 2-8`

Sarah is a fourteen-year-old slave in Maryland during the 1850s. Wanting to head north, she joins the Underground Railroad . . . but whom can she trust?

Hot Iron: The Adventures of a Civil War Powder Boy. **Written by Michael Burgan. Illustrated by Pedro Rodriquez. Stone Arch Books, 2007. 56pp. ISBN-10: 1-5988931-1-4. ISBN-13: 978-15988931-1-3.** `GR. 2-8`

Charley O'Leary joins the USS *Varuna* to fight the Confederate Army. Will this plucky twelve-year-old be able to find his brother and survive the fighting?

Isabel Soto. GR. 3-7

Isabel Soto is an archaeologist, world explorer, and time traveler. Think *Indiana Jones*, except with a Hispanic, female protagonist, and you have the basic concept down, except for the Nazis and gunfights. This new series from Capstone seeks to teach kids about historical places, eras, and cultures.

Building the Great Wall of China. Written by Terry Collins. Illustrated by Joe Staton and Al Milgrom. Capstone Press, 2010. 32pp. ISBN-10: 1-4296389-0-7. ISBN-13: 978-14296389-0-6.

> Isabella Soto travels back in time to China during the building of the Great Wall. Throughout her investigation, Izzy discovers not only how the Great Wall was created, but also why, and faces invaders while the wall is still being built.

Exploring **Titanic.** Written by Agnieszka Biskup. Illustrated by Al Bigley and Bill Anderson. Capstone Press, 2009. 32pp. ISBN-10: 1-4296389-2-3. ISBN-13: 978-14296389-2-0.

> To help with a contemporary museum exhibit, Izzy travels back in time to 1912 to find out why the *Titanic* accident was so deadly. Through (fictional) interviews with the survivors, the story comes out about the sinking of the "unsinkable" ship.

Investigating Machu Picchu. Written by Emily Sohn. Illustrated by Cynthia Martin and Barbara Shulz. Capstone Press, 2009. 32pp. ISBN-10: 1-4296389-4-X. ISBN-13: 978-14296389-4-4.

> In her latest adventure, Izzy travels back to 1475 to explore the city of Machu Picchu. While there, she meets a Peruvian boy who explains about life in that time.

Rescue in Antarctica. Written by Emily Sohn. Illustrated by Steven Butler and Anne Timmons. Capstone Press, 2009. 32pp. ISBN-10: 1-4296389-6-6. ISBN-13: 978-14296389-6-8.

> In a slight deviation from the standard format, Izzy and crew mount a rescue mission in modern-day Antarctica while discussing facts about the frozen continent.

Tracking Bigfoot. Written by Terry Collins. Illustrated by Tod Smith and Al Milgrom. Capstone Press, 2009. 32pp. ISBN-10: 1-4296389-8-2. ISBN-13: 978-14296389-8-2.

> Called in to help with an investigation, Izzy explores the history and science of tracking Bigfoot, a legendary ape-type creature.

Uncovering Mummies. Written by Agnieszka Biskup. Illustrated by Al Bigley, Cynthia Martin, and Bill Anderson. Capstone Press, 2009. 32pp. ISBN-10: 1-4296390-0-8. ISBN-13: 978-14296390-0-2.

> After a friend of Izzy's is kidnapped, she has to travel through time to various cultures to find an amulet. In the process, she learns about different types of mummies from different cultures.

Jungle Scout: A Vietnam War Story. Written by Tim Hoppey. Illustrated by: Ramon Espinoza. Stone Arch Books, 2009. 56pp. ISBN-10: 1-4342074-7-1. ISBN-13: 978-14342074-7-0.

> Former Viet Cong Lam is now a Kit Carson Scout for the Marines. It's his job to safely move the troops around land mines and booby traps. One false move could kill the entire platoon, but Lam's most difficult task may be getting the platoon to trust him.

The Last Rider: The Final Days of the Pony Express. Written by Jessica Gunderson. Illustrated by Ned Woodman. Stone Arch Books, 2007. 56pp. ISBN-10: 1-5988931-2-2. ISBN-13: 978-15988921-2-0. GR. 2-8

> Matt Edgars enjoys his job as a pony express rider, but rumors abound about a possible war with the Paiute Indians. On top of that, someone is setting fire to Express stations! Does this herald the final days of the Pony Express?

Lost in Space: The Flight of Apollo 13. Written by Gary Bush. Illustrated by Nick Derington. Stone Arch Books, 2009. 56pp. ISBN-10: 1-4342116-2-2. ISBN-13: 978-14342116-2-0. GR. 2-8

> Ramón Garza is forced to help his mother out after school at NASA after his grades begin to drop. On April 11, 1970, Ramón watches as *Apollo 13* launches; little does he know that two days later, the mission will go horribly wrong.

Mystery at Manzanar: A WWII Internment Camp Story. Written by Eric Fein. Illustrated by Kurt Hartman. Stone Arch Books, 2009. 56pp. ISBN-10: 1-4342075-1-X. ISBN-13: 978-14342075-1-7. GR. 2-8

> Annotated in chapter 5.

Ropes of Revolution: The Boston Tea Party. Written by J. Gunderson. Illustrated by Brent Schoonover. Stone Arch Books, 2008. 56pp. ISBN-10: 1-4342049-2-8. ISBN-13: 978-14342049-2-9. GR. 4-8

> A fictional story about the Boston Tea Party. Fifteen-year-old Benjamin and his best friend Joseph want to be part of the action when they hear about the Boston Tea Party, but Benjamin's boss refuses to let him leave his shop. Is Benjamin going to miss the start of the American Revolution?

Secret Weapons: A Tale of the Revolutionary War. Written by J. Gunderson. Illustrated by Jesus Aburto. Stone Arch Books, 2009. 56pp. ISBN-10: 1-4342075-2-8. ISBN-13: 978-14342075-2-4. GR. 2-8

> Although fourteen-year-old Daniel hates the redcoats and wants to fight them, his father wants him to stay and help run the blacksmith shop. Then

Daniel makes a shocking discovery. Will he put his entire family in danger to fight for what he believes in?

Standoff: Remembering the Alamo. **Written by Lisa Trumbauer. Illustrated by Brent Schoonover. Stone Arch Books, 2009. 56pp. ISBN-10: 1-4342075-3-6. ISBN-13: 1-4342-075-3-6.** `GR. 2-8`

As fifteen-year-old Cal and his mother ride across the Texas countryside, they spot thousands of Mexican soldiers approaching. Sensing trouble, Cal goes to the safest place around, the Alamo. Davey Crockett, Jim Bowie, and other soldiers are there, and they're waiting for a fight. Will this small rag-tag army be able to hold their own?

Storm of the Century: A Hurricane Katrina Story. **Written by Stephanie Peters. Illustrated by Jesus Aburto. Stone Arch Books, 2009. 56pp. ISBN-10: 1-4342116-4-9. ISBN-13: 978-14342116-4-4.** `GR. 2-8`

Hurricane Katrina is threatening New Orleans, Louisiana, and Ricky Thompson and his family must flee their city. When traffic becomes too backed up for them to escape, they take refuge inside the Superdome, a football stadium turned rescue shelter for thousands of residents.

Historical Nonfiction

Though fictional history can be entertaining, nothing beats the real thing. The books listed below bring actual historical events alive in a way that helps to convey the excitement, fear, horror, and sense of awe that permeated these events.

The 1918 Flu Pandemic. **Written by Katherine Krohn. Illustrated by Bob Hall. Capstone Publishing, 2007. 32pp. ISBN-10: 1-4296015-8-2. ISBN-13: 978-14296015-8-0.** `GR. 4-7`

Deadlier than the black plague, this pandemic that raced around the world in 1918 is detailed. From its mysterious origins to its equally mysterious end, the most fascinating aspects of this worldwide threat are examined.

The **Apollo 13** *Mission.* **Written by Donald B. Lemke. Illustrated by Keith Tucker. Capstone Publishing, 2006. 32pp. ISBN-10: 0-7368687-1-2. ISBN-13: 978-07368687-1-6.** `GR. 4-7`

A factual recounting of the *Apollo 13* rescue. After an explosion damages the space shuttle, can the crew of four astronauts slingshot around the moon and make it back to Earth, without freezing to death or burning up on re-entry?

The Attack on Pearl Harbor. **Written by Jane Sutcliffe. Illustrated by Bob Lentz. Capstone Publishing, 2006. 32pp. ISBN-10: 0-7368687-2-0. ISBN-13: 978-07368687-2-3.** `GR. 4-7`

Factual retelling of the Japanese attack on Pearl Harbor that pulled America into World War II. When the nation is desperate for oil, Japan mounts an attack on the American naval base at Pearl Harbor, Hawaii. Catching the navy by surprise, the Japanese bomb the base, ensuring America's entry into the war.

Cartoon History.

Professor, mathematician, and cartoonist Larry Gonick started this series in the pages of self-published underground comics and has graduated to full-blown trade paperback volumes of several hundred pages each. Gonnick's books have been translated into many languages, including (but not limited to) Portuguese, Greek, Czech, and Polish.

While Gonnick was looking for a publisher, he received support from Jacqueline Kennedy Onassis, who was working as an editor for Doubleday publishing and championed the books.

Though the books are very informative and entertaining, there is a lot of cartoon violence and cartoon gore (especially in the early chapters), so for this series "read before suggesting." (Harvey Award)

The Cartoon History of the Modern World Pt. 1: From Columbus to the U.S. Constitution. Written and illustrated by Larry Gonick. Collins, 2006. 272pp. ISBN-10: 0-0607600-4-4. ISBN-13: 978-00-607600-4-5. `GR. 6-8`

Shifting gears, the cartoon history series now jumps into the modern world, but with the same humor and aplomb that were hallmarks of earlier books.

The Cartoon History of the United States. Written and illustrated by Larry Gonick. Collins Reference, 1991. 400pp. ISBN-10: 0-0627309-8-3. ISBN-13: 978-00627309-8-5. `GR. 5-8`

From the first colonies to the First Gulf War, what Larry Gonick has done for the rest of the universe, he now does for the United States. If you're not careful, you're going to learn something.

The Cartoon History of the Universe Pt. 1 (The Big Bang to Alexander the Great). Written and illustrated by Larry Gonick. Main Street Books, 1997. 268pp. ISBN-10: 0-3852652-0-4. ISBN-13: 978-03852652-0-1. `GR. 5-8`

In a brief but comprehensive book, the universe is examined through the cartoon medium. Starting at the beginning of time, the book explores the history of the universe and then the history of Earth up to the death of Alexander the Great.

The Cartoon History of the Universe Pt. 2 (From the Springtime of China to the Fall of Rome). Written and illustrated by Larry Gonick. Mainstreet Books/ Doubleday, 1994. 304pp. ISBN-10: 0-3854209-3-5. ISBN-13: 978-03854209-3-8. `GR. 5-8`

> Picking up where the first book leaves off, the madcap travel through the history of the world continues, this time taking a look at religions as well as political upheavals and migrations.
>
> **Parental Advisory:** religious discussions that may be less than pious; sex; violence; war

*The Cartoon History of the Universe Pt. 3 (The Rise of Islam to the Sailing of the **Santa Maria**).* Written and illustrated by Larry Gonick. W.W. Norton & Co., 2002. 300pp. ISBN-10: 0-3933240-3-6. ISBN-13: 978-03933240-3-7. `GR. 5-8`

> Continuing in the hilarious but fact-filled vein that permeated the first two books in the series, book 3 takes the reader through the ages to the Renaissance. The dichotomies of "what I say and what I do" are played out in thought-provoking style without being overbearing.

Gettysburg. **Written and illustrated by C. M. Butzer. HarperCollins, 2008. 80pp. ISBN-10: 0-0615617-5-4. ISBN-13: 978-00615617-5-7.** `GR. 3-7`

> Butzer, a Civil War buff, presents Abraham Lincoln's Gettysburg Address in a graphic format in his first book. Working from first person accounts, including Lincoln's own notes, the events leading up to Lincoln's most famous speech are examined as well as the Address itself.
>
> **Parental Advisory:** war violence

The Great Chicago Fire of 1871. **Written by Kay M. Olson. Illustrated by Charles Barnett III. Capstone Press, 2006. 32pp. ISBN-10: 0-7368687-5-5. ISBN-13: 978-07368687-5-4.** `GR. 3-7`

> In 1871, a massive conflagration ripped through Chicago, destroying much of the city. Detailing the efforts and failings of the various fire departments of the time, Chicago would never be the same.

Biography, Autobiography, and Memoir

A relatively new area of graphic novels to younger audiences, discussing someone's life is a fascinating way to discover history and the events that shaped that life. Quite often these people have experienced difficult times or suffered horrific events, so parental review is highly suggested for any book in this section. Many titles in this section deal with famous people, famous groups, or people who are not famous but lead very interesting lives.

The Beatles. **Written and illustrated by Saddleback Educational Publishing. Saddleback Educational Publishing, 2008. 32pp. ISBN-10: 1-5990521-6-4. ISBN-13: 978-15990521-6-8.** `GR. 4-8`

> This biography of one of the greatest rock and roll bands of all times details the lives and tribulations of "the Fab Four"—John Lennon, Paul McCartney, George Harrison, and Ringo Star—from their childhoods, through their stardom, to their breakup.

Daniel Boone. **Written and illustrated by Saddleback Educational Publishing. Saddleback Educational Publishing, 2008. 32pp. ISBN-10: 1-5990521-9-9. ISBN-13: 978-15990521-9-9.** `GR. 4-8`

> Daniel Boone, American pioneer, folklore hero, and defender of the Alamo, is the focus of this biography. From explorer, to American soldier, to Indian killer, to honorary member of an Indian tribe, Daniel Boone's adventures are detailed in this fact-based book.

Elvis Presley. **Written and illustrated by Saddleback Educational Publishing, 2008. 32pp. ISBN-10: 1-5990522-1-0. ISBN-13: 978-15990522-1-2.** `GR. 4-8`

> Elvis, aka "The King," and his life are detailed in this book, from his start as a truck driver, to his rise to the position of most beloved musician in the world, to his untimely death in 1978. Also discusses his impact and influence on modern music.

Houdini. **Written and illustrated by Saddleback Educational Publishing. Saddleback Educational Publishing, 2008. 32pp. ISBN-10: 1-5990522-4-5. ISBN-13: 978-15990522-4-3.** `GR. 4-8`

> Harry Houdini, the American escape artist (1874–1926), is explored in this biography, from his early years, to his climb to fame as an escape artist, stunt performer, actor, and skeptic who set out to expose frauds purporting to be supernatural phenomena, to his death in 1926.

Kampung Boy.

An autobiographical recounting of the Malaysian cartoonist Mohammad Nor Khalid, aka "Lat," growing up in Malaya (Peninsular Malaysia) during the 1950s and early 1960s. Spread over two books, the series details Lat's childhood, first in a small village, and then in the town of Ipoh. A fascinating look at a foreign culture that doesn't involve major revolutions or horrible sacrifices.

> *Kampung Boy.* **Written and illustrated by Lat. First Second Books, 2006. 144pp. ISBN-10: 1-5964312-1-0. ISBN-13: 978-15964312-1-8.** `GR. 4-8`
>
> > In this first book by Malaysian comic creator Lat, we are introduced to a young Lat growing up in a Muslim community in the 1950s. Clean, simple illustrations and little dialogue tell the story of common events in his community that resonate with readers today. (ALA Great Graphic Novel)

Town Boy. **Written and illustrated by Lat. First Second Books, 2007. 192pp. ISBN-10: 1-5964333-1-0. ISBN-13: 978-15964333-1-1.** `GR. 5-8`

> Mat moves to the town of Ipoh, where he meets Frankie, a Chinese boy his age. Frankie and Mat become fast friends and discover American music, girls, and how to cheat in PE.

Maus. `GR. 6-8`

One of the most heart-wrenching yet powerful biographies to be committed to graphic novel format, <u>Maus</u> is the story of Vladek Spiegelman, a Polish Jew who lived through the horrors of World War II. At the same time, the book details the difficult and often contentious relationship between Art Spiegelman and Vladek, his father. A definite must read for any graphic novel reader, this series may be too intense for many younger readers. (Harvey Award, Pulitzer Prize)

Parental Advisory: intense themes, inferred violence, some graphic scenes of a disturbing nature, suicide, murder, anti-Semitism

Maus I: A Survivor's Tale: My Father Bleeds History. Written and illustrated by Art Spiegelman. Pantheon, 1986. 160pp. ISBN-10: 0-3947472-3-2. ISBN-13: 978-03947472-3-1.

> What started out as a biography of his father's survival of Auschwitz becomes a testament to and warning about the inherent need to survive. Brutal, tragic, and horrifying, yet still an uplifting testament of the human condition. This book won Spiegelman a Pulitzer Prize.
>
> **Parental Advisory:** disturbing images; violence; warfare.

Maus II: A Survivors Tale: And Here My Troubles Began. Written and illustrated by Art Spiegelman. Pantheon, 1992. 144pp. ISBN-10: 0-6797297-7-1. ISBN-13: 978-06797297-7-8.

> Vladek's story continues in the second volume of his biography as he deals with the horrors of Auschwitz, the fall of the Nazi regime, and his eventual immigration to America. Permeating the book is a sense of Art's anxiety and guilt over writing the story after his father's death, his ambivalence regarding his first book, and wrestling with the "funny-animal" metaphors.

Sundiata: A Legend of Africa. **Written and illustrated by Will Eisner. Nantier Beall Minoustchine Publishing, 2003. 32pp. ISBN-10: 1-5616334-0-2. ISBN-13: 978-15616334-0-1.** `GR. 3-6`

> A retelling of the story of Sundiata (ca. 1217–1225), a king of the Malinké, a race of Africans scattered across Western Africa. Sundiata is an ugly, crippled child, the only member of the royal family to survive the invasion by Sumanguru, a magician-king. Growing to manhood, Sundiata raises an army and overthrows the usurper, becoming the beloved, long-lived king of Mali.

To Dance: A Ballerina's Graphic Novel. **Written by Siena Cherson Siegel. Illustrated by Mark Siegel. Atheneum/Richard Jackson Books, 2006. 64pp. ISBN-10: 0-6898674-7-6. ISBN-13: 978-06898674-7-7.** GR. 3-6

Husband and wife team Siena Siegel and Mark Siegel team up to tell Siena's story of how she became a ballerina. Very kid friendly and uplifting. Highly suggested for young dancers, or those who want to be. (ALA Great Graphic Novel)

True Story, Swear to God: 100 Stories. **Written and illustrated by Tom Beland. AiT/LanetLar, 2004. 112pp. ISBN-10: 1-9320512-1-X. ISBN-13: 978-19320512-1-6.** GR. 7-8

Cartoonist Tom Beland tells short stories from his life with his "heartfelt valentine" and wife, Lily. Well written, romantic, and a nice offering of "slice-of-life" storytelling. Detailing day-to-day events, from uprooting himself to moving to Puerto Rico to be with the love of his life, Beland also discusses his childhood and measures he took to mourn his father's passing.

Parental Advisory: language

Walt Disney. **Written and illustrated by Saddleback Educational Publishing, 2008. 32pp. ISBN-10: 1-5990523-0-X. ISBN-13: 978-15990523-0-4.** GR. 4-8

Here's the story of Walt Disney, who created Mickey Mouse, animated movies, and the largest theme parks in the world. It covers from his early years, starting out with his own little studio, through what many people considered "Disney's Folly" (which is now called *Snow White*), to his innovations in filming animation and the creation of not only Disney Land, but also his most ambitious project, Disney World.

Anthologies

Anthologies are a great way to introduce readers to many different styles of graphic novels without having to buy a ton of different books. Following are some of the (few) comics anthologies for children.

Flight Explorer Vol. 1. **Edited by Kazu Kibuishi. 112pp. Villard, 2008. ISBN-10: 0-3455031-3-9. ISBN-13: 978-03455031-3-8.** GR. 5-8

Following in the footsteps of Kibuishi's anthology for adults, *Flight*, this kid-friendly book features stories and vignettes from various artists. Artistic readers will really dig this series. Includes such stories as "Jellaby" by Kean Soo, "Missile Mouse" by Jake Parker, "Zita the Spacegirl" by Ben Hatke, "Fish 'n' Chips" by Steve Hamaker, "N" by Phil Craven, and a previously unpublished story by Kibuishi, "Copper."

Golden Treasury of Krazy Kool Klassic Kids' Komics. **Written and illustrated by Various. IDW Publishing, 2010. 304pp. ISBN-10: 1-6001052-0-3. ISBN-13: 978-16001052-0-3.** GR. 3-7

Old-school comic fans will love this collection of the best comics from the early years of the genre, and new fans will delight in discovering long-lost gems from another era in this collection compiled by some of the best comics historians around.

Little Lit. `GR. 2-8`

Little Lit is aimed squarely at children. Written by some of the most recognizable artists out there, this anthology is designed to be read and enjoyed by children of all ages. These titles are highly recommended for any collection.

Little Lit: Folklore and Fairy Tale Funnies. Edited by Art Spiegelman and Françoise Mouly. Written and illustrated by Various. Raw Junior, 2000. 64pp. ISBN-10: 0-0602862-4-5. ISBN-13: 978-00602862-4-8.

> Twelve tales, some new, some retold classics, all with a slightly off-kilter feel to them. Favorite tales include Spiegelman's "Prince Rooster," about a prince who learns that he doesn't have to change the thing he likes best about himself; and Barbara McClintock's "The Princess and the Pea," which retells the classic tale with a definite leonine feel to it. Also included are activity pages and a board game (in the endpapers).

Little Lit: It Was a Dark and Silly Night. Edited by Art Spiegelman and Françoise Mouly. Joanna Cotler Books, 2003. 48pp. ISBN-10: 0-0602862-8-8. ISBN-13: 978-00602862-8-6.

> The third anthology in the series includes stories by such luminaries as Lemony Snicket, who defines the word silly as "Somewhat Intelligent, Largely Laconic Yeti"; William Joyce, who regales the reader with the story of "Art Aimesworth, Boy Crimefighter and All Around Whiz-Kid," who endeavors to isolate Giggle-illium, the silly atom; Neil Gaiman, whose dark and silly night starts with "a light and grumpy afternoon"; and Kaz, who tells the tale of a bizarre upside-down family that only rights itself when a gas explosion blows the house up, in both senses.

Little Lit: Strange Stories for Strange Kids. Edited by Art Spiegelman and Françoise Mouly. Written and illustrated by Various. Joanna Cotler Books, 2001. 64pp. ISBN-10: 0-0602862-6-1. ISBN-13: 978-00602862-6-2.

> This second collection presents more stories, this time with a strange bent. Includes the stories "Cereal Baby Keller," about an infant who eats everything (literally); "Barnaby" the first tale in the popular cartoon series from Crockett Johnson, creator of *Harold and the Purple Crayon*; and "The Several Selves of Selby Sheldrake" by Art Spiegelman, who shows us that even when we're by ourselves, we're never truly alone.

Mind Riot: Coming of Age in Comix. **Edited by Karen D. Hirsch. Aladdin, 1997. 128pp. ISBN-10: 0-6898062-2-1. ISBN-13: 978-06898062-2-3.** `GR. 6-8`

> Although it was published a decade earlier than the book *Stuck in the Middle*, this collection serves as a nice "sequel" to that book. Dealing with more teenage-themed concerns, *Mind Riot* tackles such issues as self-perception, gangs, cliques, and sexuality.
>
> **Parental Advisory:** language; sexual themes; teen angst; violence

Stuck in the Middle: 17 Comics from an Unpleasant Age. **Edited by Ariel Schrag. Viking Juvenile, 2007. 224pp. ISBN-10: 0-6700622-1-9. ISBN-13: 978-06700622-1-8.** `GR. 5-8`

> Remember how bad it was in middle school? These artists do, and they relate tales from those first, awkward years when your voice starts to crack, your body changes in strange ways, and you begin to notice (gasp!) the opposite sex. (ALA Great Graphic Novel)
>
> **Parental Advisory:** coming-of-age issues; bullying; crude humor; language

The **TOON** *Treasury of Classic Children's Comics*. **Edited by Art Spiegelman and Françoise Mouly. Abrams ComicArts, 2009. 352pp. ISBN-10: 0-8109573-0-2. ISBN-13: 978-08109573-0-5.** `GR. 1-7`

> A massive collection of comics from the 1940s to the early 1960s, aimed at kids. This book contains stories from such luminaries (most of these are Jack Kirby Hall of Fame Inductees) as Carl Barks, Walt Kelly, John Stanley, Harvey Kurtzman, Basil Wolverton, Jack Cole, and Jules Feiffer. Highly recommended (especially in this day when everything is hyperserious in comics and graphic novels).

Nate's Picks

- <u>Max Axiom</u> by Emily Sohn and Steve Erwin. Science has never been so much fun to learn about.

- *The Sandwalk Adventures* by Jay Hosler. The retellings of Darwin's teachings get absolutely hilarious, while still reiterating his core ideas.

- <u>Little Lit</u> by Art Spiegelman and Francois Mouly. Anthologies aimed squarely at kids, with enough off-kilter-ness to make it worthwhile.

Additional Book and Web Resources

Industry Awards

Much like any other genre, graphic novels have developed their own award groups over the years. Science fiction has such awards as the Hugo and Nebula, romance has the Rita, and horror has the Stoker Award, so it only makes sense that graphic novels should have their own awards. What follows is a list of current awards.

The Bill Finger Award for Excellence in Comic Book Writing

http://www.comic-con.org/cci/cci_finger.shtml

An annual award for comic book writers who were determined to have not been sufficiently honored for their work in the medium. Every year the awards committee is charged with selecting two recipients, one living and one deceased. Originally established in recognition of *Batman* co-creator Bill Finger.

Friends of Lulu

http://friendsoflulu.wordpress.com/lulu-awards/

Not only an award, but also a nonprofit organization. The Lulu of the Year is awarded for overall work from female artists and/or writers.

The Harvey Award

http://www.harveyawards.org/

Named after famed writer-artist Harvey Kurtzman, the Harvey is awarded yearly for achievement in comic books. Awarded annually at the Baltimore Comic-Con, it is similar to the science fiction/fantasy award, the Hugo, in that nominees are chosen from among their peers.

The Ignatz Awards

http://www.spxpo.com/ignatz-awards

Named after Ignatz from the comic strip *Krazy Kat* by George Herriman, this award is given to small press creators and creator-owned projects that are published by larger publishers.

Inkpot Award

http://www.comic-con.org/cci/cci_inkpot.shtml

The inkpot award is awarded annually to professionals in comic book, comic strip, animation, science fiction, and related pop-culture fields. As much as many people hate to admit it, this is a bit of a catch-all award.

Russ Manning Award

http://www.comic-con.org/cci/cci_manning.shtml

Officially known as the The Russ Manning Most Promising Newcomer Award, it is presented annually to a comic book artist whose first professional work appeared within the previous two years.

The Will Eisner Comic Industry Award.

http://www.comic-con.org/cci/cci_eisners_10nom.php

Commonly referred to as the Eisner Award, it was named after the comic pioneer Will Eisner. The Eisner is awarded annually for creative achievement in American comics. It is one of the highest accolades to be awarded yearly.

Web Sites and Databases

With the majority of comic book users and graphic novel aficionados being some sort of geek, it was really just a matter of time before they decided to start collecting information about this mediun into searchable databases. Some allow you to browse covers from all over the world; others let you monitor your entire collection and how much it may be worth.

The Big Comic Book Database

http://www.comics-db.com

A database that has been around for awhile; organizes titles by publisher.

Comic Book Database

http://www.cbdb.com

This was one of the very first databases on the Web. It doesn't seem to be getting updated much anymore, but it still has a nice glossary covering the basic information on comics and graphic novels.

Comic Book DB

http://www.comicbookdb.com

This site strives to be the be-all and end-all in comic book databases. Completely user run, it seeks to document every comic book, manga, graphic novel, writer, artist, and publisher out there, and then to cross-reference the entire mess into something that is fully searchable and comprehensive.

Comics Price Guide

http://www.comicspriceguide.com

A flashy database where you can track your entire collection and get a basic idea of how much it's worth. Also has a searchable database of covers.

Get Graphic

http://www.getgraphic.org

Originally started as a two-year project to introduce kids, parents, and teachers to graphic novels, the project just recently published its first book, made up entirely of submissions from teens in the Buffalo, New York, area. This is a great resource for teachers and librarians.

The Grand Comic Book Database

http://www.comics.org/

The Grand Comic Books Database (or GCD) is probably the biggest clearinghouse for comic book covers from all over the world. Users are constantly uploading new comic book covers: not only the newest issues that hit newsstands, but also covers from earlier eras.

The Graphic Novel Reporter

http://www.graphicnovelreporter.com

A relatively unknown, but incredibly powerful Web site that is absolutely indispensable to any librarian or teacher who is intent on pairing kids with great graphic novels. Managed by industry insiders, this is one site that you absolutely have to check out at least once.

Graphic Novels: Resources for Teachers and Librarians

http://library.buffalo.edu/libraries/asl/guides/graphicnovels/

Originally created for support of a MLS program class at the University of Buffalo, this is an indispensable site for any teacher or librarian who wants to learn more about the positive effects of graphic novels.

Make Beliefs Comix!

http://www.makebeliefscomix.com

A handy online tool that allows you to make your own comics. For a simple interface, it is actually a complex little program. The site also has writer's prompts to help generate story ideas.

No Flying No Tights

http://www.noflyingnotights.com

An absolute must visit for any graphic novel or manga that might be worth reading. As of this writing, the author was getting ready for a complete revamp of the entire Web site. Includes a section called "Sidekicks" for kids up to age twelve.

Scott McCloud's Journal

http://scottmccloud.com

Scott McCloud has become the unofficial master of comic book conventions, and his Web site is all about comic books, graphic novels, and anything to do with the medium.

YALSA "Great Graphic Novels"
www.ala.org/ala/mgrps/divs/yalsa/booklistsawards/greatgraphicnovels
forteens/gn.cfm
        At the official Web site for YALSA, the Young Adult Library Services
Association, you will find a page listing the graphic novel choices for young
adults.

Reference and Resource Books

Though this book is designed to be a guide to the genre, it is by no means a stand-
alone reference. Following are other books on the subject, written by other authors
who love the books they write about.

Getting Graphic!: Comics for Kids. **Written by Michele Gorman. Illustrated by
Jimmy Gownley. Linworth Publishing, 2007. 96p. ISBN-10: 1-5868332-7-8. ISBN-
13: 978-15868332-7-5,**
        A good starting point for media specialists in elementary school settings as well
        as children's librarians, this guide not only introduces one of the fastest growing
        genres for young readers, but also explains how graphic novels can be used for
        reluctant or slow readers and ESL learners. Works as a collection development
        tool for building a new collection as well.

*Getting Graphic!: Using Graphic Novels to Promote Literacy with Preteens and
Teens.* **Written by Michele Gorman. Linworth, 2003. 112p. ISBN-10: 1-5868308-9-
9. ISBN-13: 978-15868308-9-2.**
        Gorman's first book on getting librarians and teachers into using graphic
        novels as a tool to promote literacy. Chapters deal specifically with collection
        development, listings of graphic novels, and also details on how to integrate
        them into a school curriculum. This is an essential title for schools and public
        libraries that are considering adding graphic novels to their collections, but are
        unsure of how to proceed.

Graphic Novels: A Bibliographic Guide to Book-Length Comics. **Written by D.
Aviva Rothschild. Libraries Unlimited, 1995. 246p. ISBN-10: 1-5630808-6-9.
ISBN-13: 978-15630808-6-9.**
        In the first book to tackle readers' advisory for graphic novels, Rothschild
        described and evaluated more than 400 works in English. The book is aimed at
        especially at librarians, booksellers, educators working with teens and reluctant
        readers, and readers interested in the genre.

Graphic Novels: A Genre Guide to Comic Books, Manga, and More. **Written by
Michael Pawuk. Libraries Unlimited, 2006. 672p. ISBN-10: 1-5915813-2-X. ISBN-
13: 978-15915813-2-1.**
        The definitive guide, Pawuk's book is an exhaustive and extensive walk through
        the genre. Heavily researched and annotated, this is a must include for any
        librarian or teacher wanting to hook people up with great graphic novels.

Graphic Novels beyond the Basics: Insights and Issues for Libraries. **Written by Martha Cornog and Timothy Perper. Libraries Unlimited, 2009. 281p. ISBN-10: 1-5915847-8-7. ISBN-13: 978-15915847-8-0.**

> Designed as a sort of training manual for librarians and teachers, this book espouses the idea that not only are graphic novels a genre, but also a rather effective literary medium. Using essays by various contributors on graphic elements as well as practical matters concerning graphic novels in libraries, the book lays the foundation for a strong yet accessible graphic collection.

How-to Books

Without books, there probably wouldn't be graphic novels. The two just go hand in hand. And young fans are often inspired to try creating their own graphic novels. The books listed below discuss the "how-to" of graphic novels, from page layout, to pacing, to getting a publisher.

The Complete Idiot's Guide to Creating a Graphic Novel. **Written by Nat Gertler and Steve Lieber. Alpha, 2004. 352pp. ISBN-10: 1-5925723-3-2. ISBN-13: 978-15925623-3-5.**

> A book on how to create graphic novels for fun and profit.

Graphic Storytelling and Visual Narrative. **Written by Will Eisner. W.W. Norton, 2008. 164pp. ISBN-10: 0-3933312-7-X. ISBN-13: 978-03933312-7-1.**

> This is the book Eisner taught from at the New York School of Visual Arts. The basic setup of a panel and the composition of an image are always at the forefront of his discussions.

Making Comics: Storytelling Secrets of Comics, Manga and Graphic Novels. **Written by Scott McCloud. Harper Paperbacks, 2006. 272pp. ISBN-10: 0-0607809-4-0. ISBN-13: 978-00607809-4-4.**

> From the author of the incredible *Understanding Comics*, this book is aimed more at folks who are slightly familiar with comic book and graphic novel conventions. Discusses almost every possibility available to artists, as well as taking the reader behind the scenes.

Teaching Visual Literacy: Using Comic Books, Graphic Novels, Anime, Cartoons, and More to Develop Comprehension and Thinking Skills. **Edited by Nancy Frey and Douglas Fisher. Corwin Press, 2008. 208pp. ISBN-10: 1-4129531-2-X. ISBN-13: 978-14129531-2-2.**

> A guide for teachers to incorporate graphic novels into their lesson plans in an effort to promote literacy and reading comprehension.

Writing and Illustrating the Graphic Novel: Everything You Need to Know to Create Great Graphic Works. **Written by Mike Chinn. Barron's Educational Series, 2004. 128pp. ISBN-10: 0-7641278-8-8. ISBN-13: 978-07641278-8-5.**

> As the title suggests, this book lays out everything one needs to know about creating a graphic novel.

Appendix B

Publishing Companies

This appendix lists the various publishing companies cited in this book, along with a brief overview of the company. Where possible, contact information has been provided. Most companies are willing to supply libraries with promotional items or even galley copies of upcoming books if you contact them.

:01 Second
http://www.firstsecondbooks.com

Aimed mostly at middle-school and high-school kids, it includes a few titles for elementary-school readers. Focusing on covering multiple genres within individual books, as well as covering stories from different countries. It also has a "comics in the classroom" program for certain titles.

Active Synapse
http://www.activesynapse.com

A one-man publishing company run by Dr. Jay Hostler, PhD, the sole publisher, writer, and illustrator. Active Synapse does not publish on a regular schedule.

ADV Manga
http://www.advfilms.com/

ADV focused mostly on anime (cartoons), but had a booming publishing arm as well. Most titles are for older audiences. As of September 1, 2009, ADV has closed up shop and is no longer in business.

Albert Whitman & Company
http://www.albertwhitman.com

Children's publishing company that is famous for the <u>Boxcar Children</u> series.

Alternative Comics
http://www.indyworld.com

Independent comic book publisher. Approximately 85 percent of it offerings are not appropriate for young readers. Huge supporter and distributor of Xeric award-winning books. Jeff Mason, the publisher for Alternative Comics, also works as a criminal defense lawyer.

The Astonish Factory

http://www.theastonishfactory.com

As the Web site says, "WE CARE ABOUT CREATIONS FOR KIDS." Though its target demographic is kids, The Astonish Factory wants the stories to resonate with kids in the real world. Highly recommended for collections.

Bloomsbury USA Children's Books

http://kids.bloomsburyusa.com

An imprint of Bloomsbury USA Publishing, it is a children's publishing company, mostly focusing on traditional text-style books.

Broccoli Books

http://www.broccolibooks.com

Specializes in Japanese comics, illustration books, graphic novels, and more. A lot of its stuff is influenced by CCGs (Collectable Card Games).

Candlewick Press

http://www.candlewick.com

Children's publishing company based in Massachusetts. Focuses mostly on younger readers.

CMX

http://www.dccomics.com/cmx/

DC Comics' manga division.

Collins Publishing

http://www.harpercollins.com/imprints/index.aspx?imprintid=517984

One of many imprints under the HarperCollins publishing umbrella, Collins focuses on nonfiction books.

CrossGen Comics

One of the brightest publishers in the mid-1990s, CrossGen was an amazing publishing company that basically outgrew its financial abilities. Disney has purchased the rights to most of CrossGen's offerings, but nothing has come of the purchase so far. Most of the titles CrossGen was famous for have been hijacked by cybersquatters (people who register names for Web domains and then charge exorbitant fees to release the name), so finding reliable information is next to impossible now.

Dark Horse

http://www.darkhorse.com

The third-largest American comic book publisher, Dark Horse has cornered the market on television and movie tie-ins. Though some of its titles are decidedly not for children (mostly the movie series), on the whole, anything it publishes is worth looking at.

DC Comics

http://www.dccomics.com

The longest-running comics publisher in America, DC Comics is also the largest publisher of comic books. With such icons as *Superman, Batman, Wonder Woman, Aqua Man,* and *Green Lantern,* it's not hard to see why.

DC Kids

http://www.dccomics.com/dckids/

An imprint of comics icon and juggernaut DC Comics, DC Kids covers kid-friendly titles appropriate for all ages.

Disney-Hyperion Publishing

http://www.hyperionbooksforchildren.com

A publishing company that is solely devoted to publishing books for kids; these books make excellent additions to any collection.

Don't Eat Any Bugs Productions

http://www.donteatanybugs.net

A one man publishing company, Don't Eat Any Bugs is run and managed by Ray Friesen, one of the youngest Ignatz award winners alive. His Web site contains lots of fun stuff for visitors.

Fiery Studios

http://www.vogelein.com

Home of artist, writer, and illustrator Jane Irwin and the self-published series Vogelein: Clockwork Faerie.

Graphix

http://www.scholastic.com/graphix

A small imprint of the classroom favorite Scholastic, Graphix has a small but very popular line of comics for younger readers. Scholastic is an excellent company for classroom teaching, and is always receptive to requests.

Grosset & Dunlap

http://us.penguingroup.com/static/pages/publishers/yr/grosset.html

Another imprint of Penguin, it does a lot of movie tie-ins.

HarperCollins Books

http://www.harpercollins.com/footer/help.aspx

One of the largest publishing companies in the world, HarperCollins does not do a lot in terms of straight graphic novels. It has begun reprinting Neil Gaiman's earlier works, but as of this writing, it still does not have a straight graphic novel imprint.

IDW Publishing

http://www.idwpublishing.com

Another publishing company that caters mostly to older audiences, IDW is becoming a popular company for Hollywood to mine. Currently it holds the licenses to <u>Transformers</u>, <u>Star Trek</u>, *Doctor Who*, and *G.I. Joe*, among others.

Image

http://www.imagecomics.com

Originally created after seven Marvel Comics best-selling artists formed their own company, Image has become a large publishing company. Some titles are appropriate for younger readers, but the majority are for older audiences.

Kids Can Press

http://www.kidscanpress.com/us/ (US Website)

The largest Canadian-owned children's book publisher. Publishes books aimed at audiences from toddler to young adult.

Main Street Books

http://www.randomhouse.com/broadway

A now defunct publishing imprint that was subsumed into another imprint, Broadway Books, which in turn is an imprint of Random House.

Marvel Comics

http://www.marvelcomics.com

The second largest comics publisher in America, Marvel has quite a collection of popular characters. From Spider-Man, and the X-Men to the Fantastic Four and Ironman, Marvel is more oriented toward characters that are *different* than other people. In August 2009 Marvel became a wholly owned subsidiary of Disney.

Nantier Beall Minoustchine Publishing

http://www.nbmpub.com

Also known as NBM, this is one of the most international publishers out there, with not only American graphic novel authors, but also European and former Eastern Bloc artists and writers. Like a lot of different companies, NBM's titles range far and wide across the acceptability spectrum for children.

Olio Press

Linda Medley's publishing company; there is no Web site or central location for information on her or her work.

Oni Press

http://www.onipress.com

An independent comic publishing company, Oni offers many titles aimed at older audiences. It does have some titles for younger audiences, but any offering should be closely examined before adding it to a children's collection.

Papercutz

http://www.papercutz.com

Graphic novel company focusing on 'tweens and teens. Papercutz has quickly become a solid publishing company, starting out with <u>The Hardy Boys</u>

and <u>Nancy Drew</u>. Papercutz has made it a point to make sure all of its offerings are affordable to as many people as possible.

Philomel Books

http://www.us.penguingroup.com/static/pages/publishers/yr/philomel.html
An imprint of Penguin Publishing, Philomel is a children's book publishing company. As of this printing it only has one graphic novel that I am aware of (Brian Jacques's *Redwall*). It is a goldmine of traditional children's books, however.

Puffin Books

http://us.penguingroup.com/static/pages/publishers/yr/puffin.html
Another children's publishing imprint from Penguin Publishing, Puffin has adapted a few literary classics to graphic novel format.

Random House Books for Young Readers

http://www.randomhouse.com/kids/
The largest English-language children's trade book publisher in the world. It publishes mostly picture books, with the occasional graphic novel.

School Specialty Publishing

http://www.schoolspecialtypublishing.com
A publishing company known for textbooks, it has a series written by Mercer Mayer that is graphic novel related.

Sky Dog Press

http://www.buzzboy.net
John Gallagher writes, illustrates, and self-publishes the majority of the titles from Sky Dog Press. Some titles develop mature undertones that may not be appropriate for younger readers. John Gallagher does have a program in place to visit schools and talk about comic books.

Stone Arch Books

http://www.stonearchbooks.com
Stone Arch is one of the leading publishers of graphic novels specifically aimed at younger readers. The main emphasis of its books is that they are safe for young readers (i.e., no violence, no inappropriate content, etc.). Each and every book Stone Arch publishes also includes a discussion guide, writing prompts, and a teacher's guide for using the story in the classroom.

Tokyopop

http://www.tokyopop.com
One of the largest manga publishers outside Japan, Tokyopop has been credited with not only bringing many manga titles to American shores, but also popularizing the Korean manga style manwha. Approximately 60 percent of Tokyopop's offerings are for teenage audiences or older, so caution is urged in purchasing.

Toon Books

E-mail: mail@toon.books.com

Imprint of Raw Jr. LLC. Toon Books products are specifically aimed at readers four years old and up. Each book is designed to be read by children themselves, and each book also has what is referred to as "comics in the classroom" teaching guides for teachers to use the books in the classroom.

Top Shelf Productions

http://www.topshelfcomix.com

The publishers are Chris Staros and Brett Warnock. Well known for its inventive, controversial, and innovative graphic novels, the majority of Top Shelf's titles are nowhere near appropriate for young audiences. However, the titles produced for children are always worth checking out.

Toptron LTD T/A Fanfare

http://www.ponentmon.com

French publisher focusing on Japan's alternative comics scene. Not much else is known about this company, but caution should probably be exercised with its titles.

Villard

http://www.randomhouse.com/rhpg/villard/

This imprint of The Random House Publishing Group is not a traditional children's book publisher. Mostly focused on themes found in "pop culture," it has a couple of graphic novel titles, but does not seem poised to charge headlong into the fray.

VIZ Media LLC

http://www.viz.com

One of the biggest manga publishers on the planet, VIZ Media LLC owns the rights to such books as *Naruto, Bleach, One Piece, Inyu-yasha,* and *Full Metal Alchemist.* As with most conglomerate publishers, its offerings may need to be reviewed before adding them to a collection. Librarians may also want to check out its monthly American magazine, *Shonen Jump,* to get a good idea of what is currently making the rounds in manga circles.

W. W. Norton & Company

http://www.wwnorton.com

The oldest and largest publishing house owned wholly by its employees. Probably best known for its college text books, W. W. Norton has dabbled in graphic novels.

Author Index

Lawrie, Robin, 136–37
Lemke, Donald, 17, 80, 146, 148, 151
Limke, Jeff, 95, 96, 97, 99, 100
Lobdell, Scott, 107–8
London, Jack, 140
Loux, Matthew, 110
Lynch, Jay, 10, 81

Macchio, Ralph, 71
Manning, Matthew K., 4
Marathon Team, 111
Marsh, Robert, 129, 147
Martin, Ann M., 123
Martin, Cynthia, 141
Masters, Anthony, 124, 125, 126, 132, 133, 135
Matheny, Bill, 4
Mayer, Mercer, 109–10
McAvennie, Mike, 9
McGregor, Don, 116
McIntosh, Liz, 56
Medley, Linda, 76, 77
Meister, Cari, 126, 133, 134
Miller, Davis Worth, 67, 141
Miyazaki, Hayao, 78
Morse, Scott, 9
Mortensen, Lori, 133
Mouly, Françoise, 81, 157, 158
Mucci, Michael, 112
Mucci, Tim, 95, 143
Mukai, Natsumi, 85

Nickel, Scott, 21, 22, 58, 103, 112, 115, 119, 124
Nishiyama, Yurkio, 131–32

O'Donnell, Liam, 146, 147, 148
Olson, Kay M., 153
Omode, Akemi, 70
Ono, Toshihiro, 50, 51
Orci, Robert, 56
Orme, David, 5, 6
Owen, Erich, 22
Owens, L .L., 141

Park, Min-seo, 31
Pasko, Martin, 3
Perez, Daniel, 96
Perrin, Pat, 144
Peters, Stephanie, 148, 151
Peterson, Scott, 3
Petrucha, Stefan, 104, 105, 116, 118
Pitcher, C., 116, 124
Poon, Janice, 102
Powell, Martin, 81, 82, 94, 105, 143
Puckett, Kelly, 3

Reis, Erica, 130
Renier, Aaron, 116
Reynolds, Aaron, 16
Richardson, Roy, 140
Rigano, Giovanni, 83
Robbins, Trina, 7, 148
Ross, Alex, 2, 14, 17
Ruiz, Alfonso, 142
Runton, Andy, 90, 91

Saddleback Educational Publishing, 154, 156
Sakai, Stan, 26, 27
Salicrup, Jim, 71, 117, 118, 119
Sandoval, Gerardo, 95
Sava, Scott, 66, 77
Schrag, Ariel, 158
Schweizer, Chris, 22
Sewell, Anna, 140
Shakespeare, William, 142
Shanower, Eric, 92
Shelley, Mary, 113
Shepard, Aaron, 98
Shigekatsu, Ihara, 51
Siegel, Siena Cherson, 156
Simonson, Louise, 14
Slade, Christian, 85
Slott, Dan, 3
Smith, Andy, 109
Smith, Jeff, 73–76
Smith, Matt, 79
Smith, Tod, 112, 140, 142

Artist/Illustrator Index

Title Index

About the Author

NATHAN HERALD lives on the Western slope of Colorado with his family and is an avid fan of graphic novels for all ages. He has shared this passion with his three sons, who are now all voracious readers. He is determined to share his interest and knowledge with all those who might benefit.